80th Congress, 1st Session   -   -   -

FASCISM IN ACTION

A DOCUMENTED STUDY AND ANALYSIS OF FASCISM IN EUROPE

PREPARED AT THE INSTANCE AND
UNDER THE DIRECTION OF

REPRESENTATIVE WRIGHT PATMAN
OF TEXAS

BY

LEGISLATIVE REFERENCE SERVICE
OF THE
LIBRARY OF CONGRESS

UNDER THE DIRECTION OF

ERNEST S. GRIFFITH

WILDSIDE PRESS

TABLE OF CONTENTS

FOREWORD

By Representative Wright Patman, of Texas

The world today is faced with a dangerous manifestation of recent history known as fascism. Opinions vary as to whether this movement is economic, social, political, or philosophical, but there is marked agreement as to its objective characteristics. Briefly, fascism means the seizure and control of the economic, social, political, and cultural life of the state by a small group. Free speech, free press, free worship, and public meetings are ruthlessly suppressed. Blind obedience to the "leader" is demanded of the people and the slightest wavering means death or imprisonment to any person. Restrictive policies may be carried on against his entire family. A fascist regime is necessarily militaristic and nationalistic.

It is not my purpose to attempt a technical definition of fascism, which is given in the preface, but rather to point to some of the tendencies prevalent in society today which might lead to a resurgence of this hated movement.

To most Americans the threat of fascism vanished with the defeat of Germany and Japan in the greatest war that history has known. There is, however, a real question as to whether we defeated the evil itself in destroying its two principal exponents. Public opinion appears in general to hold that fascism is a wholly European, or at least a wholly foreign movement. Yet there are many strong symptoms of fascism in our own democratic society. True, this movement in the United States masquerades under other names than the discredited one of fascism, but whatever it may be called, its peculiar characteristics are alarmingly evident.

If we are to combat successfully such an insidious movement, many Americans must understand clearly what fascism is and what it means to the individual to live in a fascist state. At my request, the Legislative Reference Service of the Library of Congress has prepared a study of Fascism in Action as an aid to the American citizen in protecting himself and his children against this most dangerous movement of modern times.

A careful reading of this study will show what fascism in actual operation means in direct personal terms. Every person must think and act at the command of a higher authority. Every school, church, home, and business is carefully controlled by the dominant party. The concentration camp or death await the citizen who offers opposition to the regime.

To many, fascism, particularly as it operated in Germany, seemed a model of order and efficiency. It had apparently solved many of the most crucial problems of modern times. Fascist countries radically reduced or abolished unemployment, seemingly eliminated many social differences, and contrived many new devices which assisted or amused their people. But the cost to the individual was heavy.

The price was abolition of representative government, of individual liberty, of the rights of free speech, free assembly, free religion, a free press, and the principle of equality before the law.

Fascist Germany and Japan used the boasted efficiency of fascism to build mighty war machines to crush the "inefficient" democracies, but an important fact had been left out of their leaders' calculations. Democracy and efficiency, even military efficiency, are not incompatible, and the democracies decisively defeated the fascist powers and coincidentally answered one of the principal arguments in defense of fascism.

I believe we are forced to admit that fascism is today an ever-present danger to our democracy. We must consider not only how to recognize its manifestations but also what we can do to combat it. Many means can be used but no one method seems to be the real solution. Some of the most effective are described briefly below.

Perhaps the best means of fighting fascism is to recognize it, no matter under what title it masquerades. Not all "hate" organizations are necessarily fascist, but they have certain definite trends toward such a policy. If members of groups of this type can be made to realize the dangers inherent in such beliefs, a long step toward overcoming fascism will have been taken.

It is my belief that persistent and fearless exposure will kill profascist organizations and discredit the individuals who have formed them. In some cases such leaders have thousands of followers who have been attracted ideologically to them. However, there is always the possibility that exposure may attract new adherents. The present activity of the 26 defendants in the sedition trial of 1944 is a case in point. Many organizations, newspapers, radio programs, and magazines have disclosed the machinations of fascist-minded individuals and groups.

The House Committee on Un-American Activities has estimated that $100,000,000 per year is donated to propaganda organizations,[1] some of which show very definite fascist tendencies. Early in the first session of the Eightieth Congress, the chairman of this committee stated that it would conduct "the most active year" of its existence and that it would—

let the chips fall where they may   * * *   whether they fall on the Columbians, the Ku Klux Klan, or the Communists.

Many persons feel that all agreements between American firms and foreign firms should be made public. This would automatically expose attempts of foreign fascists to work through American sympathizers.

Everyone who is concerned about the means of combatting fascism in the United States agrees that our educational system offers an excellent weapon, provided that we offer its advantages to all young people regardless of their economic status or geographical location. Young people must be given the truth about democracy, and the truth about alternative forms of life. Education must not, of course, be confined to the schools, but must utilize home influences, the newspapers, the radio, and other means of public communication. Adult education must be given increased emphasis. Gov. Ellis G. Arnall

[1] U..S. Congress, House Committee on Un-American Activities, 79th Cong., 2d sess. Report No. 1996. Sources of Financial Aid for Subversive and Un-American Propaganda. Washington, Government Printing Office, 1946, p. 2.

placed first in a list of needs for a program to combat the Columbians, "a good dose of education." [2]

A prime necessity in the defeat of fascism is the maintenance of full employment. A program of full employment cannot be achieved until the pent-up demands created by wartime shortages are satisfied, but once that point is reached there must be a solution to the long-range problem. The Nation must continue to offer livelihood and hope to its citizens or they may become the prey of any demagog who offers them the promise of something better which is in reality a fascist regime.

There must be a positive policy and a definite program for raising the national income and distributing it equitably so that people can buy the products of our economy. Some writers consider this one of the most essential means for the destruction of incipient fascism.

Organized labor must be alert to the dangers of fascism. The working class has more to fear from fascism than any other group. It is significant that one of the early acts of every fascist regime is the abolition of all labor organization outside government control.

One of the most powerful means of preventing the establishment of a fascist government in a democratic country is to make certain that the existing government operates honestly and efficiently. No really strong democracy has fallen before fascism. Democracy is not to be had for the wishing, and the best efforts of every American citizen should be devoted to its perpetuation and successful operation. Democracy and efficiency are compatible, but insinuations that we must choose between democratic participation in government and efficient government often emanate from fascist sources.

Dr. Douglas M. Kelley has recently written 22 Cells in Nuremberg, a study in psychiatric terms of the Nazi defendants in the Nuremberg trials. In discussing the meaning of his findings for America he describes his discovery, upon returning to America after attending the trials, that the same prejudices expressed in the same terms that he had heard in Nuremberg were current in this country. He said:

> We can find the same ideas thinly veiled in our public press today. Even worse, we find some of our top political men, members of our highest governing bodies, making statements which would do credit to Rosenberg, Hitler, or Goebbels. * * * I am convinced that there is little in America today which could prevent the establishment of a Nazi-like state.

The fact that I requested the study of Fascism in Action does not mean that I am not equally opposed to communism in any way whatsoever. My views on the subject of communism were set forth in a letter of September 24, 1946, to Dr. Ernest S. Griffith, in the following words:

> I am opposed to communism in any form. It should be fought with every means at our command. It is obnoxious to our American democratic system of free enterprise based upon initiative, intelligence, ability, and hard work. Our system is the best in the world and although it is so much better than communism, I just can't believe that communism can get any hold in America, yet we must be on the alert and make sure that there is no formidable start toward communism.

The study of Fascism in Action, prepared by the Legislative Reference Service of the Library of Congress, is not intended as a historical description of the reasons why the fascist regimes suffered

---

[2] Edward T. Folliard, Education, Higher Standards Called Answer to Columbians. Washington Post, December 4, 1946, p. 1.

complete military defeat in the Second World War.   It has little to
do with the war, but is a comparative analysis of the way in which
those regimes operated in times of peace.   It tells the story of what
the life of ordinary citizens was under such governments.   The reader
has only to compare thoughtfully such an existence with his own to
arrive at the unqualified decision that he prefers the latter.   But he is
asked to do more than this.   Since many of us believe that there are
dangerous tendencies toward fascism in the United States today, the
present study can perform an important function in instructing the
reader in the recognition of these tendencies.   To be forewarned is
to be forearmed.   It lies within our power to defend our chosen democratic way of life against the attack of fascism, and the study Fascism
in Action is offered as a weapon in that defense.

PREFACE

This study of Fascism in Action was undertaken at the request of Representative Wright Patman, of Texas, who also indicated that its scope and method were to conform in general to the earlier study, Communism in Action (H. Doc. No. 754, 79th Cong., 2d sess.), prepared at the instance of Representative Everett Dirksen, of Illinois.

This study is appropriate because of the many similarities between fascism and communism, some of which Representative Fred E. Busbey, of Illinois, has recently listed as follows:

1. The wiping out of all independent trade-unionism with the result that those trade-unions which are permitted, exist only under the tolerance of the totalitarian state, to serve as its servile adjuncts.

2. The elimination of political parties except the ruling Nazi, Fascist, or Communist Party.

3. The subordination of all economic and social life to the strict control of the ruling, single-party bureaucracy.

4. The suppression of individual initiative, and the liquidation of the system of free enterprise, and a tendency toward government control of supercartels.

5. The abolition of the right to freedom of speech, press, assembly, and religious worship.

6. The reduction of wages and, in the case of communism, living standards.

7. The use of slave labor on a vast scale and the establishment of concentration camps.

8. The abolition of the right to trial by jury, habeas corpus, the right to independent defense counsel, and the innocence of the defendant until proven guilty.

9. The glorification of a single Leader or Fuehrer or Duce, who is all-powerful and subject neither to criticism nor removal through the ballot.

10. The utilization of a special form of social demagogy—for example, incitement of race against race and class against class—the elimination of all opposition, and the concentration of power into the hands of the ruling dictatorship.

11. The subordination of all economic and social life and the everyday needs of the population to the requirements of an expanding military machine seeking world conquest.

12. The establishment of a system of Nation-wide espionage to which the entire population is subject.

13. The severance of social, cultural, and economic contact between the people of the totalitarian state and those of other countries, through a rigorous press and radio censorship, travel restrictions, etc.

14. The open disregard for the rights of other nations and the sanctity of treaties.

15. The maintenance and encouragement of fifth columns abroad.

16. The reduction of parliamentary bodies to a rubber-stamp status automatically approving all decisions of the one-party dictatorship and the omnipotent Leader.[1]

Of course, these similarities do not erase the fact that marked differences do distinguish fascism from communism. While communism is frankly atheistic and intolerant of religion as an "opiate for the people," fascism does not in principle set itself against religion, as religion, but, rather, attacks specific religious groups and practices because they stand in the way of the full achievement of the fascist program. Communism frowns on private property, and nationalizes industries, banks, agricultural land, and all forms of property which may represent wealth. In contrast, fascism, on advent to power, reprivatizes previously nationalized businesses, encourages cartels, and develops large private property holdings, especially in industry, so as to simplify the fascist control of the economy of the land. The large property holders, by one process or another, become members of the ruling elite. Communist agriculture tends to be state owned operated, and directed, principally taking on the form of collective farms, while fascist agriculture generally is built around an agriculture class, owning or leasing its land and producing according to a state program. The list need not be expanded; suffice it to say that, as far as world politics is concerned, there is no fascist equivalent for the Communist program of world revolution (formerly the Third International), though the Axis alinement in the Second World War potentially had international aspects.

Nowhere is the similarity of fascism and communism more clearly revealed than in their very close cooperation for aggression upon other states. That was clearly demonstrated in the Russo-German treaty for the fourth partition of Poland. Recognizing this fact, the following resolution was approved by the Committee on House Administration in executive session June 19, 1947:

Resolved, That the Committee on House Administration report House Resolution 83 with the provision that the action taken by the Chairman in requesting the text of the treaty between Russia and Germany for the partitioning of Poland, as called for in the resolution by Mr. Busbey: (*Resolved,* That the Committee on House Administration, by means of a letter written by the Chairman to the Secretary of State, request the text of the treaty between Russia and Germany for the partitioning of Poland.) be included within the document proposed to be printed under H. Res. 83; and that in the event of the refusal of the State Department to respond favorably to the request of the Chairman for the text of the treaty, there be included as a part of the document to be printed under this resolution a copy of the Chairman's letter to the Secretary of State requesting the text of the treaty and also the Secretary of State's letter of refusal.

Accordingly Chairman LeCompte wrote the Secretary of State, George C. Marshall, the following letter.

JUNE 20, 1947.

The Honorable SECRETARY OF STATE,
Washington, D. C.

My DEAR Mr. SECRETARY: The House of Representatives has under consideration a resolution calling for the printing of Fascism in Action, a publication prepared by the Legislative Reference Service of the Library of Congress for Representative Wright Patman of Texas. In this connection the Committee on

[1] The Congressional Record, vol. 93, No. 107, June 6, 1947, p. A2847.

House Administration would like to make a part of that document a treaty which demonstrates the close connection which existed between Hitler and Stalin.

To that end, the Committee has instructed its chairman, by resolution, to request from you, with permission to print, a copy of the treaty between Germany and Russia which provided for the division of Poland, and about which Dewitt C. Poole wrote in Foreign Affairs (Volume 25, No. 1, October 1946, page 143) as follows:

"Poland, having been disposed of in 18 days, Ribbentrop * * * flew to Moscow * * * The new frontier between Germany and Russia was drawn with a thick red pencil—partly by Stalin himself—on a map which was then signed by him and Ribbentrop. The drawing included a mutual obligation to give advance notice of any important action in the foreign field."

We hope that it will not be incompatible with your good judgment and with the welfare and safety of this country to furnish us this material.

May I look forward to an early reply.

Very sincerely yours,

KARL M. LeCOMPTE.

Secretary Marshall's reply was:

JULY 9, 1947.

DEAR MR. LeCOMPTE: I have received your letter of June 20, 1947, requesting, on behalf of the Committee on House Administration, a copy of the treaty between Germany and Russia which provided for the division of Poland for publication in Fascism in Action.

The treaty in question was part of the German Foreign Office archives seized by Allied forces in Germany. The Department of State and the Foreign Offices of the British and French Governments have agreed that all significant documents in the German Foreign Office archives bearing on the origins and conduct of World War II should be edited for publication by historians representing the three governments. The editors are now assembling materials on the years 1937-1941, and these documents will be published as soon as the editorial work is completed.

The Department has consistently taken the position that it would be undesirable to release for publication individual documents from the documents from the German archives on the grounds that the publication of such documents out of context might be subject to misinterpretation and detrimental to the foreign relations of the United States. I hope, therefore, that your Committee will agree that the publication of this treaty should occur only in the normal course of the release of documents from the German Foreign Office archives.

Faithfully yours,

GEORGE C. MARSHALL.

While the map and the full terms of the agreement have not been released officially, the substance of the treaty, however, has already been made public by Richard L. Stokes, writing from the Nuremberg trials, on May 22, 1946, under the title of "Secret Soviet-Nazi Pacts on Eastern Europe Aired, Purported Texts on Agreed Spheres of Influence Produced at Nuremberg but Not Admitted at Trial." This article was published in the St. Louis Post-Dispatch, May 22, 1946, pages 1 and 6.

After the manuscript of Fascism in Action was delivered to Representative Patman but before the House of Representatives had voted to publish it as a House document, a number of suggestions were received for its modification. Basically and in substance the document here appears as it was originally submitted. Some changes have been made in footnotes and by way of clarification. The comparison between communism and fascism was also added to this preface lest the Communists erroneously should take any aid or comfort from the exposing of the other major form of totalitarianism.

For the most part the study was written by members of the full-time staff of the Legislative Reference Service. Those participating were:

Part I—Political:
George B. Galloway
Thorsten V. Kalijarvi
Raymond E. Manning
Howard S. Piquet
M. Loretta Stankard

Part II—Economic:
Julius W. Allen
Theodore J. Kreps
John Kerr Rose

Part III—Individual:
Hugh L. Elsbree
William H. Gilbert
Helen E. Livingston
Francis R. Valeo

The chapter on Education and Thought Control was written by I. L. Kandel, the distinguished editor of School and Society. The chapter on Labor was written by Ludwig Hamburger, formerly of the staff of Brookings Institution.

General editorial supervision was provided by Thorsten V. Kalijarvi, who also wrote the introduction and the conclusion. Editorial assistance was provided by Dudley B. Ball.

ERNEST S. GRIFFITH,
Director, Legislative Reference Service.

FASCISM IN ACTION

INTRODUCTION

WHAT IS FASCISM?

In the broad sense

Fascism in the broad sense is simultaneously a philosophy and a way of life which requires that its followers serve the state with an unwavering faith and an unquestioning obedience.[1] It makes fanaticism a virtue and weaves ideological concepts about the doctrines of race supremacy, the leadership principle, rule by an elite class, government under a single political party, the acquisition of living space, a totalitarian state, and the use of force as an instrument of national policy.[2] The roots of modern fascism, especially the German, and to a less degree the Italian, may be traced to nineteenth century thought. However, it is economically a contemporary manifestation of mercantilism; politically an apologia for world conquest; and spiritually a quasi-religious cult with special symbols and rituals.[3]

In the narrow sense

In a narrow sense fascism is the term used to describe the operation of the political, economic, and social institutions of the fascist state. That state mobilizes all physical, social, and spiritual resources and activities, compressing them into a regimented whole. Primary emphasis is placed on power.

How used here

In the following pages, when fascism means the movement in general or as a whole, it is spelled with a small "f"; when applied to Italy, it is spelled with a capital "F".

HOW IT OPERATES

What, then, are the principles, political, economic, and social, that gave rise to fascism in so many parts of the world? Where did fascism come from? What made it strong? Why such opposition to the democracies? What happened to civil liberties, equality before the law, jury trial, freedom of speech and press? Why the continual glorification of war? How did programs that enslaved people win such strong support as almost to conquer the world? What was the fifth column?

What happened to free private enterprise under fascism? To freedom of occupation? Who were the backers of fascism? How were powerful military, aristocratic, and financial interests involved? To what extent and how was fascism aided by the managers of large industrial corporations and the operators of international cartels? By

[1] Adolph Hitler's *Mein Kampf*, 1939 edition, pp. 186, 506.
[2] Raymond E. Murphy and others, *National Socialism*, Washington, 1943, pp. 3-23, also all of pt. III.
[3] Benito Mussolini, *Scritti e Discorsi*, Editione Definitiva, Milan, Vol. V, p. 386; Vol. III, p. 170 also Giovanni Gentile, *Che cosa è il fascismo?* Florence, 1925, p. 38.

1

small businessmen? By the trade unions? By large landowners? By the humble peasants?

How did it lead men to the acts perpetrated at Maidenek or Buchenwald? What was the role of propaganda? Of thought control? Of education? Why the emphasis on purity of blood and race? How did fascism in action spread hate and fear? How did it use and organize popular ignorance, indifference, envy, and nationalistic or racial prejudices?

Answers to these and similar questions will be found in the following pages.

Primacy of the people, nation, and state

All fascist thought starts from a comparatively simple idea, namely, that "a people" form a "natural community" which "becomes conscious of its solidarity and strives to form itself, to develop itself, to defend itself, to realize itself." [4] The nation and state thus become the vehicles by which a people reaches its goals.

In theory * * * the people and state are conceived as * * * inseparable * * * The state is a function of the people * * * It is the form in which the people attains to historical reality * * * [5]

In short the state is the most important power in all fascist thought and action. Everything must be subordinated to the state and must assist in promoting state ends and purposes as they are set forth in the particular fascist program and world outlook (Weltanschauung) concerned.

In practice, as will be seen in the chapters which follow,[6] this reduces itself to government by party leaders and small influential groups, such as Junkers military officials, industrialists, and revolutionary juntas.

The fascist philosophy regards the state as engaged in a conflict to achieve its ends. No one has set forth this idea more tersely or forcefully than Hitler himself when he spoke to the workers of the Rheinmetall-Borsig plant on December 10, 1940. His words were:

We are involved in a conflict in which more than the victory of any one country or the other is at stake; it is rather a war of two opposing worlds.[7]

Thus fascism is a fighting philosophy. Its state is a power state seeking at all times to achieve the greatest possible physical might. It makes no secret of that fact. Neither Mussolini nor Hitler was ever inhibited in telling the world about the powerful military machines they were building. Even in peacetime they spoke of storm troopers, the battle of grain, and the labor front.

This outlook on the world practically forces fascist leaders to use every instrument which will coerce people into obeying the dictates of government. Thus they are quick to perceive the importance of propaganda and thought control. Their ideological concepts and programs are not solely means of rationalizing acts of government, but are important devices for maximizing power.

---

[4] Ernst Rudolf Huber, Verfassungsrecht des grossdeutschen Reiches, Hamburg, 1939, pp. 156-7.
[5] Huber, pp. 165-6.
[6] See especially chapter I, "Government and Political Parties"; VI, "Organization of the Economy: Germany"; and VIII, "Labor".
[7] Adolf Hitler, My New Order, edited by Raoul de Roussy de Sales, New York, 1941, p. 874.

Subordination of the individual

Obviously the individual, his rights, privileges, freedom, and even existence itself are of secondary importance.[8] Human life takes on great value only when it serves a state purpose. In practice the fascist citizen during all of his waking moments has a role to fill, and that role is prescribed for him by the state. He is regimented in a way which defies the comprehension of the average democratic citizen. He must obey the injunctions of the state and its leaders implicitly. The state decides his living standards for him. He must submit to regulations, restrictions, rationing and substitute diets all important to the fascist controlled economy. Life consists of a multitude of duties and schedules to be met. Failure to do one's part is construed as an injury to the community as a whole and therefore punishable by penalties designed to achieve obedience and conformity. And woe to him who criticizes or opposes the government or its representatives.

Even religion does not escape regimentation. Because it causes the citizen to feel reverence for a Higher Power or Supreme Being above the state and earthly fuehrers; because it teaches faith, hope, charity, peace, humility before God but fearless defiance of earthly authorities when in conflict with Divine precepts; and because it preaches dignity of the individual, Christianity in particular becomes the object of attack. This fascistic regimentation of religion was carried to its greatest extreme in Nazi Germany. Thus the famous German General, Erich von Ludendorff,[9] exclaimed "I reject Christianity because it is international, and because, in cowardly fashion, it preaches Peace on Earth." Oswald Spengler, author of The Decline of the West, speaks of "Catholic Bolshevism more dangerous than the anti-Christian" and argues that "all communist systems in the West are in fact derived from Christian theological thought."[10] Alfred Rosenberg felt that "both the Catholic Church and the Evangelical Confessional Church, as they exist at present, must vanish from the life of our people."[11]

However, there are degrees of religious regimentation and sometimes a workable arrangement may be reached between the Church and state as was the case in Italy, Japan, and Spain. But in every instance the primary consideration is the state and such religious freedom as may be permitted is determined by the state and its leaders.

---

[8] Compare these ideas with the democratic concepts familiar to every American school child: All men are created equal. They are endowed by their Creator with certain inalienable rights. Among these rights are life, liberty, and the pursuit of happiness. To secure these rights governments are instituted among men deriving their just powers from the consent of the governed. Ours is a Nation "conceived in liberty and dedicated to the proposition that all men are created equal." The state is not the master but the servant of the individual.

In a speech at Charleston, W. Va. on February 12, 1947, Senator Robert A. Taft summarized the democratic viewpoint as follows:

"Liberty, to me means first, liberty of the individual to choose his own occupation in life and to live and conduct his business as he sees fit so long as he does not thus interfere with the liberty of others; and second the liberty of communities to govern themselves, to decide what the scope of their government actvities shall be and how their children shall live and be educated. Equality means equal opportunity to get started in life, and equal justice under law before impartial tribunals." Congressional Record, February 17, 1947, p. A582.

[9] Erich von Ludendorff, Deutscher Gottglaube. Rolf Tell, Sound and Fuehrer, London, 1939, p. 173.

[10] Oswald Spengler, Jahre der Entscheidung, Deutschland and die weltgeschichtliche Entwicklung, Munich, 1933, p. 128-9.

[11] Alfred Rosenberg in private speech at the Discussion on German Culture, Nuremberg Party Congress, 1938. Catholic Church, The Persecution of the Catholic Church in the Third Reich, Facts and Documents, London, 1940, p. 277.

The result

How then does the fascist program manifest itself? Not only are all political and economic processes and institutions centered upon building a colossus of power, but every social activity, including religious worship, is similarly oriented and directed. The army, the police, the concentration camps, education, newspapers, radio, motion pictures, all enterprises, various "4-year plans," finance, foreign trade, and last but not least, the whole of an individual's leisure time are controlled, utilized and coordinated to produce a power-mass of such overwhelming magnitude in world affairs that nonfascist states will be compelled to move along fascist-controlled orbits or be shattered into impotence.

SOME ORIGINS OF FASCIST DOCTRINES

Political

War and the absolute state. Fascist doctrines reach far back into the past. A few examples will make this clear. As for the war and power state, its background was richly furnished by the blood and iron policy of the founder of modern Germany, Prince Otto von Bismarck, who said that "force creates right; war is a natural law." In like manner, the historian Heinrich von Treitschke wrote his famous History of the German People in the Nineteenth Century around the thesis: "War is the only remedy for ailing nations."

If we look for the concept of an absolute state, which stands above all moral considerations and which possesses the power to treat its citizens without any regard for the individual, we shall find it in Professor Adolf Lasson's works. In 1868 he wrote, "A state is unable to commit any crime." [12] This only paraphrased the doctrines of Johann Gottlieb Fichte (1762–1814), the first Rector of Berlin University, who said:

* * * in relations with other States neither law nor right exists, except the right of the strongest. These relations place in the hands of the prince responsible to Fate the divine right of the Majesty of Destiny and of the Government of the world. [13]

Ethical ideas. These doctrines are far from new. During the sixteenth century, Niccolo Machiavelli wrote in his The Prince (1513): "The Prince must know how to do wrong." This idea the fascist state joins with the thought that political frontiers are merely the expression of power-political situations at a given date—a temporary front line held by the state during the lull between wars. [14] Nations are collective beings which must grow or wither, expand or decline, but which cannot stand still. [15] The struggle for redistribution of space and power is unavoidable and everlasting. Thus the state and the dictator or leader must do everything, regardless of ethical considerations, which will promote the interests of his state. The leader "must not fear to kill nor to bear the brand of infamy." [16] Treaties which stand in the way of the state must be regarded as "scraps of paper," and falsehood and deceit are the regular instruments of international politics.

---

[12] Professor Adolf Lasson, Das Kulturideal und der Krieg, Berlin, 1868, cf. Pages d'Histoire 1914–1915, No. 40, Nancy and Paris, Paroles Allemandes. Préface de L'Abbé Wetterlé, député au Reichstag, pp. 13, 14, 16–18, 29, 37, 66, 105, 129–130.

[13] As quoted from W. W. Coole and M. F. Potter, eds., Thus Speaks Germany, New York and London, 1941, p. 34.

[14] Otto Maull, Politische Grenzen (Political Frontiers), Berlin, 1928.

[15] This doctrine one observer characterizes as "nihilism pure and simple applied to international relations." See Robert Strausz-Hupé, Geopolitics, New York, 1942, p. 220.

[16] W. Fuchs, Medical Counsellor in Die Post, January, 1912, Ernest Hambloch, Germany Rampant, London, p. 65.

How thoroughly these principles were applied by Hitler will be seen if we recall that he, as the head of the German state with only apparent inconsistency, could say in 1935, that "National Socialism has no aggressive intentions against any European nation";[17] in 1936, "we have no territorial demands to make in Europe"[18] (shortly thereafter to foment the international crisis over the Sudeten lands of Czechoslovakia); in 1938, "we do not want any Czechs"[19] (annexation shortly thereafter); in January 1939, "in these weeks we are celebrating the fifth anniversary of the conclusion of the nonaggression pact with Poland. Between them and us peace and understanding shall reign"[20] (unannounced invasion came 8 months later); in September 1938, "we have called upon the constructive elements in all countries to fight in common against Bolshevism"[21] (to be followed in 1939, by a nonaggression pact hailed as a "triumph for common sense").[22]

Geopolitical. In the early part of the twentieth century the doctrine of the fascist monolithic fused politico-economic state, best typified in Germany, reached its fullest exposition in the works of a Pan-Germanic Swedish professor at Upsala named Kjellen. He maintained that the living state is manifest in five aspects: Territory or Realm (Reich), People (Volk), Economy (Haushalt or Grossraumwirtschaft), Society (Gemeinschaft), and Government (Regierung). Asserting that there was room on the European continent for only one great state, he set its bounds from Dunkirk to Riga, Hamburg to Bagdad, with an extension into middle Africa.

Kjellen's views were adopted by Haushofer and his Geopolitical Institute.[23] They became the blueprint of fascist thought in Germany and elsewhere. "The Heartland dominates the World Island and the World Island rules the World."[24] That was the geopolitical formula whether applied to Mussolini's "Mare Nostrum" or Japan's "Greater East Asia Co-Prosperity Sphere."

Economic

The economic ideal of fascism wherever it appears is economic autarchy. No imports, keep out the foreigner, substitutes (Ersatz), expansion by conquest, colonization, amalgamation, barter arrangements, cartel agreements—these are the favored activities. The era of free world trade and individualism is regarded as past. The future, they say, belongs to the giant totalitarian fortress economy.

Such ideas go back hundreds of years to the writings of seventeenth and eighteenth century English mercantilists, to Philipp Hoernigh's Oestereich Ueber Alles, Wenn es Nur Will (Austria a Ruler of the World If It Wills It), to Kameralists in Prussia and to Colbert and other mercantilists in France, Italy, and Spain.

It is Friedrich List, however, who is frequently held to have been most responsible for popularizing modern fascist or totalitarian economics. Returning from the United States where he had come under the influence of the ardent nationalism of Henry Clay and the protectionism of Alexander Hamilton, List in 1842, published The

[17] Adolf Hitler, Party Rally, September 11, 1935. Tell, p. 22.
[18] Adolf Hitler, Speech to the Reichstag on the day of the military occupation of the Rhineland, March 7, 1936. Tell, p. 17.
[19] Adolf Hitler, Speech at the Sportpalast, Berlin, August 26, 1938. Tell, p. 20.
[20] Adolf Hitler, Speech to the Reichstag, January 30, 1939. Tell, p. 24.
[21] Dr. Goebbels, at Party Rally, September 13, 1938. Tell, p. 31.
[22] Adolf Hitler, Speech on anniversary of the abortive 1923 putsch, Munich, November 8, 1939. Tell, p. 30.
[23] See A. Whitney Griswold, Paving the Way for Hitler, Atlantic Monthly, March, 1941, p. 31 ff.
[24] This phraseology is that of the English Sir Halford Mackinder in his article "The Geographical Pivot of History" published in The Geographical Journal, No. 4, April, 1904, Vol. XXII, Royal Geographical Society, London.

National System of Political Economy in which he insisted that
Germany needed complete protectionism and economic isolationism
coupled with expansion over an area reaching from the North and
Baltic Seas to the Black Sea and the Adriatic.[25]

When List's ideas were joined with the geopolitical teachings of
Haushofer they produced a program which called for a greater German
Reich in which were to be concentrated all strategic technological
skills and productivity. All other European states were to be colonies
providing raw materials, and when the need arose, low-paid labor.[26]
The famous publicist Ernst Hasse spoke as early as 1905 of filling
Germany's need for laborers to do heavy and dirty work by "our
condemning alien European stocks, the Poles, Czechs, Jews, Italians,
and so on, who live under us or find their way to us, to these helot's
occupations."[27]

So far as areas beyond fascist political dominance are concerned,
for international economic relationships is, of course, warfare, economic warfare.[28] It is waged in times of peace, as well as during
actual hostilities, only in less violent form.[29]

The economy thus built up is one of mercantilism, economic autarchy, corporate aggrandizement coupled with colonialism and imperialism, a self-sufficient area thoroughly organized and controlled,
continuously waging economic warfare.

The economic doctrines of fascism likewise run directly counter to
democratic principles. Basic freedoms such as freedom of occupation, free competitive markets, free international flow of goods, services and capital, and free private enterprise generally are either greatly
restricted or eliminated.

CONCLUSION

In conclusion, fascism in many ways is deeply rooted in ancient
ideas and institutions. Politically, it has drawn generously upon the
theories of absolutism, the supreme right of kings, dictatorship and
tyranny, ideas older than the ancient Pharaohs, Nebuchadnezzar,
Alexander the Great, and Caesar. In economic terms fascism reverts
to a mercantilism the supposed destruction of which, by Adam Smith
in his famous Wealth of Nations in 1776, is often considered to have
been the beginning of scientific economics. In cultural terms fascism
is an effort to turn back the spread of Christian concepts of the
brotherhood of man—against all liberal, humanitarian ideas which
have pioneered the emancipation of the underprivileged, racially,
culturally, and socially.

In subsequent chapters we shall see how it actually worked out—
primarily in Germany and Italy, but to a lesser extent in Spain and
Japan. Little or nothing will be said about fascism in Poland, Yugoslavia, Rumania, and certain other countries in Europe, Asia, and
South America where elements of fascist doctrine, organization, and
practice still persist.

[25] This doctrine became an obsession with geographers, e. g., Karl Ritter's Einleitung zur Allgemeinen Vergleichenden Geographie, Berlin, 1852; Friedrich Ratzel's Ueber die Gesetze des Raeumlichen Wachstums der Staaten, Leipzig, 1901; also Friedrich Naumann's Mitteleuropa, Berlin, 1916.
[26] Strausz-Hupé, p. 163.
[27] Ernst Hasse, Deutsche Politik, vol. 1, Das deutsche Reich als Nationalstaat, Munich, 1905, pp. 61–62. For a compilation of literally thousands of quotations documenting from German sources the political, economic, and social totalitarian views indicated in this chapter see W. W. Coole and M. F. Potter, editors, Thus Speaks Germany, New York and London, 1941.
[28] "Geopolitically speaking," says one observer, "Germany did not go to war in 1939; she had been at war all the time." See Strausz-Hupé, p. 101.
[29] See Arthur Dix, Wirtschaftskrieg und Kriegswirtschaft, Berlin, 1936.

PART I—POLITICAL

CHAPTER I—GOVERNMENT AND POLITICAL PARTIES

GERMANY

During the interwar period Germany was at first a parliamentary republic under the Weimar Constitution (1919–32) and then a total dictatorship under Hitler's Third Reich (1933–39). Under the ill-fated Weimar regime Germany had a parliamentary form of government on the French and English models. The chancellor and ministers were responsible to the Reichstag which was elected by universal suffrage and proportional representation. The German states (Laender) were represented in a second chamber (Reichsrat), and provision was made for direct legislation via popular initiative and referendum. A popularly elected president with broad powers was chosen for a 7-year term with indefinite reeligibility. The presidency was held in turn by Ebert and von Hindenburg, but disappeared after the latter's death in 1934. There were 20 cabinets during the German republican regime—all short-lived coalitions which broke up or collapsed from internal friction.

Described in 1919 as the "most democratic democracy in the world," the Weimar system succumbed 14 years later to a combination of circumstances. The internal weakness of the republic, its lack of inspiring leadership and popular support, bureaucratic sabotage, the multiplicity of warring parties created by proportional representation, economic depression, the humiliating treatment of Germany by the Allies, her defeat in the First World War, the harsh Treaty of Versailles, antisemitism, the influence of the reactionary upper classes and the military clique, Nazi propaganda, and Hitler's dynamic leadership—all contributed to the overthrow of the republic and the triumph of the National Socialist movement in 1933.[1] And in addition, Article 48 of the Weimar constitution provided that the President of the Reich might intervene, with armed force if necessary, to restore "public security and order" when they were seriously disturbed. He might in time of emergency abrogate certain fundamental rights, including the freedoms of speech, press, and assembly and might remove guarantees of personal liberty and property rights. Thus the National Socialist Party under the leadership of Adolf Hitler rose to power in Germany within the legal framework of the constitution.

After a series of political crises Hitler was named chancellor on January 30, 1933. The Reichstag was dissolved and, after a reign of terror, a new Reichstag under Nazi control was elected and promptly conferred dictatorial powers upon Hitler. All rival political parties were quickly outlawed, liquidated, or dissolved; their property confiscated, and their leaders imprisoned. In a series of subsequent

---

[1] For information on the support of Hitler and his party during their rise by men of wealth in Germany, see ch. VI, "Organization of the Economy: Germany."

decrees the electoral system was emasculated, the Reichsrat suppressed, the states converted into agencies of the central government, provincial and local governments reorganized, the civil service nazified, the church "coordinated," and the National Socialist Party made the only political party in Germany. In a few months the Third Reich became a one-party state, the Weimar system was destroyed, and the entire pattern of government remade.

GOVERNMENT OF THE THIRD REICH

The governmental structure of the Third Reich included the Fuehrer, the Reich Cabinet and the ministries over which they presided, the civil service, the Reichstag and the plebiscite, the courts, and the Laender.

Position of the Fuehrer

Although the Weimar constitution was never formally amended or repealed, it was largely superseded by the Enabling Act of 1933 and a series of organic laws of dubious legal validity upon which the Nazi regime based its constitutional status. These laws conferred supreme power upon Hitler who also inherited the powers of the Reich president and chancellor. He appointed and dismissed cabinet ministers and other officials, summoned and dissolved the Reichstag, commanded the armed forces, controlled the introduction and passage of all laws, and dominated Germany's foreign relations. As head of the state, leader of the Nazi Party, and "bearer of the legal will of the racial community," the Fuehrer was supreme. According to mystical National Socialist doctrine, the Fuehrer fused state, party, and people into a single amalgam. Responsible only to his conscience, he was the state and the state was the product of his will. Nazism became a political religion in which Hitler was the chief apostle, the infallible leader, and "the greatest German of all times." In such a secular theology there was clearly no place for the democratic faith in a majority rule, separated powers, or constitutional government.

Ministers and departments

Since the fascist philosophy is essentially a totalitarian philosophy, it is basic that all aspects of life must be regulated and directed to the state purpose. Therefore, while the National Socialist government accepted all existing governmental agencies, it also created a number of new ones to control hitherto unregulated areas of human activity. Notable among these new agencies were the Security Service, the Propaganda Ministry, and the Ribbentrop Bureau.

In the Third Reich cabinet government in the sense of collective deliberation and ministerial responsibility to parliament disappeared. Hitler appointed, directed, and removed members of the Cabinet at his own discretion. They were his subordinates, not his colleagues, and were personally responsible to him. Government decrees were signed by Hitler and countersigned by the minister concerned. Cabinet meetings were seldom held and differences of opinion between ministers were resolved by the Fuehrer or his deputy, Hess, who was succeeded by Martin Bornmann.

The members of the Reich cabinet were all members of the Nazi Party; the key positions were held by "old fighters" who had risen to power with Hitler. Most of the ministers were rank amateurs as far as previous administrative experience was concerned, yet many of them proved to be able organizers and executives. Under their management and Hitler's despotic and dynamic will, German economy and society were completely transformed and the country equipped for total war.

Civil service

Under the Third Reich the German civil service was completely nationalized and nazified. A series of cabinet acts and decrees converted the service into a fundamental pillar of the National Socialist state. Jews, married women, and nonsupporters of the Nazi regime were dismissed. The national, state, and local services were merged into one combined service, under uniform regulations; the traditional political neutrality of the services was negated; members were required to take an oath of fealty to the Fuehrer; and the entire service was transformed into an army of Hitler's plain clothesmen. Fear and uncertainty undermined the morale and efficiency of the service and left a lasting impress upon its ideals and methods. After the Nazis had "restored" the civil service in 1933, they enacted a comprehensive civil service code in 1937, which replaced all previous law on the subject and applied alike to national civil servants, municipal officials, school teachers, college professors, judges, et al. To be sure, many features of the old system were not changed, but its traditional foundations were shattered.

Under the 1937 law, personnel matters were handled separately by each department; there was no central civil service commission; racial purity and political reliability became additional qualifications for admission to the service; after long probation and careful examination men could become "officials" for life at 27 and women at 35; civil servants could be disciplined and dismissed for many offenses; special disciplinary courts were provided to consider removals; salary scales with periodic advances were fixed; generous noncontributory retirement provisions were made; and a Nazi-controlled union of civil servants was set up.

Reichstag and plebiscite

Nazi Germany retained an elective Reichstag to give the regime the look of legality, to rubber-stamp governmental policies previously determined, and to listen to and applaud Hitler's harangues. During the Nazi era the Reichstag increased in size to more than 800 members selected solely by the party leaders from the National Socialist Party. But it met briefly only 11 times during the first 6 years of the regime and passed only five laws. In short, the Reichstag ceased to be a deliberative assembly and served only as a sounding board and ratifier of the Fuehrer's decision.

Three types of legislation were theoretically conceivable under the Third Reich: laws passed by the Reichstag, laws accepted by popular plebiscite, and laws enacted by government decree. In practice, however, the Reichstag was seldom convoked, and plebiscites were rarely held and then only on popular proposals such as Germany's withdrawal from the League of Nations and the annexation of Austria which were overwhelmingly approved. For all practical purposes, the cabinet legislated by government decree, subject to the desires of Hitler whose will was the law.

The courts

Under Empire and Republic, German justice was administered in state courts, and judges were appointed for life by state authorities after long and special training. During the dictatorship, however, all the German courts were nationalized, state judges and officials were brought under the supervision of the Ministry of Justice at Berlin, and the administration of justice was entirely subjected to Reich control. The judiciary was "purified" by the dismissal of Jewish and politically unreliable judges who were unwilling to swear allegiance to the Fuehrer and to subscribe to Nazi ideology. Judicial independence and permanence of tenure disappeared. Justice ceased to be administered impartially and court decisions were influenced by political considerations. Under the Weimar constitution a national supreme court (Reichsgericht) had power to pass upon the constitutionality of state laws, but the Nazi decrees were ipso facto valid and not subject to judicial review.

To the old ordinary and administrative courts the Nazis added many special courts to deal with particular types of litigation. Outstanding among them was the peoples court (Volksgerichtshof), appointed by Hitler and charged with handling all cases of high treason and treason against the country, which served as a powerful weapon of party discipline.

Under national socialism the Fuehrer was the supreme source of law. Whether revealed through decree, statute, ordinance, or edict, his will was the law and by it judges and courts were bound. The rule of law in the traditional sense was completely destroyed and "justice" was administered to serve the political ends of the Nazi regime. The criminal law was entirely revolutionized and people were punished and thrown into concentration camps at the discretion of the criminal courts without having violated any statute. Due process of law was abolished, and justice was degraded into a tool of a political party.

Reich and Laender

Before the rise of the dictatorship, Germany had been a federal union composed of politically independent and administratively autonomous states whose pattern was shaped by the accidents of dynastic history. Under the Third Reich, however, the country was transformed not only from a multi-party parliamentary state into a totalitarian one-party state, but also from a federal to a unitary and centralized state. This transformation was achieved by a series of coordinating and organic acts during 1933–35, the ultimate effect of which was to reduce the once sovereign states (Laender) to mere administrative agencies of the Reich. For each state Hitler appointed and dismissed Reich regents who took their orders from the several Reich ministers and functioned as intermediary agents between the central and local governments. Hitler rewarded some of his "old fighters" by distributing these spoils of office among them. Like the French departmental prefects, the regents were the political bosses of their districts to which they applied the general policies of the Reich. The functions of government were gradually transferred from the states to Berlin, the Laender diets were liquidated, uniform Reich laws were passed in many fields formerly reserved to the states, and the Laender governments and their officials became organs of the Reich.

Prussia, the largest German state, was completely absorbed by the Third Reich. Hitler became its regent and Goering its president, responsible only to the Fuehrer. The Reich cabinet became ex-officio the Prussian cabinet and absorbed the latter's departments and administrative functions, except in the field of finance. Before 1914 Prussia controlled the Reich. After 1933 the Reich controlled Prussia whose government became an integral part of the Reich government.

Thus, the Nazis transformed Germany into a unitary state composed in 1940 of eleven Laender, each with a Reich regent. When Austria was annexed in March 1938, it was divided into seven territorial districts (Reichsgaue) each headed by a Reich regent. And when the Sudetenland was incorporated into the Third Reich in 1939, it was likewise organized into a district of the Reich with its own Reich regent. After recovery of the land lost at Versailles and the conquest of France and the splinter states, provincial governors and Nazi commissioners were appointed to administer them.

NATIONAL SOCIALIST PARTY (DIE NATIONALSOZIALISTISCHE DEUTSCHE ARBEITERPARTEI OR NSDAP)

From 1933 until her defeat by the Allies in the Second World War, Germany was a one-party state. The National Socialist Party was the only political party allowed by law, all others having been dissolved. The NSDAP became a state within the state, a public corporation exempt from the general laws of the land. Party officials acquired control of the entire machinery of government and held all its offices—national, state, and local. Party members were regarded as an elite above the common law, and were assigned duties enforceable in special party courts. Although separable in legal theory, party and state were closely integrated in practice, with the same persons performing both party and state functions. Between them they constituted the Third Reich and exercised all its authority.[2]

German citizens of pure descent, 18 years of age or over, and of tested quality were eligible for membership. Party members took an oath of fealty to the Fuehrer. Seven organizations made up the main strength of the party, of which the three most important were the storm troops (750,000), the elite guard (200,000), and the Hitler Youth (10,000,000). Affiliated with the party were eight additional auxiliary organizations, including the German Labor Front which had more than 20,000,000 members.

The internal organization of the NSDAP was described as the most complete and elaborate of any political party in the world. Its physical facilities, staffs, and financial resources were likewise unequalled. From bottom to top the party hierarchy consisted of house-groups composed of members living in the same building, blocks, cells, local groups, county and district units, with a party cabinet of 19 members and a treasurer—crowned at the peak of the pyramid by the Fuehrer and his deputy and a large staff at national headquarters. Each group at each level had its party leader, from the apartment-house janitors to the district Gauleiters, with lines of responsibility and control running up through the hierarchy. This elaborate structure was paralleled by a series of functional agencies

---

[1] An interesting illustration of this unity of party and state in practice is seen in the fact that while the party flag could be flown without the national flag of Germany, the national flag could not be flown without that of the party.

which carried on party activities in the fields of propaganda, publicity, and defense; and by a hierarchy of party courts which maintained party discipline and settled internal disputes.

During its heyday the National Socialist Party held annual party congresses at Nuremberg in September which were attended by upwards of 500,000 party members and others. These great spectacles,[3] with their colorful pageantry and symbolic ritual, were designed to evoke party fervor and impress the nation and the world with the invincibility of the Nazis. Through the indoctrination of the rising generation, the militarization of the university curriculum, and the far-flung activities of the Ministry of Popular Enlightenment and Propaganda, the Nazis undertook to control public opinion, train the future leaders of the regime, and promote the objectives of the authoritarian state. Despite its grandiose aims and impressive achievements, the life span of the totalitarian one-party state proved in the end to be as brief as the democratic Weimar system which preceded it.[4]

ITALY

Recent Italian political history falls into two periods: the liberal-parliamentary period from the achievement of Italian unity in 1870 to the Fascist revolution of 1922, and the period of Fascist dictatorship from 1922 to the Allied defeat of Italy in 1945. At the close of the First World War the government of Italy was a constitutional monarchy with a king, who as in England was a symbol but not a power; an elected Chamber of Deputies, which had absorbed all legislative power and eclipsed the nominated Senate; a powerful administration subject in principle to legislative control; with general manhood suffrage in which the electorate was free and active; and with individual rights amply secured.

CHIEF CONSTITUTIONAL FEATURES

Since 1848, the fundamental law of Italy has been the Statuto or constitution granted by Charles Albert, King of Piedmont (Sardinia). Under the Statuto the Italian government developed along liberal and democratic lines until the Fascists seized power in October 1922. Upon the outward forms of constitutional monarchy the Fascists superimposed a military dictatorship dominated by one party—the Fascist Party—ruled by one man—Benito Mussolini. Democratic government was replaced by an individual autocracy which was at once authoritarian, hierarchical, highly centralized, and antidemocratic.

Although the Statuto remained nominally in force after 1922, the Fascists revolutionized the structure and operation of the government. In place of the traditional system of separated powers, they concentrated all real power in the "chief of the government." They replaced a parliamentary democracy by a "corporative system" in which the Chamber of Corporations, composed ex-officio, represented Italians

---

[3] See ch. XII, Use of Leisure Time.
[4] Information concerning the political institutions of Nazi Germany has been obtained chiefly from the following sources: F. A. Ogg, European Governments and Politics, New York, 1939, ch. XXXVI, XXXVII, XXXVIII, and XXXIX; Civil Affairs Handbook on Germany, sec. 2, Government and Administration, prepared for the Military Government Division of the Office of the Provost Marshal General by the Office of Strategic Services; and a War Department education manual, Governments of Continental Europe, 1940, vol. 1, by James T. Shotwell et al., Government and Politics in Germany by Karl Loewenstein, pt. IV, sec. II, The Governmental Structure of the Third Reich.

on an occupational rather than on a territorial basis. They recognized only one political party—their own, and they destroyed the civil rights and personal liberties of the Italian citizen. In short, they changed the Italian constitution from a democracy to a virtual autocracy.

THE NATIONAL GOVERNMENT

During the Fascist regime (1922–45) the national government of Italy consisted of the executive, legislative, and corporative branches, each with its various councils and other organs, all of which were subject to Mussolini's will.

The executive

The executive branch comprised the King, the Duce, the Grand Council of Fascism, and the Council of Ministers or Cabinet.

Victor Emmanuel III, King of Italy and Albania, and Emperor of Ethiopia after the conquest of that country, was the nominal executive. Born in 1869, he ascended the Italian throne in 1900, and withdrew in 1946 in favor of his son, Prince Humbert.

Benito Mussolini was the actual executive. As Prime Minister and leader of the Fascist Party, Il Duce was the all-powerful dictator of Italy. Born in 1883, he was a revolutionary Socialist in his youth. After being expelled from the Socialist Party for advocating intervention in the First World War on the Allied side, he founded the Fascist movement in 1919. And he formed his first cabinet on October 30, 1922, after the successful March on Rome.

During the Fascist period, the executive power in Italy was exercised by the Prime Minister as head of the government. He was responsible only to the King and was not, as formerly, subject to parliamentary votes of confidence. Individual ministers were appointed and dismissed by the King upon his proposal. They were responsible to the King and Mussolini and functioned as the latter's agents. As head of the government, Il Duce controlled all legislative activity. No measure could come before Parliament without his approval. He could override the law in any matter that pertained to public utility institutions, issue royal decrees in the King's name, command the army and navy, dismiss judges and magistrates, and appoint only Fascists to government posts. Armed with these powers, he was the real master of Italy for almost a quarter-century.

The Grand Council of Fascism was the general staff of the Fascist regime. It was composed of 24 high officials of the Fascist Party, including Mussolini, the party secretary, the quadrumvirs of the March on Rome, the presidents of the Senate and Chamber of Corporations, seven ministers, and the presidents of the industrial and agricultural confederations. At first a party organ, the Grand Council became an organ of the state in December 1928. As the supreme organ which coordinated and integrated all the activities of the Fascist regime, it had important deliberative and advisory functions on constitutional, legislative, and party matters. Mussolini served as president of the Grand Council, called its meetings, fixed its agenda, appointed its members, and through it controlled the life of the country.

In addition to the dictator and the Grand Council, the executive branch of the Fascist government included the Council of Ministers who had jurisdiction, in 1943, over 18 ministries. Cabinet ministers were appointed and dismissed by the King on the proposal of the head of the government. Like the Grand Council, the Cabinet was Mussolini's instrument. He convoked it, presided over it, determined its personnel, and assumed as many portfolios as he chose. He also directed and coordinated the work of the ministers and adjusted differences between them. The Cabinet performed basic executive, legislative, and administrative functions. Its legislative functions were even more important than those of Parliament because it prepared and gave legal effect to the decrees and decree-laws which were eventually rubber-stamped by Parliament.

The legislative

The Italian Parliament under Fascism consisted of two chambers: the Senate and the Chamber of Deputies (which was replaced in 1938 by the new Fascist and Corporative Chamber). Neither body was popularly elected and they had virtually no real legislative power. Both houses discussed bills, usually in committees rather than in plenary sessions, and rubber-stamped the decree-laws of the executive.

The Senate consisted of about 500 life members appointed by the King usually upon the proposal of the head of the government. The nominated membership, recruited from 21 categories, included representatives of the aristocracy, bureaucracy, and liberal professions. The Senate sat as a high court of justice in cases involving high treason, attempts against the security of the state, trials of ministers, and of its own members.

The old Chamber of Deputies continued in existence until 1938, but was transformed by the electoral laws of 1923 and 1928 from a freely elected body of 535 members, chosen by manhood suffrage with proportional representation, into a corporative parliament of 400 loyal Fascist members nominated by national confederations of Fascist syndicates and certain non-industrial units. From 1,000 such nominees the Fascist Grand Council selected 400 names to be placed, as a "national list," before the voters, who could vote "yes" or "no" only for the list as a whole. Only Fascists of proved loyalty were nominated, opposition speeches in the electoral campaign were forbidden, and the Grand Council could remove any deputy. Tricolor-decorated "yes" ballots and plain "no" ballots enabled anyone to see how any elector voted. Other methods of controlling elections included murder in the case of obstreperous individuals like Matteotti, beatings, and doses of castor oil before elections. Under these conditions, the composition of the Chamber was overwhelmingly Fascist and real representative government a farce. Although the law entitled employers and workers to equal representation, the system was weighted heavily in favor of the employers and against employees and farmers.

In 1938, the old Chamber was abolished and a new Fascist and Corporative Chamber set up. The new Chamber was composed of about 650 members called "national councilors" who were appointed ex officiis by Mussolini for indefinite terms. Its membership included the head of the government, the members of the Fascist Grand Council (25), the members of the National Council of the Fascist Party (120), and the members of the National Corporative Council (500). The National Party Council consisted of the party secretary, the national directors, party inspectors, and federal secretaries. The National Corporative Council consisted of Il Duce, Cabinet members and Undersecretaries of State, certain party officers, certain party representatives in the corporations, the presidents of 9 syndical confederations, and the active members of the councils of the 22 category corporations. Every member of the new Chamber owed his appointment to Mussolini, who could remove him and who thus controlled the new body as effectively as he had the old handpicked Chamber of Deputies.

The corporative system

The executive and legislative institutions described above marked the apex of the pyramid of the Italian corporate state. Beneath them was an elaborate network of syndicates, federations, confederations, and corporations which together constituted the corporate system.

At the bottom of the pyramid were the Fascist syndical associations. These were unions at the local and provincial levels of all workers within a particular occupation. Membership was not compulsory, but was open to all citizens over 18 years of age, of "good moral and political character," and to foreigners who had resided within the kingdom for 10 years. Employers belonged to similar associations of employers. These local associations were then organized into national federations which were, in turn, grouped into confederations for nine broad segments of the economy. Thus, there were separate confederations for employers and workers engaged in agriculture, industry, commerce, and credit and insurance; and a confederation of professional men and artists which included both employers and workers. At the end of 1939, these confederations numbered 11.3 million members, of whom 2.9 million were employers and 8.4 million were workers.

The corporations were the organs which gave the corporate state its name. Although established by the law of February 5, 1934, they were in existence prior to this date as evidenced by clause VI of the Labor Charter, by the law of April 3, 1926, and by the royal decree of July 1, 1926. They were boards or councils consisting of representatives of employers, workers, the Fascist Party, and the government, formed within each of the 22 major subdivisions of the national economy. They had consultative, conciliatory, and normative powers. They advised the government on technical questions and were empowered to conciliate collective labor disputes [5] and to "enact rules for the collective regulation of economic relations and the unitary discipline of national production." They could make rules for the control of production and fair competition and fix prices for goods and services. Each corporation was composed of an equal number of workers' and employers' representatives, plus three members of the Fascist Party to represent consumers. In December 1939, the 22 corporations had 500 members divided as follows:

Fascist Party	66
Agriculture	132
Industry	132
Commerce	60
Professions and arts	58
Others	52
Total	500

[5] See ch. VIII, Labor, also ch. VII, Organization of the economy: Italy, Spain, Japan.

The functioning of the whole syndical and corporate system was carried on in accordance with the government's general economic and political program by the Ministry of Corporations. This ministry, which resembled the Departments of Commerce and Labor in the United States, granted official recognition to individual syndical associations and approved their bylaws; supervised the activities and finances of all the syndicates; drafted labor and social security legislation and recorded collective labor agreements; and served as secretariat for the 22 corporations of which the Minister of Corporations was ex-officio chairman.

The avowed aims of the Fascist corporate system were the regulation of labor relations through the negotiation of collective agreements, the settlement of labor disputes through arbitration or the decisions of governmental labor courts, and the carrying out of the Fascist economic program as a whole. During the Second World War the corporate system was extensively used to achieve a maximum of governmental control over the Italian economy.

Like other organs of the period, the corporate system was dominated by the Fascist Party. Members of the Chamber and officials of the corporations and syndicates were required to be party members and were bound by their oath of obedience to the party leader. Despite the facade of representative institutions, no free or open clash of interests or opinion was possible within the corporate structure. No important decision could be reached, no plan approved, no measure enforced that lacked the consent and support of the party hierarchy. Rather than a means for industrial self-government, the Italian syndical and corporate system was but an instrument of economic control employed by the Fascist Party and the Fascist state in the pursuit of Fascism's ultimate political ends.[6]

Provincial and local government

For purposes of local government Fascist Italy, excluding Rome, was divided into 98 provinces and over 7,300 communes. Under the basic law of 1934 these subdivisions, which once enjoyed considerable local autonomy, were subordinated to the central government. The provinces became areas of national administration and were administered by centrally appointed prefects. The prefects were the source of all provincial activity which received its impulse, coordination, and direction from them. They could suspend the local magistrates and councils, fix their size, and pass ordinances. Important subsidiary agencies of provincial government included: (1) an inspection service which assisted the prefect in supervising provincial and communal administration; (2) a prefectoral council with fiscal supervisory functions; (3) a giunta which had certain advisory and approval functions and acted as a provincial administrative tribunal; and (4) a provincial president and rectory, appointed from and removable by Rome which administered the resources and public institutions of the province.

The commune was administered by the podesta or magistrate who was appointed and removable by royal decree and who exercised both executive and legislative powers under instructions from the provincial prefect. Each commune had a council (consulta) appointed by the

---

[6] This is brought out also in ch. VIII, Labor, and particularly in ch. VII, Organization of the Economy: Italy, Spain, Japan.

prefect from persons nominated by the local syndicates, varying in size with population. Councilors held office for 5 years and could be reappointed. The council was purely an advisory body to the podesta who presided over it, framed its agenda, and consulted it on different subjects.

The basic law of 1934 also provided for the creation of joint local authorities among provinces and communes to provide for specific services or improvements, subject to the approval of the Minister of the Interior and the control of the prefect.

Rome had a special administration known as the Governatorato which was headed by a governor comparable to a podesta. The governor was appointed by the Minister of the Interior after consulting the Council of Ministers and was advised by a council of 12 members.

THE FASCIST PARTY

During the Fascist regime Italy was a one-party state. After the establishment of the National Fascist Party in 1921, all other parties disappeared and were officially abolished in 1926. In this respect Italy set the common fascist pattern of single-party politics.

Relations between the party and the state developed through successive stages. At first the party lacked official status and Parliament included opposition members. Later, responsible parliamentary government was abandoned, local and provincial Fascist federations were recognized by law, and the party's Grand Council became an organ of the state and was assigned the task of preparing electoral lists. After 1929, the internal organization and discipline of the party became matters of public law, its national secretary was appointed by royal decree, and given the status of minister in 1937, and the constitution of the party was prescribed in successive decrees. Described in an act of 1932 as "a civil militia under the order of the Leader in the service of the Fascist state," the party finally emerged as a state organ and the party officials as public officers.

Party membership, at first unlimited, was later restricted to recruits from youth organizations (Young Fascists), but later liberalized to admit outsiders. All members were required to take an oath of obedience to the leader and to serve the Fascist revolution. The total membership of the party was upwards of 3,000,000, of whom about half were adult males and half various women's and youth auxiliaries, compared with a total national population of 41,000,000. Belief in party principles, expediency, and the prospect of perquisites induced men to join. Party discipline was quite strict and occasional purges occurred.

In its internal structure the party consisted of some 10,000 local lodges or chapters (fasci di combattimento) formed in the communes on the authority of the national party secretary and grouped into provincial federations, each with a secretary nominated by the national secretary and appointed by Mussolini. Organized from the top down, the party hierarchy included the 94 Federal secretaries of the provincial federations, a National Directorate of 13 members, and other agencies and functionaries, crowned by the national party secretary and the Grand Council of Fascism—all subject to the will of Il Duce. The Grand Council had broad advisory and approval powers. Both a party and state organ, it transcended the Senate and Corporative Chamber and, with Mussolini, really ruled Italy.

Financed at first by men of wealth as a defense against socialism,[7] the Fascist Party later depended upon membership fees and annual dues, special levies and assessments which furnished it ample funds. Party discipline and prestige were maintained by a variety of rituals, celebrations, and competitions, while the populace was indoctrinated by institutes of Fascist culture, a rigid censorship, and a vigorous party press led by Mussolini's personal paper, Popolo d'Italia.[8] In short, the party was a major instrument for achieving and preserving Fascism in power, lending the regime some semblance of a democratic foundation, while meeting the needs of autocracy.[9]

SPAIN

BACKGROUND

Spain, a traditional monarchy, returned to the rule of the Bourbons after an interlude of Republican government from 1869 to 1875. The position of the monarchy was weakened during the following half century by both internal and external pressures.

The dictatorship of Primo de Rivera, 1923-30

The depression following the First World War and the defeat in the Moroccan campaign together with the increasing activities of the Spanish Communists and the break-up of the old political parties led to the coup d'état of 1923 in which Primo de Rivera took control of the government with the consent of the king. Reforms were put into effect but at the expense of human independence and freedom, and the Spanish people grew restless. The dictator, increasingly unpopular and failing in health, resigned June 1930. General Berenguer, followed by Admiral Aznar, became dictator supporting the throne. As a result of their failures, antidictatorship sentiment became antimonarchist as well.

The Republican regime, 1931-36

Fanned by Communist agitation the tame "revolution" of 1931 began when municipal elections went against the Government, and King Alphonso III fled Madrid on April 14. A provisional government drew up a new constitution which was approved by the popularly elected legislative body (Cortes). Spain was declared a "democratic republic of workers of all classes" and her foreign policy was tied to that of the League of Nations. The constitution declared that Spain had no official religion, established freedom of worship, right of divorce, civil marriage, and lay education. A coalition government of Socialist-Left Republican dominance was formed by Manuel Azaña on October 14, 1931.

The new Cortes enacted reforms in church and state relations, labor laws, provincial government, education, and distribution of land. However, continual strikes and revolts forced suspension of constitutional guarantees and led to the victory of the conservative CEDA of Gil Robles in the election of November 19, 1933. Unorganized up-

---

[7] See also ch. VII, Organization of the Economy: Italy, Spain, Japan.
[8] See ch. II, Education and Thought Control; ch. XII, Use of Leisure Time; and ch. XIV, Freedom.
[9] Ogg, ch. XLI, especially pp. 829-835. Information concerning the political institutions of Fascist Italy has been obtained chiefly from the following sources: F. A. Ogg, chs. XL, XLI, and XLII; Civil Affairs Handbook on Italy, section Two on "Government and Administration", prepared for the Military Government Division of the Office of the Provost Marshal General by the Office of Strategic Services; and a War Department Education Manual—Governments of Continental Europe, 1940, vol. 2, by James T. Shotwell et al., chs. I-VII on The Government and Politics of Italy by Arnold J. Zurcher.

risings (particularly in October 1934) protested the policies of this reactionary government. During this two-year period of lethargy and depression, of "masterly inactivity" on the part of the government, José Antonio Primo de Rivera, son of the late dictator, founded the Fascist party in Spain.

Parties of the right organized an anti-Marxist alliance while the parties of the left led by Manuel Azaña formed the Communist dominated Popular Front which was victorious in the elections of February 1936.

Revolutionary period, 1936–39

On July 17, 1936, troops in Spanish Morocco under General Francisco Franco revolted, and soon the whole country was involved in civil war. The leaders of this movement were cordially received in Rome and Berlin. Italian Fascism was seeking more glory to quiet the population, and German fascism needed a testing ground for its weapons soon to be used against France and Britain. The revolution succeeded only in certain backward areas until aided by Italian aircraft and German warships. The Republicans were untrained and unorganized, but the workers were armed and fought "with the enthusiastic strength of a mass movement." Great moral support, though little practical assistance, from the international brigades helped the spirit of the Republicans immensely. Russian contributions in men and arms, which were the first on the scene, were substantial although not on the same scale as those of Germany and Italy. The Spanish Civil War became not only a military conflict and a social struggle between reaction and revolutionary changes, but also a focal point for the clash of ideologies and of international rivalry. On September 30, 1936, the Rebel Junta formalized General Franco's de facto leadership and made him practical dictator. An edict proclaiming the end of the war was issued by General Franco on April 1, 1939, immediately after the fall of Madrid.

NATIONAL GOVERNMENT OF FASCIST SPAIN

The Falange Española Tradicionalista (FET), Franco's Fascist Party in Spain, was not the state, but it was inextricably tied to the state. During the civil war, the only government in Nationalist Spain was that of the party. "In its national services, its national council, and its Junta Política, the party possessed the semblance of a civil administration, a deliberate assembly, and a cabinet while there still did not exist any of these in the State, and when in due course these latter came into being, those of the party succeeded in various directions either in claiming for themselves functions properly pertaining to the State or in intertwining themselves with the corresponding State organizations." [10]

Program of the national government

The principal features of Franco's "broadly totalitarian" rule were: Abolition of popular suffrage and regional autonomy; continued disestablishment, equitable and graduated taxation; complete religious tolerance [11] for the Catholic Church, and a new Concordat with Rome; suppression of all "sovietic contacts" internationally and granting of privileges to "nations of related race, language, or ideology."

[10] The Spanish Political Situation, The World Today, Chatham House Review, London, November 1945, vol. 1, p. 215, Royal Institute of International Affairs.
[11] See ch. XIII, Religion.

Powers of the head of state

An indication of Franco's supreme power was given in some of his titles. These included Generalissimo of the Armed Forces, President of the Cabinet, Chief of State, Premier, and El Caudillo (national chief of the party). By a decree of August 3, 1939: "The chief (assumes) in its entire plenitude the most absolute authority. The chief is responsible only to God and history."

Cabinet and administration

A council of National Defense governed nationalist Spain during the first weeks of the revolution and was replaced on October 1, 1936, by the Technical Council of State (Junta Técnica). There were committees for ministries and two secretariats, one to direct foreign relations and one to act as liaison between the council and the head of state. On January 30, 1938, the Junta Técnica was replaced by a Cabinet of 11 ministers, similar to other European cabinets. Franco, as President of the Cabinet, was to coordinate the work of the ministries. This task he turned over to the Vice President who was also minister in charge of Morocco and Spain's colonial possessions and of the organization of supplies. Franco himself held three portfolios as supreme commander of the Army, Navy, and Air Force. The Minister of Foreign Relations was responsible for negotiating a new Concordat with the Holy See. The Home Department supervised reconstruction in devastated areas. A new Ministry of Public Order was created. For a short time the Ministry of Labor was called significantly "Syndical Action and Organization."

All Cabinet Ministers were ex-officio members of the National Council of the FET and some of them were also members of the Junta Política of the party.

The FET had 13 national services or executive branches which paralleled and sometimes overlapped the ministerial departments.

Cortes

Spain's Cortes or unicameral legislative body had 238 members. The Cortes had been declared "the superior organ of participation of the Spanish people in the tasks of the State," and its duties were "the preparation and elaboration of the Laws, without prejudice to the sanction pertaining to the Chief of State." Individual members could not introduce bills and no law was effective without the approval of the Chief of State. Committees might suggest subjects for legislation to the President of the Cortes; and, if the Government approved, they were submitted to the entire body.

Ministers, party officials, civil governors and mayors, university heads, presidents of learned bodies and members of the supreme court were ex-officio members of the Cortes. El Caudillo appointed 50 members. One-third of the members were elected by the syndicalist associations, and were evenly divided among employers, technicians, and laborers.

Syndicates

By the charter of labor, published by the state on March 9, 1938, vertical syndicates were created to incorporate all factors of the country's economic life.

The vertical syndicate is a corporation in public law formed by combining into a single organism all the elements devoted to fulfilling the economic process within a particular service or branch of production, arranged as a hierarchy under the direction of the State. Its officials will all be active members of FET. It will study problems of production, propose solutions to them, and intervene, through specialized bodies, in the regulation of conditions of work. Its policy will chiefly be carried out through the State.[12]

Local government

Fascist Spain abrogated regional autonomy and revised all legislation granting provincial and municipal home rule. The Government appointed all the members of provincial deputations and civil governors of the provinces, and the mayors and councilmen of the municipalities.

Courts

At the base of the hierarchy of courts were 9,364 municipal courts. Above these were 551 tribunals of first instance or lower courts, 50 provincial high courts, and 15 regional high courts. At the apex was the Supreme Court. The courts were frequently used for political purposes, and the independence of the judiciary had never been proclaimed. Special tribunals were set up to prosecute enemies of the state. There were no provisions against ex post facto laws. All judges were required to pledge allegiance to El Caudillo and, therefore, to the party.

POLITICAL PARTIES

Merger of Falangists and Traditionalists

On April 19, 1937, the two main nationalist groups, the Falangists and the Traditionalists, were fused into a single party under the leadership of General Franco. The militias of the two parties were united, and all other political parties and organizations were abolished. The party was called the Spanish Traditionalist Phalanx and the Committee of Attack of the National-Syndicalists (Falange Española Tradicionalista y de las Juntas de Ofensiva Nacional-Sindicalista or FET). The merged party was essentially Falangist in character; the Traditionalists or Carlist Requetés added only a long history and a Catholic background. The fascist Falange was not in absolute control of either party or state because the party remained a coalition though dominated by this group. Franco kept check on the party by giving members only ex-officio membership in organs of government. The army was Franco's partner in being identified with both the party and the state. Thus Franco could slough off either in order to escape responsibility.

Structure of FET

The FET constitution declared that the party had "an Imperial and a Catholic mission," and directed the party to create and maintain syndical organizations under a military chief, and establish a close connection between the party and the army by setting up a special military section within the party.

A secretariat (Junta Política) of 12 members aided Franco in policy making and administration. Half of its members were appointed by the head of the state and half were elected by the national council.

The number of members on the national council varied from 25 to 100 after its establishment in August 1937. The members, who were nominated by the head of the state, met once a year to discuss national problems selected by the leader.

---

[12] E. Allison Peers, Spain in Eclipse, 1937–43, London, p. 119.

Membership in local units of the FET was voluntary. Members were either militant Falangists or provisional members. The latter had to be approved for militant membership in 5 years or leave the organization.[13]

CONCLUSION

Fascism being synonymous with totalitarianism assigns all powers to the state. Upon attaining control fascist parties immediately create a centralized government with a leader at its head, which leader is given absolute powers. The supremacy of the state over all groups and individuals is quickly achieved. Frederic Austin Ogg describes it as follows:

In the Fascist conception, what existed first was a "movement"; to achieve its objects (one of which was to suppress parties), the movement took on the name, form, and technique of a party; in turn, the party became inextricably interlocked with the Government—an organ of the state; and the ultimate product was what is known in general as the "regime." [14]

Wherever possible fascist groups seek to accomplish their governmental changes within the laws of the state. If that is not possible, they simulate legality for their actions. Thus the German Constitution may have been violated by Hitler when he combined the two offices of Chancellor and President, but article 48 of that same constitution gave the President powers to suspend the laws and constitution in times of emergency and thus opened the door of legality to most of Hitler's acts. That was also true of Mussolini. He acquired control seemingly within the framework of the Italian constitution.

Fascist states tolerate only a single party—the fascist party itself. All opposition—individual and group alike—is silenced. The following chapters describe the regimentation of all human beings and activities which follows upon that silence.

The nineteenth and early twentieth centuries were characterized by the spread of democracy, which was accompanied by a minimum amount of government. Several fields, such as thought control and the use of leisure time, had not been subjected to government exploitation. The fascist states have seized upon these and have improvised new governmental agencies for their regimentation. Fascist adventures in these and all other realms of human activity have not been guided by chance, but by the firm determination to bring everything within the state under its supervision and direction, to serve the state and its avowed purposes. Fascism means total regimentation and regulation.

---

[13] Information concerning the political institutions of Fascist Spain has been obtained chiefly from the following sources: R. L. Buell, et al., New Governments in Europe, section "Spain under the Republic" by Bailey W. Diffie and Charles A. Thomson, New York, 1937, pp. 404–476; E. Allison Peers, Spain in Eclipse, 1937–43, London, 1943; Council on Foreign Relations, Inc., Political Handbook of the World, 1946, New York, 1946.

[14] Ogg, pp. 829–30.

CHAPTER II—EDUCATION AND THOUGHT CONTROL

IMPORTANCE OF THOUGHT CONTROL IN FASCIST COUNTRIES

Nowhere have fascist countries been more successful than in the field of thought control. Nowhere have they demonstrated more clearly how completely integrated in terms of a common purpose are all fascist actions. To them the beliefs and views of people both at home and abroad are of the utmost significance. The totalitarian state—because of its very nature—must regulate education, art, literature, radio, the cinema, press, and public platforms. At home the desired frame of mind is achieved through regimentation and direction, consisting chiefly of excluding undesirable influences and creating acceptable ones by using a number of familiar devices of public opinion control.[1] Abroad the object sought is a favorable background for the spread of fascist ideas and for the accomplishment of fascist foreign programs and acts,[2] often summarized as psychological warfare.

A power device

The institutions for moulding, directing, and manipulating public opinion become instruments of power for they constitute a form of coercion. They are the means by which thought is directed into the desired channels.[3]

Where old institutions, such as the press section of the Foreign Office in Germany, are at hand, they are adapted to work in the approved direction. In the past, however, fascist governments have had to create most of the agencies of thought control, such, for example, as the German Ministry of Propaganda, the German Ministry of Education, and the Italian cinema control, LUCE. Fascism has been exceptionally prolific in improvising these agencies. All have been designed to bring about unity of thought and action.[4]

Aims of fascist revolutions

Fascist revolutions—like revolutions in general—have two objectives: (1) They seek general acceptance of their advocated ideologies. (2) They strive for permanence in the hope of having the fascist form of life adopted as the form of life both at home and abroad.

No surer way of accomplishing these objectives has been found than by shaping the thinking of at least one generation of young people during its formative years. Hitler in Germany and Mussolini in Italy both believed that the rising generation, taught in this way, would accept Fascism and National Socialism without question or

---

[1] Eugen Hadamovsky, Propaganda und Nationale Macht, Oldenburg, 1933. The whole work is referred to, but p. 132 ff. especially useful here.
[2] An effective and short summary of this subject as applied to Italy may be found in Harwood L. Childs, Propaganda and Dictatorship, Princeton, 1936, pp. 50–53.
[3] See Thorsten V. Kalijarvi, ed., Modern World Politics, 2d ed., New York, 1945, ch. 16.
[4] See Josef Goebbels in the Frankfurter Zeitung, February 16, 1939.

objection. Thus the two revolutions and their attendant governments and ideologies were to be permanently established. Education immediately assumed a most important political significance.[5] It was no longer only a way of making young people grow in mind and body, but henceforth it was to become a program for inculcating the young with the desired attitudes and beliefs, and an instrument for the accomplishment of state purposes.

Totalitarian concept of education

Totalitarian education reduced to its simplest terms was from this time on to have two objectives: (1) To eradicate and kill off all competitive and inimical ideas; and (2) simultaneously to foster the fascist ideology, its institutions, and its form of life everywhere. This inescapably meant rigid state control of education, a condition which John Stuart Mill in his Essay on Liberty deplored in the following words:

A state-controlled system becomes a mere contrivance for moulding people to be exactly like one another * * * in proportion as it is efficient and successful, it establishes a despotism over the mind, leading by natural tendency to one over the body.

In addition, totalitarian states, particularly Nazi Germany and Fascist Italy, conceived of education not merely as the process carried out formally in schools and universities, but included under it every experience that affected the mind. Hence, even more attention was devoted to extrascholastic and informal agencies—such as youth organizations, and all types of leisure and recreational activities of children, youth, and adults—than to formal education.[6] Both formal and informal education were directed to conditioning the people to implicit and unquestioning obedience and submissiveness to the will of those in power. In Nazi Germany the principle inculcated was that "Hitler is the law and will of the people," and in Fascist Italy that "Il Duce is always right". In Japan the emperor was worshipped, and in Spain El Caudillo was given an exalted position.

The essence of education in totalitarian states was best expressed in the central doctrine of Nazism—Gleichschaltung, whose connotation is inadequately conveyed by the usual English translation "coordination." The Nazi state was defined as "the national condition in which every human being thinks and acts in a way coordinated with the thoughts and acts of every other human being." Or as defined by Goebbels, Gleichschaltung was to be the normal condition of Germany which "is to have only one goal, one party, one conviction, and this state organization is to be identical with the state itself. Revolutions know no compromises. The state must stand for the principle of totality."[7] Translated into popular slogans, Gleichschaltung was expressed simply in two forms: Du bist nichts; dein Volk ist alles (you are nothing; your people is everything), and Gemeinnutz geht vor Eigennutz (the common weal comes before personal weal).[8] Hence everything that made up life was part of an organic whole, derived its meaning from the whole, and proceeded to

---

[5] Harold Goad and Michele Catalano, Education in Italy, Rome, 1939, pp. 1-15; also C. H. Abad, Fascist Education in Italy, Current History, vol. 36, July 1932, pp. 433-437.
[6] See ch. XII, Use of Leisure Time.
[7] Frankfurter, Zeitung, February 16, 1939.
[8] Lest this slogan mislead readers in thinking that this is the same as the phrase "promote the common welfare" in the American Constitution, the fact should be emphasized that the Nazi party officials were the sole judge of what was "Gemeinnutz."

it.   In the words of the leading philosopher of Nazi education, Ernst Krieck:

> State, religion, language, economy, law, society, culture, science, education, school * * * stands, therefore, in organic interdependence with all other aspects of life and its expressions.[9]
> The epoch of "pure reason" of "objective" and "free science" is ended.[10]

What this meant in its practical results and without its philosophical refinements was tersely expressed by Robert Ley, Nazi Minister of Labor, when he said:

> Since the Nazis came into power the only private life remaining is at night when you are asleep.   You are a soldier of Hitler as soon as you awake.

Italian Fascism, which decried "the putrescent corpse of liberalism," regarded the state as an organism which "transcending the brief limits of individual life represents the imminent spirit of the nation." Gleichschaltung in Fascist Italy became "everything for the state; nothing outside the state; nothing against the state," which was translated into the popular slogan, painted on every wall throughout Italy, credere, obbedire, combattere (believe, obey, fight).

One other aspect of totalitarian ideology must be mentioned if the educational practices are to be understood, and that was the attack on accepted religions.   Alfred Rosenberg was the leading proponent of a movement back to Nordic religion.   How far the efforts to wean youth from their religious affiliations or to emphasize their "religious duty (to) Adolf Hitler and God as synonymous" [11] were successful is not known, but the Hitler Youth did attempt to organize its activities at times when its members should have attended Sunday school or church services and did include in its program celebrations which were supposedly a return to Rosenberg's idea of a Nordic religion. Mussolini failed, but not for want of trying, to replace religious instruction in schools by a simplified philosophy of a religion and to secure control of Catholic youth organizations.   Failing in that effort, prayers were written for schools and youth organizations to inculcate loyalty to Mussolini as God's gift to Italy.[12]

THE EDUCATIONAL STRUCTURE

Germany

The Weimar Republic had introduced radical changes in the educational system of Germany.   It provided a common school of 4 years (Grundschule) for all pupils; it increased the opportunities for secondary and higher education and introduced a new type of secondary school (Aufbauschule), more closely articulated with the elementary

---

[9] Ernst Krieck, Nationalpolitische Erziehung, 7th ed., Leipzig, 1932, pp. 9ff.

[10] Ibid., pp. 1, 16.

[11] See the account of Kurt Kietzke's Deutsche Schulgebete in the Friends of Europe, June, 1939, p. 509. A detailed account of this aspect was presented in M. Power's The Nazi Persecution of Christianity, New York, 1940; also, I. L. Kandel, The End of an Era, New York, 1941, pp. 77 ff.

[12] See ch. XIII, Religion.   This aspect, particularly of National Socialism, was already noted in the title of one of the first pamphlets issued after the Nazi Revolution, Hitlerism, Why and Whither, Some Aspects of a Religious Revolution by Dr. George Norlin, Friends of Europe Publications, Pamphlet No. 22, London, n. d.   "It is difficult," wrote Dr. Norlin, "without being on the ground to appreciate the fact that Hitlerism is itself a kind of religion."   Ambassador William E. Dodd referred to Fritz Brennecke, the Nazi Primer, translated by Harwood L. Childs, New York, 1938, as "The Bible of a Political Church."

schools than the types inherited from the Imperial regime. More
important, however, than the change in organization was the new
spirit introduced in administration and in curriculum and methods.
In administration decentralization was encouraged; local authorities
were given more autonomy in educational matters; the organization of
parents' councils and of teachers' councils was promoted. The
curriculum, which in each state had been prescribed before the First
World War, began to be published in the form of guides to teachers
(Richtlinien) on the basis of which teachers drew up the courses of
study in each school or group of schools. The starting point in the
curriculum of the elementary school was the immediate environment
of the pupils, and the method of instruction was the activity method.
Elementary education was child centered (vom Kinde aus). Activity
methods were advocated also in the secondary schools and teachers
were urged to use all subjects of instruction to promote better understanding of German culture. Finally, the Weimar Constitution
provided that education should be conducted "in a spirit of national
culture and international conciliation." The efforts of the Weimar
Republic were wrecked for three reasons: (1) Sufficient time was not
allowed to change the outlook of teachers from traditional authori-
tarianism to the new ideals of republicanism; (2) a large majority
of secondary school teachers were kept on in the schools and they
were not only class conscious but many had served as officers in the
Kaiser's army; (3) the authorities were too tolerant of the use of the
multiplicity of youth organizations for political ends, a tolerance of
which the National Socialists took advantage in their own organization of youth in 1926.

The first task undertaken by the Nazis after the revolution was to
eliminate all elements of liberalism from all educational institutions.
A new direction was given by the organization in 1933 of an exposition
of books suitable for children and youth, all of which were directed to
inculcating the spirit of war-mindedness, heroism, and sacrifice, and
a few to criticisms of the Versailles humiliation.[13] Since there was as
yet no national ministry of education, a new course of study for the
teaching of history was issued for the whole of Germany by Wilhelm
Frick, Minister of the Interior, in which the idea of the heroic world
viewpoint was emphasized and which, starting with prehistory, came
down through the ages to the disintegration of the German people
through the disgrace of Versailles and the Liberal-Marxist philosophy
of the Weimar Republic.[14]

In 1934 a Ministry of National Education was created with control
over education throughout the Reich which deprived the States of
the autonomy they had always enjoyed. From the Ministry down,
a hierarchy of officials was established on the leadership principle
(Fuehrerprinzip);[15] local authorities were shorn of the powers which
they had enjoyed under the Weimar Republic; parents' and teachers'
councils were abolished. Teachers' associations, which had always
been vigorously active, were disbanded; and all teachers were required
to join the National Socialist Teachers' Organization. Curricula and
courses of study were again rigidly prescribed and were dominated by
Nazi ideology.

[13] For a list of the books see I. L. Kandel, The Making of Nazis, New York, 1935, pp. 18 ff.
[14] Kandel, The Making of Nazis, pp. 66 ff.
[15] Hans Bernhard Brausse, Die Fuehrungsordnung des deutschen Volkes, Hamburg, 1942.

The organization of the school system started with a common foundation school (Grundschule); at the end of the 4 years the majority of the pupils continued for another 4 years in the elementary school (Volksschule), while a minority entered secondary schools or at the age of 13 passed from the elementary school to the secondary school (Aufbauschule), mentioned earlier. One important and long-overdue reform, which the Republic had been unable to secure, was the replacement of the multiplicity of secondary school types by two for boys (Gymnasium and Oberschule) and one for girls (Oberschule), in addition to the Aufbauschule. At the same time, in 1938, the length of the traditional 9-year secondary course was reduced to 8, so that young men could complete their professional studies earlier, marry, and produce children. The aim of girls' education was defined by Hitler as "indispensably to be that of the future mothers."

Organization, however, is relatively unimportant. More enlightening were the new emphases in education. The special characteristic of Nazi education was the utilization of all subjects for purposes of indoctrination. The chief emphasis was placed on biology, the peculiar vehicle for instruction in the race theory and racial purity on the "blood and soil" (Blut und Boden) principle; history for inculcating the ideal of heroism and the common interests of the Nordic stock; geography with a stress on living space (Lebensraum), and the lands and colonies which Germany had lost and must regain; and physical education for hardening (Verhaertung) as a preliminary to military training. No opportunity was missed in other subjects, such as arithmetic and mathematics, physics and chemistry, and literature, to inculcate the Nazi ideology.[16]

The aim of education, however, was not the development of intellectual interests or intellectual training so much as indoctrination and propaganda. From all reports, it was clear that intellectual standards declined to the extent that school principals were urged to overlook poor work if a student was engaged in youth activities. This was even clearer in higher education where the traditional student organizations were disbanded and replaced by the German Student Corporation (Deutsche Studentenschaft), entrusted with the task of seeing "that all students fulfill their duties to the people, state, and university," a task extended also to the supervision of and reporting on professors. It was this organization that laid down the principle that "a good political record is better than a scholastic record."

Even under the Imperial regime the ideal of academic freedom in the universities had been carefully protected. The Nazis destroyed it. Ernst Krieck stated that "academic freedom is absolute nonsense"; while another Nazi philosopher of education, Alfred Baeumler, said that "the scholar must be replaced by the soldier type." The universities were completely deprived of their autonomy; professors could be dismissed, retired, or transferred by a special committee in Berlin. Candidates for university teaching posts (Dozenten) were no longer appointed by their colleagues but by the same committee, and after appointment were required to spend 3 months in an academy for Nazi indoctrination.

[16] For samples of arithmetic problems to inculcate the ideas of race purity, war- and air-mindedness, etc., see Kandel, The End of an Era, pp. 202 ff.; and for examples in physics and chemistry of war, see p. 282. Examples from other subjects are given in Kandel, Education in Nazi Germany, pp. 28 ff, London, 1938.

The Nazis did not intend to look to the products of secondary schools and universities for the future leaders in political, military, and other Nazi affairs. For the selection and training of future leaders special schools were established under the direct control of the National Socialist Party. These schools were the National Political Educational Institutions (Nationalpolitische Erziehungsanstalten or Napoli), the Adolf-Hitler-Schulen, and the Ordensburgen; admission to these latter was by careful selection on physical and racial grounds and proven loyalty to the party. According to an English Board of Education report on Physical Education in Germany (1937), "it is capacity for action rather than capacity for contemplation that counts" both in the selection and training. The chief emphasis in all three types of schools was on physical development and strict discipline of military character, and instruction in race theory, biology, history, economics, and politics. It was through these schools, according to Rauschning, that Hitler hoped to produce "those fearless, vigorous, commanding, and cruel young men with the strength and beauty of young beasts." [17]

Italy

Education in Fascist Italy had many of the characteristics of Nazi education, but it never achieved the same degree of ruthless efficiency. The first leaders in the reform of Italian education after Mussolini came to power were idealists and many of them liberals who had been associated from the beginning of the century in a movement for cultural nationalism. Not for some years was Mussolini quite clear about the interpretation that he would give to Fascism. When Giovanni Gentile, the Italian Minister of Education, began his reform in 1923–24 it was with the intention of making the system more efficient by introducing a certain measure of centralization, applying the activity methods in elementary education, and improving the quality of secondary education by adopting severe entrance and leaving examinations, whereby the number of students would be reduced and the rest receive the education best fitted to their abilities. He also hoped by these measures to check the overproduction of and, therefore, unemployment among intellectuals. Except for the Hegelian concept of the state, there was not much in Gentile's reform that was Fascist, and it was for that reason that he was virtually dismissed and replaced by a Minister of Education who could interpret Fascism better.

By 1928, all teachers were expected to be loyal to Fascism, and many had become members of the party. Liberal professors, such as Gaetano Salvemini, were dismissed, and the universities lost their autonomy. State control was intensified and centralization established with a hierarchy of officials responsible to the Ministry. Teachers were forced into the single organization (Associazione Fascista della Scuola). In 1928, the state began to prepare, publish, and distribute elementary school textbooks and to prohibit the publication of secondary school textbooks without the approval, which meant a rigid censorship, of the state. This step was deliberately taken to impress the spirit of Fascist revolution on pupils and students. The race theory and the teaching of military science in secondary schools were later adopted in imitation of the Nazis.

[17] See also Johannes R. Becher, Deutsche Lehre, London, n. d.; George F. Kneller, The Educational Philosophy of National Socialism, New Haven, 1941; Raymond E. Murphy and others; National Socialism, Washington, 1943; Alina M. Lindegren, Education in Germany, Washington, 1939.

The Fascist school system [18] included maternal schools, attended, where available, by children from 2 to 6; elementary schools for children from 6 to 14, but owing to an inadqeuate supply of schools the majority of children had little more than 5 years of elementary education; the more fortunate had the opportunity of attending trade schools or entering secondary schools—teacher-training, technical, scientific, or classical—provided they could pass the difficult entrance examinations. Except in history, there was not the adaption of subjects to ideological ends as in Nazi Germany. An Educational Charter (Carta della Scuola) was issued by the Grand Council of the Fascist Party in 1939 to inculcate education more thoroughly with Fascism and to tie curricular and extra-curricular (or Youth) activities together. From the age of 10 or more, attention was to be devoted to manual work and preparation for vocational training, with opportunities for able students to enter the secondary schools. The war broke out before the charter could be put into effect.

Other Fascist countries

Education in other fascist countries was moulded on the same pattern as that of Germany and Italy. Thus in pre-Second World War Japan, an oriental and non-European country, the state exercised a rigid control over a highly centralized system of education, vesting supreme power in the Minister of Education.[19] The Imperial Rescript on Education, issued in 1890, which established the educational system in force in Japan at the outbreak of the First World War, said in part:

* * * always respect the Constitution and observe the laws; should emergency arise, offer yourselves courageously to the State; and thus guard and maintain the prosperity of Our Imperial Throne coeval with heaven and earth.[20]

The Minister of Education was charged with all matters relating to art, science, literature, and religion. He was not only the highest authority on educational matters, but assisted the Parliamentary Vice Minister in the conduct of political affairs. Among his many duties was that of directing and supervising the Superintendent-General of the Metropolitan Police on matters under his control. The Minister also had political functions when dealing with local mayors and governmental officials. That Japan's form of education was fascist is evident by the names of the following institutions: Bureau of Thought Supervision, Government Research Institute of National Culture, Protection and Encouragement of Educational Work.[21]

A study of Spain,[22] Yugoslavia, Bulgaria, and Poland, would reveal the same molding of educational institutions to state ends. So important were educational institutions considered that the first objects of attack by new fascist governments were students and professors who refused to accept the new regime. Book burning had a political purpose.

[18] See Goad and Catalano; H. R. Marraro, The New Education in Italy, New York, 1936; Partito Nazionale Fascista, La Cultura Fascista, Rome, 1936; Herbert W. Schneider, The Fascist Government of Italy, New York, 1936, ch. 7, pp. 144–146.
[19] General Survey of Education in Japan, issued by the Japanese Department of Education, Tokyo, 1935.
[20] Printed before title page of General Survey of Education in Japan.
[21] A useful survey giving the organization of the Japanese school system is Education in Japan, Kenkyasha, 1938; also H. L. P. Keenleyside and A. F. Thomas, History of Japanese Education, Tokyo, 1937.
[22] For an account of Spanish education see Gonzalo Galvez Carmona, Nuestra Pedagogia, Granada, 1938. In Spain the falange burning of alleged Communist and Nihilist books was preceded by the earlier Communist burning of churches and nuns.

Germany

Although Nazi and Italian dictatorships used education to promote their ideologies, they placed the chief emphasis for indoctrination and propaganda not so much on the schools as on youth organizations. One reason for this was that, despite supervision and control, formal education was still wedded to the tradition of intellectual training. What the dictators and the parties wanted was emotional conditioning which would produce unquestioning followers. As Hitler put it, it is the duty of a German "to learn to be silent, not only when he is blamed justly," but "to learn, if necessary, to bear injustice in silence"; or, in the words of the decalogue for young fascists, "days in prison are always merited." Education, according to Hitler, must be directed "not at pumping in knowledge, but at the breeding of absolutely healthy bodies."

The Hitlerjugend, organized in 1926, had 1,000,000 members between the ages of 14 and 18 in 1933, and the number had increased almost eightfold when the war broke out. In 1933, all other youth organizations were abolished and their place taken by the Hitlerjugend, of which Baldur von Schirach was made the leader directly responsible to Hitler. The organization consisted of the Deutsches Jungvolk (boys from 10 to 14), the Hitlerjugend proper (boys from 14 to 18), the Jungmaedel (girls from 10 to 14), and Bund Deutscher Maedel (girls from 14 to 18). The aim of the organization was the development of Nazi character and physical efficiency in the early years and military training and indoctrination in National Socialist world outlook. Leaders were selected from the youth themselves; later, special training was provided for potential leaders in the schools.[23] The winter months were used for meetings in clubhouses with a uniform and prescribed program of study; the other months were devoted to physical and military training for boys, and for girls to physical training and courses in first aid, child care, and dietetics. The Hitlerjugend was more than a youth organization; it was a political-military institution (politisch-soldatische Erziehungsgemeinschaft) for political indoctrination and military training. At the age of 18, members were admitted to the party, and after 6 months of compulsory labor service (Arbeitsdienst)[24] and 2 years of military training became eligible for admission to the Storm Troops (Sturmabteilung or S. A.) or the Elite Corps (Schutzstaffel or S. S.)[25]

The best summary of the machinery for development of the Nazi mentality is contained in a statement by Robert Ley, Minister of the Labor Front:

We begin with the child when he is three years old. As soon as he begins to think he gets a little flag put in his hand; then follows the school, the Hitler Youth, the S. A., and military training. We don't let him go; and when adolescence is past, then comes the Arbeitsfront, which takes him again and does not let him go till he dies, whether he likes it or not.[26]

In an interview with a French journalist Mussolini made an almost identical statement in 1935:

We have been bending every effort to better the education and instruction of the young. We take the little Italian as a child and fashion his thoughts and

[23] Referred to on p. 9.
[24] See ch. VIII, Labor.
[25] See Kandel, The Making of Nazis, pp. 106 ff.; and Brenneke, The Nazi Primer.
[26] Kandel, Education in Nazi Germany, 1938, p. 8.

s?ntiments in harmony with the great ideas of his country at the same time as we
s rengthen the body with military exercises. Our organization extends into the
citizen's whole life and our Dopolavoro are not sufficiently known abroad. In
these clubs 3,000,000 workers come after their work for recreation, rest, and
instruction.[27]

Italy

The Fascist organization of youth began in 1926, with the creation
of the Balilla for the moral and physical training of Italian youth from
6 to 18. In 1929 the Balilla was placed under the Ministry of Education. In 1930 the organization was extended by the addition of the
Young Fighting Fascist Groups (Fasci giovanili di combattimento).
Finally, in 1937 the whole system was reorganized into the Italian
Youth of the Littorio or G. I. L. (Gioventú italiana del Littorio),
with the motto "Believe, obey, fight" replacing the earlier motto of
Balilla, "The Book and the Musket.". The number of members in
1938 was 7,577,381, bound by oath to obey the Duce's order and devote
strength or life to the cause of the Fascist revolution. The organization supervised physical education in the schools; provided moral,
premilitary and sports education to its male members, and physical
training and instruction in domestic economy and child care to the
female members; organized summer camps, excursions, and cruises;
and promoted cultural activities in political training, music, drama,
and national competitions in these fields and in sports and athletics.
Special courses were established to train directors and leaders with
an Academy of the G. I. L., and a Center for Political Studies. For
university students there was a separate organization, the G. U. P.
(Gruppo Universitario Fascista), with aims similar to those of the
G. I. L. At the age of 21 the university students and the Young
Fascists entered the Fascist Party or the National Militia, and the
Young Fascist Girls the Women's Fascist Groups.[28] For adult
workers Mussolini, in 1925, established the Opera Nazionale Dopolavoro, a further extension of the system of control which extended
from the cradle to the grave.[29]

PROPAGANDA

Extent

Having viewed the regimentation of education, there remain to be
considered some of the other ways in which Fascism exercised thought
control over its subjects. Not chance, but necessity, made all programs, methods, and techniques for manipulating views vital to fascist
governments. Mussolini in speaking of the control of theaters, literature, and lectures said that his party must "create what one may call
spiritual imperialism." [30] Wilhelm Weiss, head of the Reich Association of the German Press, observed in speaking of the theater:

* * * what is decisive is the question for which side the battle is waged on
the stage. The standpoint of Art as Art, is, according to our view, not tenable.
Both art and the critic serve a higher ideal, the ideal of national honor and the
ideal of a truly German culture.[31]

[27] New York Times, October 7, 1935.
[28] See Renato Marzolo, The Youth Movement in Italy, Rome, 1939.
[29] See ch. XII, Use of Leisure Time.
[30] Benito Mussolini, Scritti e Discorsi, Milan, vol. VI, pp. 373–75.
[31] Frankfurter Zeitung, December 17, 1935.

Goebbels, head of the Propaganda Ministry, announced:

The Government intends to determine what is serviceable or expedient for People and Nation. Decisions in the sphere of art leadership can be made only by statesmen and not by the artist.[32]

Captain Weiss in another connection is reported to have said before the German Press Chamber of Dessau:

The critic must be constantly aware that what he sees on the stage is politics in the broadest sense of the term. A journalist dealing with art questions must have today a primarily political standpoint * * * the old idea that there is good and bad art must be removed.[33]

From these brief comments and from what has already been said about education, it will be apparent that totalitarianism in all of its aspects can be summarized as a creed or an all-embracing religion, whose tenets, ritual, and priesthood are determined by the fascist rulers in terms of what they consider to be the interests of the state. The essential character of both National Socialism and Fascism was succinctly described by Goebbels when he said:

The Nazi Party is a political church, where for hundreds of thousands of years German people will be trained to be true National Socialists. We are the political pastors of our people.[34]

Fascist religion viewed facts as relatively unimportant, but considered their interpretation of the utmost significance. News became only one part of the story. The most important part was the interpretation. News was slanted, directed, rationed, and monopolized by the rulers to their own ends. Another way of putting it is that news was the skeleton on which the flesh and sinews of interpretation were hung.[35]

The term propaganda

Since fascist governments call thought control propaganda, it is significant to note that propaganda is not exclusive with them, but is characteristic of the age in which we live. For the most part all propaganda, fascist included, deals with political, social, economic, and religious questions. Fascist propaganda differs from other types in that (1) it usually emphasizes the race idea which is based on the theory that the earth is inhabited by different races of people, who differ in quality one from the other; (2) is world-wide and possesses world-wide ambitions; (3) is thorough and efficient (that was particularly true of Nazi propaganda); and (4) has the power of the state behind it. The sovereignty of truth is ridiculed and skeptical methods of inquiry, which permit the individual to come to his own conclusions, are repressed.

The full significance of these characteristics will be appreciated when one recalls that modern propaganda has been evolved as a result of changes in economic and military techniques. Large-scale production and mass consumption have brought high-pressure advertising. Modern world politics depends to a large degree on the mass opinions of politically conscious peoples. In the same way that modern advertising is an economic weapon of modern giant enterprise, propaganda is a part of the political strength of a state [36] to be set alongside

[32] Frankfurter Zeitung, May 22, 1939.
[33] New York Times, March 16, 1937.
[34] Quoted by Brenneke, Nazi Primer, p. 256.
[35] Frankfurter Zeitung, February 16, 1939.
[36] Kalijarvi, ch. 1.

its army, navy, and air force. The high degree of organization and the efficiency of fascist propaganda makes it a particularly valuable political weapon to those governments. In theory totalitarian governments represent the will of the people.[37] In practice totalitarian states set the standard to be followed and then enforce conformity with it. Propaganda thus is simultaneously an instrument of national policy and of war which a state ignores at its peril.

Totalitarian governments, which are always organized for war, logically develop and keep careful control over all thought-shaping and directing agencies at all times. Thus they have an advantage over democracies which are particularly vulnerable to and have no defense against fascist propaganda in times of peace, precisely because they uphold freedom of speech and press.

Totalitarian governments protect themselves against hostile propaganda by fighting it with their own. Hence prewar German propaganda had relatively little effect upon Soviet Russia, since the propaganda agencies of both countries were highly developed and both were prepared for a war of words and thoughts.

The machinery

Some idea of the extent to which fascist control over thought is exercised may be gained by a brief glimpse at the largest and most effective propaganda agency the world has ever seen, namely, the Nazi National Ministry of Popular Enlightenment and Propaganda. Dr. Goebbels' Ministry developed most features of public opinion control with a thoroughness characteristically German.

Division I: Legislation and Legal Problems, Budget, Finances; and Accounting; Personnel Administration; Ministerial Library; National Chamber of Culture; Council of Commercial Advertising (Werberat der Deutschen Wirtschaft); Fairs and Expositions.

Division II: Coordination of Popular Enlightenment and Propaganda (Positive Weltanschauungspropaganda); Regional Agencies of the Ministry; German Academy of Politics (Deutsche Hochschule fuer Politik); Official Ceremonies and Demonstrations; National Emblems; Racial Questions; Treaty of Versailles; National Literature and Publishing; Opposing Ideologies; Youth Organization; Business and Social Politics; Public Health and Athletics; Eastern and Border Questions; National Travel Committee (Reichsausschuss fuer Fremdenverkehr).

Division III: Radio; National Broadcasting Company (Reichsrundfunk-Gesellschaft m. b. H.).

Division IV: National and Foreign Press; Journalism; Press Archives; News Service; National Association of the German Press (Reichsverband der Deutschen Presse).

Division V: Cinema; Moving Picture Industry; Cinema Censorship; Youth Literature Censorship.

Division VI: Theater, Music, and Art; Theater Management; Stage Direction; Design; Folk Art.

Division VII: Protection against Counter-Propaganda at Home and Abroad.[38] Thirty-one regional offices carried out the work of the national organization. Its philosophy was epitomized by Eugen Hadamovsky, the Third Reich broadcasting director in 1933, when he commented that "Propaganda is will to power and victorious only as the tool of an idea." [39]

The Ministry was buttressed by a host of detailed regulations governing the supervision and functions of press, radio, film, stage, art, literature, and the lecture platform. In 1934 a decree was passed "protecting National Socialist literature", and setting up a commission which examined books and certified for distribution those which

[37] Huber, pp. 163–165.
[38] Quoted from Childs, ed., Propaganda and Dictatorship, ch. II by Fritz Morstein Marx, pp. 19, 20
[39] Hadamovsky, p. 148.

were "unobjectionable." Obviously the "unobjectionable" ones were those which carried forward the aims of National Socialism and did not offend any of its regulations or leaders.

The picture would not be complete if attention were not called briefly to the institutions and improvisations adopted by other fascisms, Italy's in particular. There, news was controlled by the Fascist Press Syndicate; the cinema by LUCE (L'Unione Cinematografica Educativa); radio by Ente (Ente Italiano per le Audizioni Radiofoniche); and many other activities by the Dopolavoro.[40] In addition the Fascist faith was carried forward through a number of cults such as those of (1) hero worship, (2) violence, (3) action, and (4) Romanism. Censorship was heavily relied upon.

Coordination with other state activities.

It should be remembered that fascist thought control agencies and regulations are always supported by the state and all of its agencies, the secret police, the Volksgericht, the Special Tribunal for the Defense of the State, and similar institutions. The techniques and procedures used have been publicized too widely to require repetition here. They range from censorship, canned editorials, and news releases to book burning, and even physical violence and murder.

In the foreign field.

In keeping with their world-wide interest, fascist countries extend their propaganda into the international field. In times of peace their work abroad is devoted chiefly to creating a friendly attitude for fascism. Mussolini was especially successful in this field. Agents of the government are directed to cultivate all groups likely to be favorably predisposed. Funds are supplied generously. Germany's AO (Auslandsdeutsche Organisation) was amply supported with money, personnel, and materials with which to carry on its activities.[41]

Thus the aim is to prepare the ground abroad so that when a crisis arises the Quislings, the Seyss-Inquarts, and the fifth columns are ready to go into action. Propaganda materials, such as films, literature, and lecturers, are supplied in abundance. Information bureaus, railway agencies, and steamship companies are drafted into the network and are given positive parts to play. When war comes, the fascist state therefore has its propaganda machinery all ready for action. To all intents and purposes it is a war machine.

Both in peace and war, the propaganda program of fascist governments is one of divide and conquer.[42] Seeds of hate are sowed. Class is divided against class. Religious, racial, political, and economic minorities are pitted against each other, and animosities are exploited. Before the totalitarian armies attack, the enemy must be "softened up." Fear, hate, doubt, suspicion, and distrust are exploited. During the Second World War Germany used this type of propaganda against France, Poland, Norway, and Denmark. Perhaps the most notorious case of fascist "softening up" was that which preceded the Nazi acquisition of Czechoslovakia. After the victim state has been suitably "softened up," the fascist force moves in. It is greeted by its

[40] Best summary, La Cultura Fascista.
[41] See ch. III, Foreign Policy; also Murphy, particularly pp. 22, 46.
[42] Ladislas Farago and L. F. Gittler, eds., German Psychological Warfare, New York, 1941; U. S. Office of War Information, Divide and Conquer, Washington, 1942; Ewald Banse, Germany Prepares for War (Translated by Alan Harris), New York, 1934.

'Quislings and fifth columns which assure complete and immediate success with a minimum expenditure of time, manpower, and personnel.[43]

It is true that this study is not concerned with the operation of propaganda during the Second World War, with Lord Haw Haw, Axis Sally, the jamming of broadcasts, and the operation of secret radio broadcasting units in the belligerent states. However, it should be emphasized that fascist propaganda techniques both in war and in peace are alike. War merely brings on an intensification of peacetime activities. It should also be noted that the secret radio, press, films, and literature, which occasionally make their way into fascist countries in peacetime, in spite of rigid controls, only serve to accentuate the completeness and the effectiveness of the censorship and thought direction.

Obviously there has been no consistency of experience among fascist countries. Each has had its own institutions, its own experiences, and problems. Spain, in April 1947, was still a novice in the field, and her institutions in a substantial measure followed the Italian pattern. Pre-Second World War Japanese propaganda institutions, in spite of their older non-European background, bore considerable similarity to the German propaganda agencies. This may have been due to the long military background of both countries. Other former fascistic propaganda agencies, such as those of Antonescu and Pilsudski, were not developed as highly as those of Germany, Italy, and Japan. Nevertheless, it is safe to say of them as of fascisms in general that they followed the pattern of thought control already described. Everything physical, spiritual, and intellectual had to be controlled for the state and its myriad purposes.

CONCLUSION

Democratic people, who cherish freedom of thought, beliefs, and religion; who consider knowledge to be worthy for its own sake; who speak of pure science; and who consider scholarship and knowledge as open roads to the truth, will always have difficulty in understanding the underlying approach of fascism to the whole field of thought control. Perhaps the idea may be most tersely and illustratively put in the words of Walter Frank who says that true National Socialist scholarship lies "in learning to fight; in fighting to learn; and in fighting and in learning alike to form the soul of the Nation."[44] Krieck said, "We stand before a task which demands heroic, fighting, soldierly, militant scholarship. Wissenschaft becomes for us weapon and tool for the building up of the voelkisch-political community."[45]

The whole field of thought control is one of conditioning for conflict. It is not profound nor intellectual, but streamlined, efficient,

---

[43] Kalijarvi, ch. 9. This description applies primarily to Germany and Italy. Spain had not reached this stage when the fascist powers were defeated in the Second World War. However, the Spanish intentions were clearly set down in Ramiro de Maeztu's "Defensa de la Hispanidad," 1934, the thesis of which was adopted by Franco Spain and its supporters in the Spanish Catholic world. These intentions and their attendant programs were decried by the Uruguayan statesman, Pedro Manini y Rios, when he publicly withdrew his approval of the Franco regime on January 18, 1942, and denounced it because of its "persecutions," "violent reprisals," dictatorial character, foreign policy in harmony with the Axis and its "incredible claims" to the restoration of Spain's "hegemony over what was the empire of Charles V." See William B. Bristol, "Hispanidad in South America," Foreign Affairs, vol. 21, January 1943, pp. 314-315.
[44] Otto Kreppel, Nationalsozialistisches Studententum und Studentenrecht, Koenigsberg, 1937, p. 11.
[45] Krieck, p. 86.

effective, emotional, passionate, romanticist, political, and filled with the exploiting of prejudices and hate. Fascism is a psychological, not a rational force. It is built upon the support of the masses as they are directed under a system of fuehrership. The philosophy is one of faith, belief, regulation, uniformity, and constraint. Fascist thought is national-mindedness to the nth degree based on a political foundation. Its sole consideration is the success and survival of the fascist state, to that end everything must be surrendered—objectivity, logic, consistency, and even truth itself.

CHAPTER III—FOREIGN POLICY

NOTE.—In 1945 and 1946 the United States Department of State sent a special interrogation mission under Dewitt C. Poole to question prominent leaders in Germany concerning German foreign policy under national socialism. This chapter has utilized the results of these interrogations. Thus it is possible here to set forth the operation of fascist foreign policy based upon information, views, and observations of those who were party to its formulation and operation.[1]

COMMON CHARACTERISTICS OF FASCIST FOREIGN POLICIES

Since foreign policy is but the extension of national efforts beyond a country's frontiers in order to meet domestic needs, it is not surprising that fascist states should act abroad as they do at home. Born, as a rule, in disturbed conditions, fascism profits by the same disturbed conditions in international affairs.

There has been a tendency in some quarters to regard all fascist states as alike and even to consider that a conspiracy for world control once may have existed among them.[2] In the light of available material, this is not so. However, the spirit of fascism of one country has so much in common with that of another country that fascisms everywhere tend to arouse mutual sympathy and understanding. The following discussion will show that fascist dictators have come together on occasion in response to mutual needs, but that at no time did anything like an organized conspiracy exist among them.[3] Moreover, individual dictators like Mussolini, Hitler, and Antonescu[4] might out of mutual regard for one another undertake certain acts in common. But they also have refused to take concerted action, as did Franco when he demurred at entering the Second World War on the side of the Axis Powers.[5]

Nor does mutual regard always mean trust among fascist dictators, nor prevent them from "holding out" on each other. Thus Hitler did not notify Mussolini about his annexation of Austria in the Anschluss;[6] and Mussolini notified Hitler only the day before the Italian troops were sent into Greece (October 28, 1940) that he was embarking on Ciano's War.[7] Italy was always in the dark on Nazi

[1] An illuminating discussion of the material to be found in these interrogations was given by the chairman of the Commission, Dewitt C. Poole, in Light on Nazi Foreign Policy, Foreign Affairs, vol. 25, October 1946, pp. 130–154.

[2] See Eleuthère Nicolaus Dzelepy, L'Alliance des Fascismes, Paris, 1934; Gerhard Schacher, Berlin and Rome in Central Europe, Contemporary Review, London, vol. 151, January 1937, pp. 38–45; The Economist, vol. 135; Robert Dell, Paying Ransom to Hitler, Nation, vol. 144, February 27, 1937, pp. 234–236.

[3] Relations Between Italy and Germany Have Been Growing Noticeably More Cordial, English Review, vol. LXIII, December 1936, pp. 623–4; Fascist Alliance, New Republic, vol. LXXXIX, December 9, 1936, pp. 159–160.

[4] State Department Mission, Interrogation, Dr. Hermann Neubacher, Wiesbaden, October 5, 1945. Dr. Neubacher, the roving Nazi ambassador in the Balkans, was closely associated with Rumanian affairs.

[5] State Department Mission, Interrogation, Hans Heinrich Dieckhoff, Lenzkirch, Schwarzwald, November 7, 9, 1945; also his Memorandum, Berlin, June 25, 1945.

[6] State Department Mission, interrogation, Paul Otto Gustav Schmidt, Oberursel, October 19, 22–26, 1945. Dr. Schmidt was the Chief of the Ministerial Bureau (BRAM), 1939–44. In the latter year he became Chief of POW and the Civilian Internee Section. As a skilled interpreter he was present at most of the major developments in German foreign relations under the Nazis. His interrogation was one of the most extensive and at the same time fruitful conducted by the Commission.

[7] State Department Mission, interrogation, Neubacher. Dr. Neubacher was involved in the Greek affair.

war plans.[8] Hitler failed to notify Japan of his pact with Soviet Russia (August 23, 1939), and Japan did not notify Germany of its attack on Pearl Harbor.[9] All of these acts were in direct contravention of treaties existing among the parties whereby they promised to keep each other informed about important political matters.

Thus, when the fascist dictators did act in unison, it was usually to attain common objectives, although occasionally, as when Hitler extricated Mussolini from the Greek war, one dictator might rescue another to save himself.[10]

There are a number of characteristics which fascisms have in common. Let us examine them.

Dynamic and aggressive

One of the stamps of fascist foreign policy is its dynamic and aggressive character.

At first dictators tend to be careful and cautious. Hitler promised President Hindenburg that he would accomplish his program peacefully,[11] and his first year was marked by a tolerance and concessions to Russia [12] which were totally lacking subsequently. Mussolini's foreign policy was weak and exploratory during the first few years of his rule,[13] and it was not until the Corfu incident in 1923, that he took a strong stand. Franco in Spain in April 1947, had not yet lost that caution.[14] However, once fascist rulers feel themselves secure, their foreign policy becomes more and more aggressive. Cautious Mussolini became aggressive in 1923, took a firm stand in the case of Hungarian arms shipments, and challenged the world in the Ethiopian crisis, after which time he was both belligerent and acquisitive.[15] Hitler began his crisis politics in international affairs only a few months after he became Chancellor,[16] because he was surer of his control over Germany in the early stages than was Mussolini over his control of Italy.

Expansionist

Fascist foreign policy is also expansionist in character.[17] More will be said on this point later. It is enough here to call attention to Germany's claims to Lebensraum, Ostraum, and colonies; Italy's claim to living space, a revival of the old Roman empire, Nice, Corsica, Tunisia, and the Adriatic;[18] Japan's demands for an oriental Monroe

[8] Italy Kept in Dark on Nazi War Plans, excerpt from Ciano Diary, reprinted Washington Star, June 22, 1945.
[9] State Department Mission, interrogation, Herbert von Dirksen, Wiesbaden, September 8-13, 1945. Von Dirksen was German Ambassador to Russia from 1928-33, to Japan from 1933-38, and to England from 1938-39.
[10] Interrogation, Neubacher; also Luigi Mondini, Prologo del Conflitto Italo-Greco, Rome, 1945.
[11] State Department Mission, interrogation, Horace Greeley Hjalmar Schacht, Wiesbaden, September 25, 1945. Dr. Schacht, the President of the Reichsbank, joined with Schleicher to persuade Hindenburg to give Hitler a chance at the chancellorship.
[12] Interrogation, von Dirksen. Von Dirksen testified that Hitler made a conciliatory start by granting an extension of time on the payment of the Russian debt to Germany. He accompanied this act by a conciliatory speech.
[13] H. Arthur Steiner, Foreign Governments and Politics, American Political Science Review, vol. 25, February 1931, pp. 146-152.
[14] But that it was kept in check by world events may be readily seen by reference to Bristol, Roucek, Interrogation Schmidt.
[15] See for example French Powder, Italian Matches, Literary Digest, vol. 106, July 12, 1930, p. 10; Robert C. Binkley, Franco Italian Discord, Current History, vol. 32, June 1930, pp. 529-533; and E. W. Polson Newman Mussolini's Foreign Policy, Fortnightly Review, vol. n. s. 128, July 1930, pp. 59-68.
[16] Interrogation, Schmidt.
[17] Claude Jeantot, Germany and the World, Living Age, vol. 349, September 1935, pp. 19-23; L. B. Namier, Germany Looks Toward Austria, the same, pp. 23-26; Herr Hitler's Thirteen Points, Politics in Review, vol. 2, April-June 1935, pp. 29-31; Mildred S. Wertheimer, Aims of Hitler's Foreign Policy, Foreign Policy Reports, vol. 11, June 5, 1935.
[18] In addition to the references in footnote 15, see Louis Aubert, France and Italy, Foreign Affairs, vol. 9, January 1931, pp. 222-242; Sir John Marriott, England and Italy, Fortnightly Review, vol. n. s. 138, No. 824, August 1935, pp. 194-202; B. W. Patch, Anglo-Italian Rivalry in the Mediterranean, Editorial Research Briefs, vol. 1, April 13, 1937.

Doctrine, acquisition of Manchuria, and attainment of the objectives of the Tanaka Memorial;[19] Spain's Hispanicism;[20] Poland's acquisition of Teschen; and Hungary's claims to Translyvania and Podkarpatska Rus, to mention only a few.

Improvised

Since fascist foreign policy is usually revolutionary, it is marked by improvisation.[21] The fascist leaders suspect the old foreign office officials and tend to disregard them and their advice.[22] For that reason particularly, fascist foreign policy lacks continuity and consistency, and is marked by abrupt changes and turns.[23] First one line is tried, and if it does not work, then another is tried, the first being dropped without hesitation. No clearer instance can be found than Hitler's abandonment of his anti-Russian campaign to enter into a treaty with Stalin, and then 2 years later to attack Soviet Russia.[24]

Reflects domestic struggle

As a reflection of the domestic struggle for control the same techniques are used abroad by fascist leaders as at home. Espionage of many sorts (often one observer is charged with observing another) is engaged in.[25] Sometimes these practices result in serious complications as they did in the Helmuth case. The end result is confusion of authority and uncertainty as to who is the legitimate representative of the fascist state.[26]

A contagious force

Fascism in foreign policy is a powerful and contagious force. It plays upon mass psychology; and since it possesses dramatic appeal, it induces emulation. Thus, a similarity is to be found in the foreign policies of the European fascisms prior to the Second World War. A study, for example, of the home grown fascist movements in Poland, Hungary, Bulgaria, and Rumania reveals a striking similarity of attitude, program, and purpose to that of Germany. The means of combatting Bolshevism were perfected in one state in terms of what it observed and copied from the others confronted with the same problem. The same copying will be found in their economic policies.[27] The success of Mussolini, Hitler, and Tojo in their dealings with the democracies furnished the smaller fascisms with object lessons in dynamic and aggressive diplomacy.

---

[19] The expansionist aims of Japan are discussed in Kalijarvi, ch. 28; the Tanaka Memorial, New York, 1942.

[20] K. S. Robson, Third Winter of the Spanish Civil War, Nineteenth Century, vol. 124, No. 742, December 1938, pp. 666–676; Ernest Bock, Spain and the Axis, The Contemporary Review, vol. 161, March 1942, pp. 148–153.

[21] Interrogation, von Dirksen.

[22] State Department Mission, interrogation, Andor Hencke, Wiesbaden, November 19, 1945. Hencke was the Undersecretary of Foreign Affairs in the German Foreign Office in charge of the Political Division. See also State Department Mission, interrogation, Paul Giese, Berlin, February 1–April 15, June 10, 1946. Giese was Amtsrat in the foreign press division of the Propaganda Ministry.

[23] Poole, especially the introductory part and conclusions; also T. P. Conwell-Evans, Continuity of German Foreign Policy, The Nineteenth Century, vol. 132, No. 785, July 1942, pp. 33–38.

[24] Poole.

[25] The Career of Heinrich Himmler, Reproduction Branch SSU; also State Department Mission, interrogation Captain Dietrich Niebuhr, Wiesbaden, November 10, 1945, gives an excellent chart showing the various agencies engaged in spying and secret service; State Department Mission, Walter Schellenberg, the chief of Amt VI, Nuremberg, December 19, 1945.

[26] State-Department Mission, interrogation, Hans Heinrich Dieckhoff. Helmuth Case. Osmar Alberto Helmuth was an intermediary through whom Argentina attempted to purchase arms from Germany during the Second World War. Helmuth was arrested by the British at Trinidad because of a leak in information, due it is now suspected to friction between the Foreign office under Ribbentrop and the Security Service (Sicherheitsdienst) under Himmler, for the latter of which Helmuth was working.

[27] See ch. V, Foreign Trade, VI, Organization of the Economy: Germany, and VII, Organization of the Economy: Italy, Spain, Japan.

WHO MAKES THE FOREIGN POLICY IN A FASCIST STATE?

Foreign policy in fascist states is usually made by the dictator. In Germany Hitler made the German foreign policy, and Ribbentrop merely tried to do what he thought Hitler wanted.[28] Similarly, Mussolini was directly responsible for Italian foreign policy.[29] The same can be said for Horthy in Hungary,[30] who removed chancellors who did not please him. Pilsudski and Beck in Poland set the course of their states in international affairs, as did Antonescu in Rumania and as did Tito in 1947 Yugoslavia. On the other hand the Spanish foreign policy was set by the Falangist Party and was voiced by Serano Suñer;[31] and in Japan the military clique determined the policy to be pursued.

OBJECTIVES OF THE FOREIGN RELATIONS OF THE PRINCIPAL FASCIST STATES

Germany

The foreign policy of National Socialist Germany had several objectives;[32] (1) to fight and eradicate the rival system of communism, and as a corollary to check Russia everywhere, especially in eastern Europe and the Balkans;[33] (2) to extend German economic and political control over the Balkans and eastern Europe, which upon the subjugation of Czechoslovakia gave rise to a new imperial politics and an extended economy (Grossraumpolitik and Grossraumwirtschaft);[34] (3) to remain on friendly terms with Great Britain; (4) to be on the aggressive always and never to lose face at home (Nazi foreign policy was in a major measure designed for home consumption and drawn up with an eye to its effect upon the German people. In no other way can the dramatic actions in the case of the Anschluss, the march into Czechoslovakia, the war upon Yugoslavia, and Hitler's 10-day limit forced upon Chamberlain at Munich be consistently explained); (5) to secure Lebensraum or the acquisition of enough territorial space in which the German race could grow, move, and spread[35] (it also meant an expanded area in which German industrialists would have a preferred position. Thus, if they did not actually have a monopoly of trade, they would control the market, and be the sole buyers of the colonial products); (6) to achieve autarchy or economic self-sufficiency; (7) to regain the lost German colonies including not only the pre-First World War colonies, but also the "lost German colonies" in Switzerland, Belgium, and Denmark;[36] (8) to make the world secure for Germans everywhere, which was supported by racial corollaries so familiar that they need no repetition

[28] State Department Mission, interrogation Bernd Gottfriedsen, Kassel, September 10–11, 1945. Gottfriedsen was secretary to Ribbentrop. See also State Department Mission, interrogation Hencke, October 23, 1945; Jeantot, pp. 19–20. Paul Schwarz, This Man Ribbentrop, New York, 1943.
[29] Galeazzo Ciano, The Ciano Diaries, 1939–43, Garden City, 1946.
[30] State Department, interrogation, Nicholas Horthy von Nagybanya, Wiesbaden, September 12, 1945.
[31] The Suñer Mission, The Economist, vol. 139, October 12, 1940, pp. 459–460.
[32] W. M. Jordan, Great Britain, France, and the German Problem, 1918–39, London, New York, 1943, reviews the situation up to the outbreak of the Second World War.
[33] Otto Kriegk, Krieg oder Frieden? Weltpolitik zwischen Nationalsozialismus und Bolschewismus, Berlin, 1939; Hans Rothfels, Ostraum, Preussentum und Reichsgedanke, Leipzig, 1935.
[34] Patch; The Russo-German Feud Regarded as a Farce, The Economist, vol. 124, August 29, 1936; Manchester Guardian, September 18, 1936, p. 230; Herr Hitler's Thirteen Points.
[35] R. C. K. Ensor, Mein Kampf and Europe, International Affairs, vol. 18, July-August 1939, pp. 478–496; Henry C. Wolfe, Hitler Looks Eastward, Atlantic Monthly, vol. 159, February 1937, pp. 239–246.
[36] Towards a New Empire, Review of Reviews, vol. 86, June 1935, pp. 34–38; George Glasgow, Germany and Colonies, Contemporary Review, London, vol. 151, April 1940; Ferdinand Kuhn, Vast Empires and the Nazi Threat to Them, New York Times, May 26, 1940, p. 5; Felix Wirth, German Colonial Ambitions, Contemporary Review, London, vol. 163, January 1943, pp. 36–39.

here;[37] (9) to reject the League of Nations and the whole system of collective security;[38] (10) to free Germany from foreign encirclement;[39] and, (11) to establish the National Socialist Weltanschauung and world interest beyond challenge.[40]

These will show the trend of German thinking.[41] It was supported by the concept that a totalitarian state must be armed to the teeth; the state must be purified of Jews; an alliance must be found with the weaker partner, Italy, and with Britain; sufficient territory must be acquired in order to make the Reich a world state;[42] and the 1914 borders would not answer German needs in 1933–39.[43]

Italy

Italian foreign policy prior to the Second World War had as specific aims:[44] (1) to acquire sufficient living space for the cramped Italian people, which was to be accomplished by territorial changes in Europe and by the acquisition of a new colonial empire; (in Europe the cry was principally for Nice, Savoy, and Corsica;[45] in Africa it was for the expansion of Libya, the securing of Tunis, the conquest of Ethiopia, and for such further concessions as could be extracted from France and Great Britain); (2) to make the Adriatic Sea an Italian lake by bringing Albania, Greece, and Yugoslavia under Italian domination;[46] (3) to make the Mediterranean Sea safe for Italy, which would entail[47] (4) bringing Italy out of her isolation as an island, and would result in (5) Italian opposition to Great Britain;[48] (6) to fight communism everywhere;[49] (7) to develop the Italian Navy and air force and to make Italy a great power;[50] and (8) to make Italy strong vis à vis France since it was chiefly at her expense that the Italian territorial ambitions on the European continent could be achieved.[51]

The Italian foreign policy aims were built about the needs of a strong military state with a growing population,[52] which demanded room to expand and economic resources with which to develop its greatness.[53]

Spain

In this company Franco's Spain was a relatively minor power. However, the objectives of its foreign policy[54] even in 1947, were: (1)

[37] Herr Hitler's Thirteen Points; Wertheimer; Frederick L. Schuman, The Conduct of German Foreign Affairs, Annals of the American Academy, vol. 176, November 1934, pp. 187–221; and in the same volume by the same author, Third Reich's Road to War, pp. 33–43; Reich Will Defend Minorities Abroad, New York Times, January 18, 1938, p. 16; Karl Ludwig von Oertzen, Deutschland ohne Sicherheit, Munich, 1934.
[38] Heinrich Rogge, Hitler's Friedenspolitik und das Volkerrecht, Berlin, 1935.
[39] Encirclement: Myth and Reality, The Spectator, June 30, 1939, pp. 1116–1117; Encirclement, London Times, July 12, 1939, p. 15; James Leslie Brierly, Encirclement, London, 1939.
[40] Hans Volz, Von der Grossmacht zur Weltmacht, 1937, Berlin, 1938.
[41] Wertheimer.
[42] Paul Kirn, Politische Geschichte der deutschen Grenzen, Leipzig, 1944; Franz Alfred Six, Das Reich und Europa, eine politisch-historische Skizze, Berlin, 1943; same author, Europa, Tradition und Zukunft, Hamburg 1944.
[43] Berlin, Deutsches Institut fuer aussenpolitische Forschung, Europa; Handbuch der politischen, wirtschaftlichen und kulturellen Entwicklung des neuen Europa, Leipzig, 1943.
[44] Barbara Ward, Italian Foreign Policy, Oxford, 1941.
[45] Virginio Gayda, Italiens Kampf um Lebensraum, Berlin, 1942; V. K. Sugareff, Italian Penetration of the Balkans, Current History, vol. 33, November 1930, pp. 218–222; Marriott; Patch; The Economist, vol. 136, July 29, 1939, pp. 205–206; Geoffrey Theodore Garratt, Mussolini's Roman Empire, Harmondsworth, 1938.
[46] John Oliver Crane, Italy and the Adriatic, Rome, 1933.
[47] Stephen King-Hall, Mediterranean Problem, New York, 1938.
[48] Patch.
[49] La guerra contro la Russia bolscevica, Rome, 1941.
[50] Patch.
[51] Virginio Gayda, Italien und Frankreich, Berlin, 1939.
[52] Virginio Gayda, Che cosa vuole l'Italia?, Rome, 1940.
[53] Dino Grandi, L'Italia fascista nella politica internazionale, Rome, 1930.
[54] These had been laid down at an earlier date and listed in Camilo Barcia Trelles, Puntos cardinales de la política international española, Barcelona, 1939.

to oust communism and to fight it where it may be encountered; (2) to acquire living space; (3) to secure control over Morocco, Gibraltar, and north Africa;[55] (4) to unify Spain and the Spanish people; (5) to spread the concept of the cultural unity of the Spanish race in terms of Hispanidad;[56] and (6) to develop a new order for Spain. Here are the first three points of the Falange Española Tradicionalista.[57]

1. We believe in the supreme reality of Spain. To strengthen it, elevate it, and improve it is the urgent collective task of all Spaniards. In order to achieve this end, the interest of the individuals, groups, and classes will have to be remorselessly waived.

2. Spain is a destined unity in the universe. Any conspiracy against this unity is abhorrent. Any form of separation is an unpardonable crime. The existing Constitution, insofar as it encourages disunity, commits a crime against the destiny of Spain. For this reason we demand its immediate abrogation.

3. We have a will to empire. We affirm that the full history of Spain implies an empire. We demand for Spain a preeminent place in Europe. We will not put up with international isolation or with foreign interference. With regard to the Hispano-American countries, we will aim at unification of culture, of economic interests and of power. Spain claims a preeminent place in all common tasks, because of her position as the spiritual cradle of the Spanish world.

Japan [58]

The Japanese foreign policy prior to 1941 had as its chief purposes: (1) to bring to an end Western control in the Orient; and (2) to supplant Western influence by Japanese influence, thus creating (3) the much publicized Japanese Greater East Asia coprosperity sphere. Elsewhere in the world the Japanese (4) would open the trade marts to Japanese industry. The Tanaka Memorial,[59] however, went even farther and stated it to be Japanese objectives (5) first to conquer China, then (6) to defeat the United States, and finally (7) to establish Japanese hegemony of the world.

Regardless of the weight given to the Tanaka Memorial and its program, the Japanese objectives were similar to those of Germany and Italy. They were based upon a strong military and naval machine, the need for territorial expansion, the desire for economic self-sufficiency, and the spread of Japanese influence by challenging to war those powers which stood in the way of her achieving her objectives.

General

The examination of the foreign policies of other fascist states would show that as far as objectives are concerned there is a definite pattern which they seem to follow. Based upon racial unity and predominance, they seek territory for expansion and growth, attempt to establish self-sufficiency at home and economic penetration abroad, and in most cases are strongly anticommunistic.[60]

---

[55] Carlos Ibañez de Ibero, El Mediterráneo y la cuestión de Gibraltar, San Sebastian, 1939.

[56] Samuel Eijan, Hispanidad en Tierra Santa, Madrid, 1943.

[57] Robson, Third Winter of the Spanish Civil War, p. 673.

[58] Kalijarvi, ch. 28.

[59] The aims of the Tanaka Memorial had been discussed freely prior to 1927, but it was not until that year that it became public property.

[60] The conflict with communism is a struggle for power since ideologically and in practice there is comparatively little difference between communism and fascism.

GERMANY

THE ORGANIZATION OF FOREIGN AFFAIRS UNDER NATIONAL
SOCIALISM

The most extensive organization for the formulation and conduct of fascist foreign policies was set up in Germany. Not only was it most extensive, but we know most about it. For these reasons it will be described as the arch type of its kind.

The Foreign Office (Auswaertiges Amt)[61]

The German Foreign Office was the historical and functional agency of the German Government for the administration of its foreign affairs. Organized on both functional and geographical lines, it had been reorganized in 1936, to make it more efficient. In spite of this, from the outset it failed to command Hitler's confidence because he distrusted the practiced and experienced diplomat. Baron von Neurath was its head in 1933. Later he was replaced by Joachim von Ribbentrop.[62] During the national socialistic experiment in Germany, the Foreign Office continued to have charge of German diplomats abroad, but its wings were clipped and other agencies replaced it in many areas. Moreover the ambassadors' powers were reduced.

Ribbentrop Bureau (Dienststelle or Buero Ribbentrop) [63]

This agency was a Nazi improvization on foreign affairs, set up in 1934, to enable Ribbentrop to perform foreign policy functions outside the recognized Foreign Office of the German Government. Ribbentrop claimed this agency was essential to building a broader basis for peace with England and France than was possible through the Foreign Office. In 1935–37, it reached the height of its power, employing a staff of 60 people. It was to all intents a substitute foreign office for Ribbentrop. After Ribbentrop became Foreign Minister, the Bureau declined in significance and was not influential when the Second World War broke out. In form and organization it was patterned after the foreign office.

Foreign Policy Office of the National Socialist Party (Aussenpolitisches Amt der NSDAP) [64]

This was the party office under Rosenberg, which interested itself in foreign relations. It never had great power because Rosenberg was regarded as theoretical and visionary. But it did contribute to confusion in the administration of Nazi foreign policies.

---

[61] The following State Department Mission interrogations give a good perspective on the operation of the *Auswaertiges Amt:* Andor Hencke, Wiesbaden, October 23, 1945 and November 19, 1945; Baron Oswald von Hoyningen-Huene, Wiesbaden, October 11, 1945; Hans Thomsen, Wiesbaden, October 10, 1945; Hans Treutzschler von Falkenstein, Wiesbaden, October 25, 1946; Fritz Adalbert von Twardowski, Wiesbaden, October 3, 1945; Dr. Edmund Veesenmayer, Wiesbaden, October 5, 1945; Dr. Hermann Neubacher, Wiesbaden, October 5, 1945; Baron Constantin von Neurath, November 10, 1945; Friedrich Wilhelm von Prittwitz und Graffen, Wiesbaden, November 3, 1945; Otto Reinbeck, Bad Toels, February 4, 1946; Joachim von Ribbentrop, Nuremberg, September 21, 1945; Paul Otto Gustav Schmidt, Wiesbaden, November 12, 1945; Heribert von Stempel, Oberursel, November 18, 1945; Werner Stephan, Bremen, May 3–27, 1946; Hans Heinrich Dieckhoff, Lenzkirch, Schwarzwald, November 7, 9, 1945 including his Berlin Memorandum of June 25, 1945; Herbert von Dirksen, Wiesbaden, October 11, 1945; and Berndt Gottfriedsen, Kassel, September 10–11, 1945.
[62] Interrogations, von Ribbentrop; Schmidt.
[63] State Department Mission, Interrogations, Berndt Gottfriedsen, Paul Otto, Gustav Schmidt, and Joachim von Ribbentrop.
[64] Interrogation, Gottfriedsen, also Schuman.

Foreign Organization of the Ministry of External Affairs (Auslands-organization der Aussenministerium) [65]

This organization, known as the AO, was headed by Ernst Wilhelm Bohle. It was a party device, which aimed to hold together German citizens abroad by organizing them into a single district *(Gau)*. For several years prior to 1945, it occupied 300 rooms at Berlin-Wilmersdorf, Westfaelischestrasse 1. Eighteen or nineteen of its offices were concerned with propaganda and cooperation with Nazi sympathizers in other countries. But in addition to these there were other offices concerned with personnel for Nazi offices, teachers abroad both on elementary and advanced levels, Hitlerjugend, the press, race questions, administrative matters concerned in the operation of AO, refugees, indoctrination of officers, and the conduct of German students abroad. The AO was consulted on many questions of foreign policy including the selection of ambassadors, the operation of embassies, and the foreign policies to be pursued with regard to the countries in which members of the AO lived. It was the bane of many an ambassador's existence. In organization it was lined up according to subject matter and geography. The United States fell into Landamt VI.

Related agencies [66]

Several other German agencies, either directly or indirectly touched upon foreign relations. The Ibero American Institute (Ibero-Amerikanisches Institut) was a social group which had some influence on the relations with Brazil, especially under Colonel von Faupel. The German Foreign Institute (Deutsches Auslands-Institut) was a research agency and was helpful to Hans Luther before he became ambassador to the United States;[67] but as an established agency it was eschewed by Bohle and his AO, and consequently by the Party. The Association for Germans in Foreign Lands (Volksbund fuer das Deutschtum im Ausland), originally powerful and designed to hold together ethnic Germans abroad, lost power when Bohle refused to let it be amalgamated with his AO in 1938. Then the German Public Assistance Center (Volksdeutsche Mittelstelle) designed to help returning Germans, was checked by Bohle, who refused to let it assist his AO. In addition there were German Railways, AO sea trip (Seesfahrt), AO ship voyage (Schiffahrt), NS (National Socialist) Womans Organization (Frauenschaft) of AO, the German Labor Front (Deutsche Arbeitsfront) of AO, all more or less tied into activities abroad.[68] It would be a mistake to attribute to these any concerted program except to hold the Germans together and to promote the program of the state in some form or other. But, as will be apparent, they added to the multiplicity of agencies and organizations interested in and charged with the formulation and operation of German foreign policies.

---

[65] Interrogations, Gottfriedsen; Ernest Wilhelm Bohle, Oberursel, September 5, 6, 7, 8, 1945. Bohle was the Secretary of State for Aussenministerium and chief of the Auslandsorganization. Also see National Socialism, prepared by the Division of European Affairs, Department of State, Washington, 1943.
[66] Interrogation, Bohle.
[67] State Department Mission, Interrogation, Dr. Karl Stroelin, Oberursel, September 18, 19, 21, 1945.
[68] Interrogation, Bohle.

Office of Colonial Policies (Kolonialpolitisches Amt) [69]

This office in charge of Franz Ritter von Epp had as its duty the formulation of plans looking toward the reestablishment of a German colonial empire. Its activities were encouraged by German military victories in the West, but as the war went on it faded into insignificance and at last withered out of existence.

Secret services [70]

As noted elsewhere the domestic scene and the foreign scene were ridden with secret services. Over and above the regular attachés the military services maintained a secret service, the (Abwehr) Military Intelligence. Representatives were to be found in almost every large German Embassy. In addition to this, Himmler was the head of Secret Military Police (Geheime Feldpolizei) and the Secret State Police (Geheime Staatspolizei) through which agencies he maintained a special section, Office No. VI, Amt. VI of the Headquarters of the National Security Service (Reichssicherheitshaúptamt), whose duty it was to spy abroad. [71]

It was this Office No. VI (Amt. VI [72]) which was represented in many embassies and which was responsible for negotiating with Argentine authorities [73] (instead of the Embassy) for the sale of German arms to Argentina through the medium of Osmar Alberto Helmuth, [74] an act which led to the breaking of diplomatic relations between Germany and Argentina during the Second World War. It was the general practice for representatives of the Security Service (Sicherheitsdienst) to operate independently of the established diplomatic officers. [75]

Even big business engaged in economic espionage through its representatives abroad and was headed by Max Ilgner's well-known Berlin NW 7.

Propaganda [76]

Soon after Ribbentrop became Minister of Foreign Affairs, Goebbels extracted from him the right to appoint his own representatives to Washington, London, and Buenos Aires. In 1942 this list was extended to cover Stockholm, Cophenhagen, Bucharest, and Rome. While these representatives were sent solely for propaganda purposes, the interpretation of what composed propaganda was so broad that Goebbels' men actually exerted an influence on the operation of German foreign policy. The Propaganda Ministry was also organized to deal with the domestic and foreign press and in that way exerted further influence.

Goering and special missions

It was a conspicuous feature of Nazi foreign policy to send emissaries to foreign capitals who started political conversations or negotiations, often without inform-

---

[69] Interrogation, Gottfriedsen; also Felix Wirth, "German Colonial Ambitions," Contemporary Review, London, vol. 163, January 1943, pp. 36-39.
[70] State Department Mission, interrogation, Captain Dietrich Niebuhr, Wiesbaden, November 10, 1945; interrogation, Dr. Theodor Paeffgen, Wiesbaden, October 19, 1945; interrogation, Walter Schellenberg Nuremberg, December 19, 1945; interrogation, Erich Schroeder, Hohensasperg, February 5, 1946; interrogation, Karl Gustav Arnold, Berlin, November 20, 1946; interrogation, Ulrich von Gienanth, Wiesbaden, October 9, 1945.
[71] Interrogation, Niebuhr.
[72] Interrogation, Paeffgen. See also ch. VI, "Organization of the Economy," footnote 67.
[73] Interrogation, Schellenberg.
[74] Interrogation, Helmuth.
[75] Interrogations, Giese; Arnold; Paeffgen.
[76] See ch. II, Education and Thought Control; interrogations, Stephan; State Department Mission, interrogation, Frau Hanna Brauweiler, Berlin, January 29-June 7, 1946; interrogation, Giese.

ing the accredited officials—the Ambassadors. Ribbentrop in particular used to send members of his personal staff to foreign capitals to collect information and to negotiate. And Goering, Goebbels, and Rosenberg followed his example.[77]

When affairs were at their worst just before the outbreak of the Second World War, Goering sent as his special emissary Fritz Wiedemann to try to reach an understanding with the British. As a result Wiedemann fell out of favor with Hitler.[78]

Not only were emissaries sent, but occasionally one of the Nazi leaders carried on the relations with a foreign country for Germany. Thus Goering was the key to Polish and German relations, especially during Pilsudski's life.

It was not strange then, from the standpoint of German foreign policy, that Rudolf Hesse should have flown to Britain during the war to carry on negotiations on his own in hopes of bringing about an understanding between Germany and Great Britain. Unorthodox as it was, it was characteristically national socialism in action.

Foreign representatives and the party [79]

While at the outset the diplomatic officers of the Foreign Office were not subject to pressures to become members of the Party, they were eventually urged by von Neurath himself to join. At first there were relatively few changes made in the staff of the Foreign Office. When Ribbentrop became Foreign Minister, he introduced only a few of his own men into the Foreign Office. Among those who did accompany him were Baron Steengracht, Hewel, Abetz, and Stahmer.[80] However, by 1940–41 the Party began to take a stronger hold on the Foreign Office and Party members began to permeate the staff. Noteworthy Party appointments were made to the Balkan States, chief among them were A. H. Beckerle to Sofia, Hans Ludin to Slovakia, Siegfried Kasche to Zagreb, von Killinger to Bratislava, Dr. Erich Benzler to Belgrade, Dr. Edmund Veesenmayer to Budapest, Dr. W. A. J. Fabricius to Budapest, and Dr. H. Neubacher as Special Envoy.[81]

Attentat of July 20, 1944

The strained relations between Hitler and the Foreign Office became even more troubled after the attempt on Hitler's life on July 20, 1944, because several of the old-line diplomats were believed to have been involved.

Operation of an Embassy

Former Ambassador to Russia, Japan, and England, Herbert von Dirksen, commented on the effect of the multiplicity of agencies concerned with German foreign policy as follows:

Yes; that was dreadful * * * The embassies in Spain and Japan became so ausblasiert (blown up) with all kinds of extraordinary personnel that the poor Ambassador hardly knew what was going on. The Polizei Attachés in particular were not only cooperating with the local police but carrying out all sorts of secret jobs of their own.[82]

---

[77] Interrogation, von Dirksen.
[78] Interrogation, von Dirksen; Dieckhoff.
[79] Interrogations, Hencke; Veesenmayer; Neubacher; Twardowski; Tannenberg.
[80] Interrogation, Gottfriedsen.
[81] Interrogation, von Gienanth.
[82] Interrogation, von Dirksen.

In Spain, where the German Embassy numbered 500 at one stage, Ambassador Dieckhoff resigned because of the frustration of his official work due to activities going on behind his back in his own Embassy. Von Meynen and von Thermann had the same experience in Argentina.[83]

Summary and results

A birds-eye view of German foreign policy in organization and operation shows that the struggle for power of the Nazi leaders at home was carried over into foreign affairs. Goering, Goebbels, Himmler, Rosenberg, Hesse, and Bohle vied with Ribbentrop and the Foreign Office for a hand in foreign affairs.[84] Hitler set the main lines of policy by wish and intuition, and the many leaders, agencies, and agents concerned with these policies confused them in operation and frustrated each other. Himmler purchased the Mannfred Weiss works in Rumania so that he would be free of Goering in the manufacture of airplanes.[85] He also reached out with his SD and military intelligence (Abwehr) into foreign affairs to establish the control which would make it possible for him to take over if Hitler died. Both actions embarrassed the regular German diplomatic officials. Other Nazi leaders were similarly looking forward to further controls and power, and hoped to achieve them by dabbling and meddling in foreign relations. The end results were contradiction, paradox, conflict, inefficiency, lack of coordination, and frustration. If the case for dictatorship is efficiency in government, then national socialism in foreign affairs was a contradiction of that thesis, for it was inefficient.

GERMAN FOREIGN POLICY IN OPERATION

Having observed the organization and machinery for the formulation and conduct of foreign affairs in Germany, it remains to observe the course of German foreign policy under national socialism.[86]

1934

The first challenge of the Nazis to the traditional system of international relations came in the withdrawal from the League of Nations, an act which caused no reaction in Germany.[87] This was followed in June 1934, by the blood purge, which Paul Winkler says Hitler ordered after a 2-day conference with German industrialists and bankers in order to rid the Nazi Party of "liberal" elements. It lowered German prestige abroad and revealed the character of Nazi thought and policy. Hard on the heels of this act came the assassination of Chancelor Dollfuss (July 25, 1934)[88] which simply carried over the technique of the blood purge into the field of international affairs. The Foreign Office, well acquainted with sentiment abroad, was disturbed at these events, but could do nothing about them, even though German stock

[83] Interrogation, Dieckhoff.
[84] Interrgoations, von Prittwitz und Gaffron; Schmidt.
[85] Interrogation, Veesenmayer.
[86] Interrogations in footnote 61, especially Schmidt.
[87] Walter Truckenbrodt, Deutschland und der Völkerbund, die Behandlung reichsdeutscher Angelegen-heiten im Voelkerrechtspolitische Lage Deutschlands, Berlin, 1936.
[88] Interrogation, Schmidt.

was rapidly declining throughout the world.[89]   The immediate effect of these excursions into the use of force resulted in the Franco-Soviet Consultative Pact of December 5, 1934.[90]   It was defensive in nature and should have been a warning to the Nazis, but it only made them more obdurate and stubborn than ever.[91]

1935

Again in 1935, in the Saar plebiscite, the Nazis interpreted the German victory as a party victory, although the party had had nothing to do with it and although there had been no correspondence nor any consultation between the Saarlanders and the Foreign Office.[92]   Pressing this advantage, Hitler announced that Germany intended to create a new air force and would institute universal conscription (May 2, 1935).[93]   Again the answer of France and Russia to this was the conclusion of a mutual assistance pact.   And again it had no effect on the Nazi leaders.   Then came the mission of Simon and Eden to Berlin in the spring of 1935, from which the Anglo-German naval agreement eventually resulted.   Like the invasion of the Rhineland it was not in accord with the peace treaties and with the system of collective security; but no one protested in this case.[94]

The tempo of events was gradually being stepped up.   Next Mussolini embarked upon his Ethiopian war.   He did not give Hitler advance notice of his action, but the Fuehrer greeted the Italian venture with enthusiasm and promised unqualified German support for Italy.[95]   Later Mussolini at the Munich Conference admitted that Italy could not have carried on the war for a week if the League of Nations' oil sanctions had been effective.

1936

The reoccupation of the Rhineland and its remilitarization had been anticipated by Germany in a communique of February 21, in which Hitler denounced the Franco-Soviet Pact of Mutual Aid[96] as incompatible with the Locarno Treaties and with the League of Nations Covenant.   The German generals were not happy with the venture because it was too risky.   They did not have their new Army ready; but Hitler went ahead with remilitarization in spite of them.[97]   The League condemned Germany.   Shortly thereafter Ribbentrop went to London with a 19-point peace proposal suggesting a 25-year peace pact, an air pact, and an eastern Locarno; but these came to nothing.

Then on November 14 Hitler denounced the international control of the Rhine, Danube, Elbe, and Oder rivers.[98]

A few months' respite was followed by the formation of the Rome-Berlin axis agreement of October 25, 1936.   It rested upon no specific agreement, but upon an instrument providing for general cooperation between Italy and Germany.   The joint recognition of Franco was

[89] Interrogation, von Neurath.

[90] Memorandum by the German Government respecting the Franco-Soviet Treaty, the treaty of Locarno and the demilitarized zone in the Rhineland, London, 1936.

[91] Interrogation, Schmidt.

[92] Wertheimer.

[93] Interrogation, Schmidt.

[94] Interrogation, Schmidt.

[95] Robert Menzies MacGregor, Order or Disorder?, London, 1939; Documents Relating to the Italo-Ethiopian Conflict, Ottawa, 1936.

[96] K. K. Kawakami, Germany and Japan Today, International Conciliation, April 1936.

[97] Germany and the Rhineland, Royal Institute of International Affairs, London, 1936.

[98] Interrogation, Schmidt.

the first manifestation of its operation in the political sphere.[99] It was subsequently amplified by the Anticomintern pact, which was a Ribbentrop instrument, in the creation of which the Foreign Office had no part. Although it was of no particular significance, it did anticipate the Tripartite Alliance pact of September 27, 1940,[100] and had as purpose the rallying of Italy and Japan to Germany's assistance in the case of a war with Russia.

Meanwhile, Hitler was making it known that Germany wished to secure colonies, and he desired western Africa particularly.[101] When he talked these matters over with the British Minister of Foreign Affairs, Henderson, the latter was apparently willing to make only qualified concessions contingent on an over-all settlement of issues between England and Germany, including the latter's return to the League of Nations. The negotiations were therefore unsuccessful.

1938

Next came the Anschluss with Austria. The union of the two countries was generally accepted as inevitable; but when it came, it was handled as a party affair in which the Foreign Office had no part.[102] When Schussnig held his meeting with Hitler at Berchtesgaden on February 21, 1938, the sessions were stormy in view of Schussnig's unwillingness to accept Hitler's proposals. The invasion (Einmarsch) of Austria was an improvization, which stunned the world and created opposition even in Great Britain, where the union had been sympathetically expected.[103] It was not the act, but the way in which it was carried out that aroused animosity. Italy had not been consulted, and Hitler was gratified that this time Mussolini did not take action as he had at the time of the assassination of Dolfuss. Italian tacit cooperation led to Hitler's visit to Rome on May 3–10, which resulted in a fascist review of the European situation.

The next adventure revolved about the Sudeten problem and the negotiations leading to Munich.[104] When the Czech-Soviet pact of mutual assistance was entered into in 1935, it brought the possibility of Russian use of Czech flying fields as air bases for attacks on Berlin, because the Czech flying fields were located only an hour's distance from the German capital. In 1937, Goering told ex-President Hoover that Czechoslovakia was like an appendix, "and when you have appendicitis, you cut it out." Measures for the march into Prague were drawn up as early as March 1938. A propaganda campaign was launched to foment discord in Czechoslovakia. In hopes of preventing war over Czechoslovakia, Lord Halifax made a fruitless mission to Hitler at Berchtesgaden, which was followed by the unsuccessful trip of Chamberlain to the same place on September 15, 1938.[105] Another session was held at Godesberg on September 22, and it, too, was un-

[99] German-Italian Agreement, Manchester Guardian, vol. 35, October 30, 1946, p. 344; Hunger Breeds War, The New Statesman and Nation, vol. 13, Jan. 2, 1937, pp. 3–4; A Hitler-Franco Pact in 1938 Reported by Royalist Agent, Christian Science Monitor, May 20, 1941, p. 4.
[100] Interrogation, Schmidt.
[101] Franz Borkenau, The New German Empire, New York, 1939; Du Maroc au Cameroun, Paris, 1941.
[102] Interrogation, Schmidt.
[103] R. B. Mowat, The Crisis in Central Europe, The Nineteenth Century, vol. 123, No. 734, April 1938, pp. 394–404.
[104] Interrogations, Hencke; Field Marshall General Wilhelm Keitl, Wiesbaden, October 20, 1945.
[105] Interrogation, Hencke.

productive.[106] Then came Munich, when Mussolini presented his proposal for a compromise arrangement, which was accepted in modified form, and the world believed that peace had at last been secured.[107]

1939

Now Czechoslovakia and all eastern Europe were under Nazi domination.[108] Russia had been rebuffed, and a period for the consolidation of conquests had set in. But Hitler refused to rest or to consolidate his gains. Relations with Czechoslovakia grew worse in spite of the concessions on the Sudeten issues. Between September 1938 and March 1939, German foreign policy toward Czechoslovakia was one of condescension. The march into Prague took place on March 14-15, 1939, when President Hacha was on a visit to Berlin.[109] Many of the career experts of the Foreign Office were stunned. Most of the informed Germans were likewise stunned. This tour de force was gratuitous,[110] because German control over truncated Czechoslovakia was complete. This dramatic stroke aroused the world. The march showed clearly the Nazi "inexorable progression from demands based upon ethnographical grounds to the theory of Lebensraum." It marked a great divide in history,[111] for after this point national socialism was committed to a program which could end in only one of two ways: (1) A complete Nazi victory and domination over the world with all the program of national socialism implied; or (2) ultimate loss of face and eventual defeat. Before the march into Prague peaceful consolidation of gains with improved foreign relations was possible for Germany. After March 5, 1939, Nazi Germany had thrown the challenge so clearly to Britain, France, and the rest of the world that there was no alternative but preparation for eventual war.[112]

Tension increased. During the turmoil surrounding the investment of Czechoslovakia, Hitler seized Memel on March 22, 1939.[113] The first ultimatum to Poland was delivered on March 21, 1939, calling for a return to Germany of Danzig and demanding an extraterritorial corridor for Germany through the Polish Corridor. Poland, supported by England, balked.

Now England began countermeasures. She built a system of nonaggression treaties giving guaranties of mutual assistance to the states around Germany. These treaties included Poland (March 31 and April 3). France too offered similar guaranties to the smaller European states, and signed treaties with Greece and Rumania (April 13). During the next few weeks Henderson tried to come to terms with Hitler. Goering and Ambassador Dirksen tried to avert a conflict with Britain. These measures failed because Hitler refused to budge from his demands on Poland.[114]

Meanwhile, the Anglo-French negotiations with Russia were not going too well.[115] In August 1939, Germany turned to Russia in order

[106] Interrogation, von Dirksen.
[107] Interrogation, Oertzen.
[108] Gerhard Schacher, Germany Pushes Southeast, London, 1937.
[109] Interrogation, Hencke.
[110] State Department Mission, Interrogation General Heinz Guderian, Wiesbaden, October 4, 1945.
[111] Interrogation, Schmidt; Karl Olivercrona, England eller Tyskland, Lund, 1940.
[112] Germany—What Next? Harmondworth, Penguin, 1939; Sir Arthur Willert, England's Duty, Atlantic Monthly, vol. 59, January 1937, pp. 96-104.
[113] Interrogation, Schmidt.
[114] Willert.
[115] Interrogation, Schmidt.

to neutralize her in the coming conflict. Success took the form of a Soviet-German Pact on August 23, 1939, which laid at rest the rivalry of the two countries over the Baltic issues and over all other problems.

Hitler was now free to follow a completely aggressive course,[116] and as a result increased his pressure on Poland until conflict became inevitable. When the British ultimatum followed by the declaration of war was·communicated to Hitler, he could not believe them because he had been so sure that decadent Britain and France would not fight.[117] However, once war was declared, eastern Europe was divided between Russia and Germany, as Poland was subjected to a fourth partitioning arranged by special treaty between Stalin and Hitler.

The War, 1939–45

When the war broke out, the Nazis did not like the Italian neutrality, and when Mussolini finally entered the conflict on June 10, 1940, the Germans considered his act as "hopping on the band wagon" so that he would be able to share in the spoils without fighting.[118] During the war many peace feelers were extended by Germany in the hopes of retaining what she had won. Hitler, however, made them only when they were to his advantage. Since he would listen only to that which he liked and wanted to hear, he completely underestimated the United States,[119] and he refused to take the advice of his generals and refrain from war with Russia. He had planned the attack on the Soviet Union long in advance, although action was first set in motion in August 1940.[120] The Tripartite Alliance was of no value. The Axis did not cooperate in strategy, and the Nazis misunderstood the significance of the Allied strategy and conferences. The program of improvization failed to stand the test of actual conflict, and defeat attended the war.[121]

Summary

A review of the organization and operation of Nazi foreign policy from 1933 to 1945 makes several points clear.[122] (1) Since Hitler made the foreign policy of Germany, and Ribbentrop echoed him,[123] Berchtesgaden became the emotional center of an incalculable and unpredictable German foreign policy. (2) While at first, national socialist objectives met a favorable reception in some responsible circles, especially on the theme of encirclement of Germany, these views changed

[116] Interrogation, Schmidt. Russia too was free to force treaties of protection on Latvia, Lithuania, and Estonia, and later on Finland. Subsequently she absorbed the three first into the Soviet Union and then went to war against Finland, when she could not induce her to abandon her sovereignty by treaty and military arrangements.

[117] Paul Herre, Deutschland und die europaeische Ordnung, Berlin, 1941; Robert Gilbert Vansittart, Lessons of My Life, New York, 1943; Pierre Deboeuf, Hitler a menti, Lille, 1944; Arthur Pillans Laurie, The Case for Germany, Berlin, 1939; Friedrich Stieve, What the World Rejected; Hitler's Peace Offers, 1933–39, Washington, 1940.

[118] Carlo Sforza, L'Italia dal 1914 al 1944 quale io la vidi, Rome, 1945.

[119] Interrogations, Schmidt; von Dirksen; Guderian.

[120] Elizabeth Knaust in Goebbels Framed the Stalin Pact, The American Mercury, vol. 49, No. 194, Feb., 1940, pp. 135–142, states that the preparation for the pact began in 1936 under Goebbels' direction, and that she was in charge of the files which pertained to that arrangement. She further states that Hitler knew nothing about it. This should be set against the interrogations of Schmidt, Hencke, and others, which indicated that Hitler was very much in the know and that the idea of the pact was another Nazi improvization.

[121] Andrzej J. Krzesinski, Nazi Germany's Foreign Policy, Boston, 1945.-

[122] The best survey is Poole; also see State Department Mission, Interrogation, Wilhelm Keppler, Wiesbaden, October 23, 1945; Axel, Freiherr von Freytagh-Loringhoven, Deutschlands Aussenpolitik, 1933–39, Berlin, 1939.

[123] Poole; Interrogation, Schmidt; Claude Jeantot, Germany and the World, Living Age, vol. 349, September 1935, pp. 19–23; Mowat.

after Munich.[124] (3) German efforts to divide Europe into crusading blocs were at first unsuccessful, but with the Spanish Civil War the Axis Powers and Russia faced each other squarely in Spain with most of the European states trying to bring the opposing forces together.[125] (4) It was impossible to depend on Hitler's statements. On January 30, 1937, Hitler stated in the Reichstag, "The time of so-called surprises is over.[126] Yet surprise came after surprise, each followed by a protest that it constituted the last German demand. (5) Hitler continued to make offers of peace, but most of them were rebuffed because to accept them could only mean loss of power or vital possessions by the acceptor.[127] (6) Hitler's lack of knowledge of the rest of the world made it impossible for him to understand the Anglo-Saxon and democratic countries.[128] (7) The Foreign Office was deliberately bypassed in most of the major events.[129] (8) Nazi foreign policy was therefore the continuation of Nazi revolutionary techniques in world affairs. These were not averse to assassination, murder, kidnapping, double-crossing, and bloodshed, and the use of military force if success attended the violence.[130]

Reaction to German foreign policy [131]

The first reactions to national socialist demands and actions took the form of efforts to conciliate and appease the Nazis by making concession after concession.[132] There were offers of colonial concession by both Britain and France in the hopes of averting war.[133] But once Nazi diplomacy was in full swing, it aroused more and more determined opposition abroad. Europe set about rearming.[134] The Russians developed the most powerful defense of which they were capable.[135] The British were first conciliated by the naval pact, but soon entered into political and diplomatic rivalry with Germany which ended in the formation of guaranty treaties with Germany's neighbors. France followed Britain's lead in this respect. As the Axis Powers seemed to grow nearer each other and become more belligerent, the rest of Europe and the United States grew more sympathetic toward each other and joined in efforts to checkmate the specter of war which was rapidly taking on concrete shape.[136] President Roosevelt sounded out the smaller states to learn which of them feared German aggression. Hungary, Rumania, and Poland, began quarreling over the spoils in Czechoslovakia. Other countries seeing this were determined not to yield to further German pressure.[137]

[124] T. P. Conwell-Evans, Between Berlin and London, Nineteenth Century, vol. 119, No. 707, January 1936, pp. 57–68; The encirclement of Germany, Commercial and Financial Chronicle, vol. 142, February 15, 1936, p. 1026.
[125] Interrogation, Schellenberg; also Dell.
[126] The exact words were, "die Zeit der sogenannten Ueberraschungen abgeschlossen ist."
[127] Stieve.
[128] Poole; also State Department Mission, Interrogation, Karl Ritter, Oberursel, Sept. 3, 1945.
[129] Interrogations, Giese; Hencke.
[130] S. M. Marvey and B. Zoborski, German Menace to Europe through the Ages, n. p., 1944.
[131] Paul B. Taylor, Problems of German-American Relations, Foreign Policy Reports, vol. 14, No. 9, July 15, 1938. pp. 98–108.
[132] Wertheimer; interrogation, Schmidt.
[133] Interrogation, von Dirksen.
[134] Willert.
[135] Joachim Joesten, Storm over Northern Europe, Contemporary Review, London, pp. 454–460.
[136] Vansittart; Walter Bastian, Widerspruechc? Warum sie Hitler nicht glauben, Leipzig, 1940.
[137] Interrogation, Horthy, Sept. 12, 1945.

OPERATION OF OTHER FASCIST FOREIGN POLICIES

ITALY

The Italian policies bore a striking similarity to the German in their operation. We have already commented on the early stages elsewhere. On December 24, 1925, Mussolini was made responsible for foreign policy solely to the King. In April 1933, Mussolini called for territorial changes in Europe consisting of: (1) a German corridor through the Polish Corridor; (2) the return to Hungary of Transylvania, Temesvar, Grosswarden, and Klausenburg; (3) the cession of "Krain" to Austria; (4) the independence of Crot'a; and (5) an Italian protectorate for Bosnia, Montenegro, and Albania.[138] In May of 1934, he sought land in Somaliland and Eritrea. In September, he sought further expansion in Africa, and on November 19 he reached a friendship accord with Austria. The next summer (1935) he embarked upon the Ethiopian conquest and in the fall challenged Britain in the Mediterranean.[139]

By 1936 the Italo-British rivalry in the Mediterranean replaced the Polish Corridor and the Rhineland as centers of disturbance.[140] That same year saw a Japanese-Italian agreement óver concessions in Ethiopia. In 1937, Italy [141] and Britain were discussing a mutual pact which was signed in 1938; but Italy continued to expect periodic friction with Britain and constant friction with France. Then Mussolini took the leading and most aggressive part in the intervention in the Spanish Civil War.[142] Italian propaganda flooded the Arab states. Mussolini tried to mobilize the Mediterranean area under Italian leadership, and he demanded a voice in the control of the Red Sea similar to that which Italy exercised in the Mediterranean. In 1938, while Hitler was making his excursions, Italy held the key to European peace, and Mussolini used it in an effort to open concessions in Tunisia, Corsica, and Nice (November). In January 1939, Djibouti was added to the list. When the invasion of Czechoslovakia took place, the Axis worked in complete accord, and as Hitler pushed ever eastward, Italy worked her end of the Axis to secure concessions in the Mediterranean.[143]

OTHER FASCISMS

In 1947, Spanish foreign policy had not developed to the same degree as had those of Germany and Italy by 1939. Besides, the world setting in 1947 was far less propitious for international fascism than it had been eight years earlier.

Japan after the First World War acquired some of the mandated islands which had belonged to Germany. The Washington Arms Conference accorded her a Navy, third in rank in the far eastern waters. The 5–5–3–3 formula satisfied her as long as it halted further building of the navies of Britain and the United States. When the formula no longer could profit Japan, she abandoned it.

[138] Mussolini Challenges Britain, Washington Post, November 2, 1936, p. 7.
[139] Documents Relating to the Italo-Ethiopian Conflict.
[140] Patch; Kuhn; Virginio Gayda, Italia e Inghilterra; l'inevitable conflitto, Rome, 1944.
[141] Agreement between the United Kingdom and Italy, Rome, Apr. 16, 1938, London, 1938.
[142] Vera Micheles Dean, European Diplomacy in the Spanish Crisis, Foreign Policy Reports, vol. 12, No. 18, Dec. 1, 1936, pp. 222–232.
[143] New York Times, Apr. 9, 1939, p. E-4.

Twice after 1918, Japan invaded China, the second time to wage war against the Chinese until the end of the Second World War. During the interlude between the two World Wars, the Japanese Government grew more and more aggressive, walked out of the League of Nations, shelled American and British ships, machine gunned the British Ambassador, stripped occidental subjects, became a member of the anticomintern pact, and generally challenged the western countries. Japanese trade entered Africa, Latin America, the United States, Europe, and the world at large. Japanese industries sought world markets and new sources of raw materials.[144]

Enough has been said to show that the fascist pattern of foreign policy is much the same wherever it is encountered. What Germany did on a grand scale, other fascist countries have done on a smaller scale.[145] They have been guided by much the same motives and feelings. The same need for growth, the same feelings of having been unjustly treated, and therefore finding it necessary to rectify the injustices,[146] the same talk of the necessity for fighting may be heard among them all.

As a single illustration, take the following statements from the three dictators of Germany, Italy, and Spain.

Hitler said:[147]

When peoples are fighting for their existence on this planet, and they are thus faced with the fateful question of "To be or not to be," all considerations of humanity or aesthetics collapse into nothing.

Mussolini said:[148]

Words are beautiful, but rifles, machine guns, ships, aeroplanes and cannons are still more beautiful.

Franco said:[149]

Life means fighting; nations reach their historic climax in fighting; if they rest on their laurels, they are overrun.

CONCLUSIONS

What conclusions can be drawn about fascist foreign policy?[150]

1. The dictator formulates and determines foreign policy, which thus reflects his strengths and weaknesses.

2. Established agencies for the conduct of foreign relations are frequently relegated to the background and made impotent. This results in a conspicuous lack of correlation of foreign policies both in formulation and in execution.

3. Revolutionary methods as practiced at home are translated into international affairs resulting in secretiveness, duplicity, and contradictory actions. This is destructive to confidence between states and thus militates against a stable international order.

4. Many agencies are set up to do the same thing and the overlapping duties and functions of these agencies cause confusion and frustration in the administration of fascist foreign policies.

---

[144] See Ch. VI, and VII Organization of the Economy, Germany; and VII "Organization of the Economy, Italy, Spain, Japan."
[145] The Suñer Mission, The Economist, vol. 139, October 12, 1940, pp. 459–460.
[146] Ernest Hambloch, Italy Militant, London, 1941.
[147] Mein Kampf, English edition, ch. VI, p. 81.
[148] Newman.
[149] Ernest Bock, Spain and the Axis, The Contemporary Review, London, vol. 161, March 1942, pp. 148–153.
[150] Gerhardt Eisler and Albert Norden, The Lesson of Germany; a Guide to her History, New York, 1945.

5. In Germany those who set, controlled, and executed foreign policies were amateurs and dabblers.[151]

. 6. Fascist foreign policy lacks continuity and correlation.

7. Generally it lacks informative background for decisions. Therefore, it is inefficient, paradoxical, and self-contradictory since crucial steps are taken capriciously, intuitively, and individually

8. Fascist foreign policy tends to become a crisis policy, which gathers momentum as it progresses. In the case of Hitler, he was able to deal with only one point at a time, thus intensifying each crisis in which he was involved.

9. Fascist foreign policy is world-wide. It is quick to claim threats to the security of the fascist state no matter where they may appear to arise, and it tends to take aggressive action on the basis of such claims wherever it is possible to do so.

---

[151] Interrogation, Schmidt.

CHAPTER IV—FINANCE AND FISCAL POLICY

INTRODUCTION

The approach to public finance in a totalitarian state is strongly influenced by the approach to the whole economy. Finance is merely one of the instruments for making the economic resources of the country available to carry out the policy of the regime, which is, naturally, presented as the best policy for the country. There is a remarkable resemblance between the financial technique used in the fascist countries, particularly Germany, and that used by many of the capitalist countries during the war. We find the same underlying policy, which was to curtail as much as possible the purchasing power of the civilian population so as to leave a larger proportion of the national income for meeting the national emergency; the same increase in currency circulation, with the counteracting controls to prevent inflation; more or less the same restrictions on private investments and the movement of capital in general; the same trend in taxation; and, to some extent, the same use of the central banks.

This resemblance is not at all surprising, in view of the fact that there is not a great choice in the methods of financing a modern war or preparations for it. In the case of a totalitarian regime, like that of the U. S. S. R., where the government has complete control of the economy, there is less dependence on financial technique, since the government is in a position to determine, at the source, the distribution of the national income; the government also has complete control over wages and prices. In the fascist countries where private ownership was preserved, a semblance of traditional financial methods had to be maintained; but many of the financial terms used acquired new meanings.

Policies and experiences with respect to the monetary system, banking, corporate finance, taxation, and debt, are briefly reviewed here for Germany, Italy, and (to a very limited extent) Spain. A strong currency was a passion with the Germans (who still had not forgotten the wild inflation of the 1920's) and they succeeded very well. There were substantial increases in the amount of money in circulation in all the countries, but only in Italy did the increase get quite out of hand. Strict control was exercised over banking and the financial operations of corporations in general. Deficit financing was a characteristic of fascist finance. Notwithstanding large rate increases, the efficient tax system of Germany and the inefficient tax system of Italy were both unable to cope with expenditure demands. Borrowing was extremely varied in nature, and some compulsion was resorted to. On the other hand, no bond drives, as we came to know them, were conducted in Germany. The debt of all three countries increased tremendously.

MONETARY SYSTEM [1]

The currency of Germany remained strong all during the reign of Naziism, whereas the currencies of Italy and Spain depreciated substantially. Strong controls made possible a success in Germany that was not evident either in Italy or Spain. Spain underwent the smallest actual increase in monetary circulation (if issues of the Republican government are disregarded), Germany came next, while Italy suffered most of all.

Germany's currency during the war included paper Reichsmarks and Rentenmarks, and subsidiary coins made largely of aluminum, copper, zinc, and silver, and special money issued to soldiers. The monetary unit was the Reichsmark which contained 100 pfennigs, equivalent to 40.3325 cents in United States currency. In September 1944, the United States Government fixed an exchange value of 10 cents. By law, the gold standard was in operation in Germany, but reserve requirements adopted in 1924, were eliminated in 1933. In 1938, gold coins were required to be sold to the Reichsbank. Though the doors were opened wide to any type of war financing by way of paper currency that was desired in 1939, extensive and effective controls kept German currency at a very high level, so high in fact that international trade was difficult. Total circulation of Reichsbank and Rentenbank notes increased from RM 4.1 billion at the end of 1933 to RM 5.9 billion at the end of 1937, RM 35.2 billion at the end of 1943, about RM 56.6 billion as of the end of February 1945, and RM 65-70 billion at the end of the war. Of these totals, between half a billion and one and one-half billion Reichsmarks were issued by the Rentenbank and the balance was issued by the Reichsbank.

In Italy, paper money in circulation consisted of notes of the Bank of Italy, and notes of small denomination issued by the state treasury. There were also silver, nickel and steel alloy, and bronze coins. The lira, which was divided into 100 centesimi, was the monetary unit. As revalued in 1936, the lira's gold content was the equivalent of 5.2631 cents. Gold reserve requirements were eliminated "temporarily" in 1935. The actual gold reserve in September 1946, was 523 million lire. Changes were made in the official rate from time to time, but in 1941 the 1936 rate was restored. With the Allied occupation of Italy, the exchange value of the lira was 100 to the dollar. In February of 1946, there was a revaluation downward to 225 lire to the dollar, and in early 1947, a further decline to 378 to the dollar. Note circulation fell from about 18 billion lire at the end of 1927, to 13 billion at the end of 1933. It rose gradually to 19 billion lire in December 1938, 31 billion by the end of 1940, and 73 billion at the end of 1942. As Fascism approached its collapse, the financial front gave way, the government failed to cover its deficits either from revenue or from loans, and had to resort to the printing press on a large scale. In June 1945, 350 billion lire (including about 65 billion of Allied military currency) were in circulation, and by March 1946 the total had reached 384 billion (including 92 billion of Allied military currency).

---

[1] Most of the information for this section is taken from the following sources: (1) U. S. Treasury Department. Germany—Preliminary Report on Selected Financial Laws, Decrees and Regulations, 1944, (mimeographed); (2) Annual Reports of the Bank for International Settlements.

Spanish currency consisted of paper pesetas issued by the Bank of Spain, and coins made of aluminum, tin, and copper. The peseta was divided into 100 centimos. Before the Civil War, the peseta had a gold parity of 32.66 cents. There have been several readjustments since. In early 1947, the peseta was valued at 9.132 cents. Bank of Spain notes totaled 4.8 billion pesetas at the end of 1935, about 13.5 billion at the end of 1941, about 16.4 billion at the end of 1943, and 22.8 billion as of the end of 1946. Notes issued by the Republican Government during the Civil War were repudiated. The bank had gold reserves of 1.2 billion pesetas and silver of 550 million pesetas as of October 31, 1946.

BANKING

Summary

Germany and Italy had well developed banking systems while that of Spain was comparatively less advanced. All had central banks that were the tool of the government. In Germany and Italy, banks generally conducted their activities in accord with policy determinations other than their own. They became collectors of the people's savings which found their way into government obligations or investments directed by the state. German banks became an important instrument in controlling the finances and resources of conquered areas during the war.

Germany [2]

Summary.—Germany had a variety of types of banks, with the Reichsbank at the top. The joint stock banks were the big private banks that financed private industry. They were often a combination of commercial bank, investment bank, and investment trust. In the era before the 1930's banks were (on the whole) subject to very little government control. As a result of the banking crisis of 1931, and the government financial aid which was given at that time, the system was virtually nationalized on the eve of Hitler's coming to power. Although later "reprivatized," the banks remained subject to government domination. In addition, numerous government-owned and operated banks were organized for special purposes. During the war, banks generally became not much more than administrators of accumulated savings and capital. They funneled the savings of their depositors into government bonds. They did not make their own decisions as to what use their funds should be put. With the spreading conquest by German arms, there was hardly a bank left in Nazi-controlled Europe that was not a subsidiary of the German banking system.

General.—In Nazi Germany, the many types of banks, though not legally nationalized, were subject to strict control. Some of them were more directly under control of the Laender than the Reich. The Reichsbank was the bank of first importance, and under the immediate direction and control of the Fuehrer. General control of banking was lodged in the Ministry of Economic Affairs which exercised its powers through the Reich Banking Control Office or through the Reichsgruppe Banken. In addition, a very substantial body of legislation

[2] Most of the information for this section is taken from the following sources: (1) Treasury study and Bank for International Settlements reports cited in footnote 1; (2) Kenneth Mackenzie, The Banking Systems of Great Britain, France, Germany, and the United States of America, London, 1935, pp. 169–174; Otto Nathan, The Nazi Eeconomic System, Durham, 1944.

applied to specific types of banks on the Reich or Laender levels. A Reich postal savings system was introduced following the Anschluss with Austria in 1938.

The Deutsche Reichsbank stood at the apex of the German bank system. It had offices throughout the Reich, exercised the primary privilege of note issue, operated as a bankers' bank (although it also received substantial commercial and industrial deposits), and functioned as banker to the Reich. Though previously independent of the Reich Chancellor, under the Nazis it became a tool of the Government. The revised law itself declared that the bank "shall act for the attainment of the objectives set by the National Socialist government." The law under the Nazis also limited ownership of shares in the bank to German nationals eligible to citizenship and legal persons or concerns within the Reich. As of the end of 1944, about 96 percent of its assets were government obligations.

Other banks closely identified with the German Government were the Rentenbank, the Gold Discount Bank, and numerous government-owned and operated banks organized for special purposes. The Rentenbank was established in 1923, to assist in stabilizing the currency, by issuing new currency secured by a mortgage on agriculture. The desired result was obtained, and though it had been intended to abolish the bank and retire the rentenmarks issued by the bank, both continued. The Gold Discount Bank was originally established to finance exports. Numerous government owned and operated banks were organized from time to time to hold government interests in banking and industrial enterprises, provide credit to cooperatives, and finance numerous other activities. Some of the banks were affiliated with or subdivisions of the Reichsbank, some were under the Ministry of Economic Affairs, some were under other ministries not normally concerned with finance or banking, and some were under the control of the Laender.

Joint stock banks were among the principal financial institutions of the country. They were encouraged by the Government in many ways because of their great resources for supplying the credit demands of industrialists. They did a considerable business as banks of deposit and discount, and also conducted other kinds of ordinary banking operations. A large portion of their deposits were on time, this enabling them to invest in industrial concerns to a greater extent than would be otherwise possible.

Other types of banks and their operations were, briefly, as follows:

Private banks.—These banks carried on banking in its more simple forms long before the advent of the joint stock banks which absorbed many of them.

Cooperative banks.—Made loans to small traders, shopkeepers, landowners, and farmers.

Mortgage banks.—Granted loans on the security of mortgages on improved real estate, or land in the process of development.

Savings banks.—These banks, which were either privately or municipally owned, carried both savings and checking accounts. They were the real local banking institutions, and were mainly under the supervision of the Laender. During the Second World War, they were important as collectors of savings for investment in war bonds.

A tabulation of deposits among German banks as of December 31, 1943, is given below.[3]

[In billions of Reichsmarks]

	Total deposits [1]	Savings deposits only [2]
Six large joint stock banks	24.5	4.4
Savings banks [3]	79.0	66.9
Postal savings banks [4]	4.8	4.8
Credit cooperatives [4]	22–23	17.0
	131	[5] 93.0

[1] Giro and savings deposits.
[2] The figures in this column are included in the first column.
[3] The average amount of individual savings is reported to have risen from RM 521 in 1939 to RM 985 in 1942 and RM 1,195 in 1943.
[4] Partly estimated.
[5] The total of all savings deposits in the country were estimated at RM 97 billion.

Role of banks as instrument of fascism.—On the eve of the National Socialist revolution, the German banking system had become virtually nationalized. It became so because the government had to step in to prevent a banking and industrial collapse incident upon the banking crisis in the midst of a world-wide depression. The property rights which the government acquired in the banks as a result of aid furnished to the banks were relinquished as the banks found themselves able to repurchase their interests. However, the pattern of control which was to become characteristic of the Nazi economy was also followed with respect to banks. In practice, the banks were stripped of their power to decide which services they would render, and the actual services they did render depended upon the general situation in the economy. The capital market all but disappeared.

During the war, the banks became mere administrators of accumulated savings and capital, and executors of the capital expenditure and general credit plans of the state. The savings of the people flowed into the banks (strict controls made other use impossible), and from there it was automatically invested in Treasury bills and bonds. The banks were not permitted to make their own investment decisions. These were dictated by the Government, which also fixed the interest rates. All was done to give effect to the military program.

The international role that banking played in marching behind the advancing German armies presents an intriguing if somewhat sordid picture. A start had been made in taking over the banking systems of Austria and the Sudetenland, but as the war progressed most of the financial resources of Europe were held by the Reichsbank or the six large joint stock banks. Hardly a bank remained free of the German banking system. The United States Office of War Information described further aspects of the process in this way:

Chiefly the Nazis have obtained control over the resources of Europe by reaching over and above all business to get a monopolistic grasp on the purse strings of industry. With the banks of the conquered nations in their hands, Nazi plutocrats hold power of life and death over Europe's business. They direct the flow of money into Nazi-controlled or Quisling enterprises; or they freeze off capital and credit from business houses that refuse to "cooperate." Furthermore, European banks normally control industrial enterprises through share ownership; thus, control of a bank means operating control of an industry.[4]

[3] Bank for International Settlements, Fourteenth Annual Report, 1943–44, p. 210.
[4] Press release for papers of May 16, 1943.

Looking back on the role of German banks during the war, our office of military government has declared:

Under the Nazi regime, the banking system played an indispensable part in financing war. Its great money-creating efficiency made it possible to provide the huge funds needed (for) the rearmament and aggression, without causing obvious inflation such as that which ruined Germany during the last war. The banks, and particularly the central bank or Reichsbank, also provided technicians to assist in looting the occupied countries without which Germany could not have continued to fight. Individual German banks established or used existing agents to exploit all Europe, both for private profit and for the good of the Nazi regime. "Respectable" German bankers were used to preserve Nazi assets in Switzerland and the other neutral countries.[5]

Italy [6]

Summary.—There were several types of banks in Italy. The Bank of Italy (the single bank of issue) stood at the top. There were three "national interest banks" so designated because of their coverage of the entire country through branches, five "public law banks," about 350 small commercial banks, about 100 savings and agricultural and credit banks, and about 2,000 small cooperative, "popular," and rural banks. In addition there were post office savings banks which (in 1941) had deposits nearly twice those of savings banks. One result of the financial crisis of 1931, was the removal of industrial financing as a function of the banks. This function was transferred to special institutes which became instruments for carrying out Mussolini's economic policies. In general, bankers lost much of their independent position under fascism. They became a conduit of capital into channels prepared by the government.

General.—The Bank of Italy, the sole bank of issue, managed the monetary and rediscount policies of the country, and supervised indirectly the entire banking system. Participation in the capital of the bank (which had been private until 1936) was only nominal, and was held by other banks, insurance companies, etc. The bank became principally a bankers' bank in 1936, although it still made advances on securities.

The "National Interest Banks" were the three biggest commercial banks operating by means of branches throughout the country. They exercised the classical functions of intermediate agencies for making payments and granting credit, and also did a large scale business through affiliated concerns in foreign countries. Though managed as joint stock companies, their stock was transformed into registered bonds held only by individuals or bodies of Italian nationality or by foreigners who gave up voting rights at meetings.

The five "public law" banks (the Bank of Naples, the Bank of Sicily, the Banca Nazionale del Lavoro, the Istituto di San Paolo, and Monte dei Paschi di Siena) were large commercial banks which also carried on an important savings and mortgage business. They had no stockholders and distributed no dividends. Government officials and representatives of local bodies participated in their management. The Banca Nazionale del Lavoro was owned outright by the Government.

[5] Office of Military Government, United States Zone, Reports and Information Branch, European Theater, Weekly Information Bulletin, January 5, 1946.
[6] Most of the information for this section is taken from the following sources: (1) Giuseppe Bianchini, Italian Banking Reorganization, The Banker, London, vol. 43, September 1937, pp. 226–232; (2) V. Azzolini, Italy's Monetary Policy, The Banker, London, vol. 43, September 1937, pp. 223–225; (3) A. Philip Woolfson, M Day, Banking and Finance, Cambridge, Mass., 1940; (4) Statesman's Year Book, 1946.

Bank deposits in Italy had a rapid rise during the war due largely to the heavy borrowing by the Government from the central bank and the commercial banks. The table below sets out the course of deposits from December 1938 to May 1945:[7]

	December 1938	December 1942	May 1945 (estimate)
Time deposits:			
Commercial banks	34. 7	67. 0	240. 0
Postal banks	29. 1	59. 3	150. 0
Total	63. 8	126. 3	390. 0
Index	100	198	612
Demand deposits:			
Commercial banks	25. 0	68. 1	315. 0
Postal banks	1. 3	3. 4	15. 0
Total	26. 3	71. 5	330. 0
Index	100	272	1255

Role of banks as instrument of Fascism.—The Italian Government supervised and inspected banks and laid down general policies for them to follow. It controlled the use made of savings, collected and directed them into those branches of national activity where they were needed most. An official Fascist publication compared credit to the lifeblood of a body whose circulation was regulated by the state.

It is still private enterprise—

the report continued—

which accumulates capital and creates the organs through which it is distributed, but in the totalitarian state the purpose served is the collective national and not a private interest * * *.[8]

The various kinds of banks were organized into federations, which were entrusted with the representation of their general economic interests, and the various federations in turn were grouped in the Fascist Confederation of Credit and Insurance Firms.

The financing of industry in Italy was taken away from commercial banks as a result of the financial crisis of the depression of the late 1920's and early 1930's, and made a function of institutes created by the Government. Among the more important of these were the I. M. I. (Istituto Mobiliare Italiano) created in 1930, and the I. R. I. (Istituto di Ricostruzione Industriale) in 1933. At least seven other institutes or similar organizations were set up to operate in particular fields. All were empowered to issue debentures against loans, some of which were guaranteed by the Government.

Spain [9]

Banking in Spain as late as 1947 was not a well-developed business. In fact, there were comparatively few banks throughout the country. There had been, however, a series of specialized credit institutions founded by the state. Banking legislation going back to 1921 took the firm attitude that banks were public servants subservient to the general welfare of the community. The Bank of Spain stood at the center of Spanish finance. It was a privately owned bankers' bank and fiscal agent for the Government. As of November 1944, about 71 percent of the bank's assets consisted of Government obligations.

---

[7] William D. Grampp, The Italian Lira, 1938–45, Journal of Political Economy, vol. 54, August 1946, p. 323.
[8] Fascist Confederation of Industrialists, Fascist Era Year XVII, Rome, 1939, p. 65.
[9] Most of the information for this section is taken from the following sources:
(1) League of Nations, Money and Banking, 1942–44, p. 176; (2) Report of the Bank of Spain, 1936–1941, Federal Reserve Bulletin, vol. 29, May 1943, p. 399; (3) Annual Reports of the Bank for International Settlements.

During the revolution, two institutions were functioning as the "Bank of Spain." One was controlled by the Government of the Republic and the other by the Nationalist Government. Both issued peseta notes in counterpart of advances to their respective governments to finance domestic war expenditures. The Republican Government used the bulk of the bank's gold and silver reserves for payments abroad. After the revolution, all note liabilities and a large part of the deposit liabilities of the bank under the Republican Government were repudiated. Savings bank deposits in popular savings banks in Spain at the end of 1942 amounted to 8.4 billion pesetas distributed over 5.4 million accounts. Deposits in post-office savings banks amounted to 125,000,000 pesetas in 1943. By a decree of late 1941, the post-office savings bank opened a savings account with an initial entry of 1 peseta for every Spanish child born.

CORPORATION FINANCE [10]

Germany and Italy exercised very strict control over investments, directing them into channels that best served the interests of the state. In both countries, corporations were firmly regulated, dividends were limited, stock exchanges were closely supervised, and speculation in stocks was severely discouraged.

Germany, in 1937, in order to centralize control of corporations, required all with a capitalization of less than RM 100,000 to dissolve; new corporations had to have a capitalization of RM 500,000; the powers of stockholders were drastically reduced, while the powers of boards of directors were increased. Control of stock exchanges was transferred from the Laender to the Reich Ministry of Economic Affairs, and listings on the exchanges were limited to large stock issues. Price control, which was introduced for securities in 1943, had the effect of substantially curtailing all trading. Price control also proved very useful in connection with the administration of the decree relating to registration and compulsory sale of privately owned securities which had been adopted in late 1941. When securities were bought by the Government—and the Government did become a large stockholder in industrial enterprises—treasury notes were issued in exchange therefor, and these were deposited in a blocked account with the Reichsbank. Substantially all securites not bought by the Government had to be deposited in special banks (as originally adopted in 1937) and ultimately with the Reichsbank. A limitation on distribution of cash dividends to 6 percent (8 percent in some cases) was imposed in 1934, as a measure to prevent stock speculation and the resulting diversion of funds from the capital market to the stock market. Declared dividends in excess of legal cash dividends at various times were either heavily taxed or directed to be invested in Government bonds or tax certificates.

---

[10] Most of the information for this section is taken from the following sources:
(1) Nathan work cited in footnote 2; (2) Treasury study cited in footnote 1; (3) Bruno G. Foa and P. G. Treves, Italian Finance and Investment, Economica, London, vol. 6, August 1939, pp. 270–295; (4) Thaon di Revel, Italian State Finances, The Banker, London, vol. 43, September 1937, pp. 217–218; (5) Bank for International Settlements, Twelfth Annual Report, 1941/42, p. 194; (6) Lawyers' Directory, 1947, p. 1791.

In Italy, important controls over the volume and direction of investment were in effect prior to the late 1930's, but it was then that the world-wide depression, the Ethiopian War, sanctions, and the drive for self-sufficiency and armaments provided strong reasons for control. The requirement of licenses for establishing new industrial plants and extensions was inaugurated to prevent undue excess capacity, but this was later turned into a weapon for checking otherwise undesired investment. Stock exchanges were placed under the control of the Council of Ministers and the Inspectorate. Corporations with a capital under 1 million lire were required to transform themselves into limited liability companies. Aliens were forbidden to subscribe to the shares of a corporation without the permission of the Government. Bonds of corporations in excess of paid-up shares had .to be secured by a mortgage or government securities. A 6 percent dividend limitation imposed as an inflation preventive during the Ethiopian War was replaced by a progressive tax on dividends. Other measures, to discourage trading in stocks and particularly speculation, included a transfer supertax of 4 percent of the sales price of the securities and a tax on capital gains.

GOVERNMENT FINANCE

Summary

The fascist countries resembled the democracies in at least one respect—namely, the continuous running of financial deficits. Neither Germany, nor Italy, nor Spain showed a surplus of receipts over expenditures for many years, even before the war. Very considerable increases in revenues were experienced by each country, but expenditures advanced at a faster pace than did revenues.

Germany

The budget in Nazi Germany was a tool for carrying out policies that had previously been determined by agencies other than the Ministry of Finance, which created and executed the budget. The Reichstag, of course, formerly had a place in the budget process, but with the growth in the power of the Fuehrer, the Reichstag was excluded from participation in the budget enactment—as it was from legislation generally. For practical purposes, there was no publication of budgetary details after the Nazis took power.[11] The obvious purpose of such secrecy was the concealment of rearmament expenditures.

Tax revenues were divided roughly as follows. In the beginning of the Nazi regime, a depression period, income taxes produced about one-fifth of all tax revenues. This proportion increased gradually to one-fourth, and as the war drew to a close to more than one-third. The tax on corporations grew from practically nothing to nearly one-fourth in 1944. The turnover tax was fairly constant, ranging usually around one-fifth to one-sixth of the total. The taxes on beer, tobacco, sugar, and customs duties, which produced more than one-third of all tax revenues in 1933, declined to a point where they paid about one-fifth.

Revenues from taxes imposed by the Reich rose continuously from RM 6.6 billion in the fiscal year 1933, to RM 44.1 billion in fiscal 1943.

---

[11] The result is that there are a great many estimates which vary widely. Most of the statistics given in this chapter are taken from publications of the League of Nations, the Bank for International Settlements, an article by Richard W. Lindholm, German Finance in World War II, American Economic Review, vol. 37, March 1947, pp. 121–134, and Otto Nathan's study cited in footnote 2.

Declines to RM 39.8 billion and RM 36.8 billion were experienced in fiscal years 1944 and 1945. Other receipts mainly from war contributions of the Laender, communities, etc., occupation costs, and administrative receipts increased rapidly from RM 4.5 billion in fiscal 1940 to RM 37 billion in 1944. The occupation costs themselves, which amounted to about RM 84 billion through September 1944 (of which France paid about two-fifths), were very severe burdens on the conquered territory. The table below gives a 3-year wartime picture of the sources of German receipts 1940–42:

Analysis of German Finance, 1940–42 [1]

	Reichsmarks (billions)
Internal finance:	
Taxation and other internal revenue	108. 9
Nonbank borrowing:	
Savings issues	1. 0
Other (residual item)	34. 4
Total taxation and nonbank borrowing	144. 3
Borrowing from savings banks	43. 1
Total other than commercial banking system	187. 4
Borrowing from commercial banks	22. 8
Borrowing from central bank	12. 8
Total from banking system	35. 6
Total expenditure internally financed	223. 0
External finance:	
Current revenue	40. 2
Borrowing	14. 5
Total externally financed	54. 7
Total expenditure	277. 7

[1] Bank for International Settlements, Thirteenth Annual Report, 1942–43, p. 269.

The Nazis also made use of private or quasi-public organizations for the performance of certain functions previously performed by the Government or new functions directed to be established. It has been estimated that expenditures for these purposes equaled between 15 and 20 percent of the total income from taxes and customs. A list of these groups would include the Hitler Youth Organization, NS Public Welfare, and the Winter Relief, and such affiliates of the Nazi Party as the storm troopers, the elite guard, the Labor Front, the Organization of Government Officials, the Students Organization, and the private Reich Aerial Defense Association, all of which performed certain public functions. In addition there were such quasi-public organizations as the Reich Food Estate for the control of agriculture, the Organization of Industry for the control of industries, and the Supervisory Agencies for the control of foreign and domestic trade. All obtained funds from special theoretically voluntary (but actually compulsory) contributions, collections, and fees outside of public budgets. Some surpluses found their way into the Reich Treasury.

Expenditures have been difficult to determine.[12] It is war expenditures, however, that interest most people, and estimates in many

[12] "Publication of expenditure figures was completely discontinued, obviously to suppress information on war preparation which such figures might have revealed." Nathan, p. 276.

cases bear little resemblance to one another. Roughly, it seems that about two-thirds of total expenditures were for war in the years just preceding the beginning of the Second World War. With the war itself, this proportion increased so that for fiscal 1945 about four-fifths of all expenditures were for war. In the 6 years beginning April 1, 1939, and ending March 31, 1945, it is estimated that RM 514,000,000,000 were spent for war out of a total of RM 687,000,000,000, or about 75 percent.

Italy [13]

For many years, Italy had operated at a deficit. The world depression left that country comparatively unaffected for a while, and it was not until the end of 1931 that it hit with full force. It reached its peak in the years 1932–33. A continued deficit had been experienced beginning with the 1932 fiscal year right on through the Second World War, and up to April 1947. Expenditures fluctuated slightly during 1931 to 1935, and then started sharply upward with the Ethiopian War and sanctions. From 1936 through 1944, deficits were annually just about equal to war expenditures. Over this period estimated expenditures for war approximated 400,000,000,000 lire or 57 percent of total expenditures of 709,000,000,000 lire. Revenues, excluding loans, amounted to 306,000,000,000 lire or about 43 percent of all, expenditures in this 9-year period. In the war period itself Italy financed less of its war expenditures by taxation than did most other belligerents. Revenues were slightly in excess of one-third of the total expenditures. Total Government expenditures in 1943 constituted about 80 percent of the national income, as contrasted with about 60 percent in the United States. After 1944, the greatly depreciated lire was reflected in greatly increased expenditures. In fiscal 1945 expenditures were 368.1 billion lire, and in 1946, they were 366 billion. Receipts for these years were 94.9 billion and 221.1 billion lire, respectively.

The table below gives a picture of Italy's sources of revenue in the years just before military collapse.[14]

	Financial years ended June 30—		
	1940–41	1941–42	1942–43
	(Millions of lire)		
Direct taxes	8,914	9,548	10,817
Indirect taxes and duties	8,954	11,127	11,330
Customs and indirect taxes on consumption	6,328	6,135	6,132
Monopolies	4,499	6,017	8,213
Lotteries	519	584	673
Main sources of revenue	29,215	33,412	37,166
Repayments and consortiums	700	1,298	1,217
Miscellaneous revenue	4,118	3,508	4,644
Total ordinary revenue	34,033	38,218	43,027
Recovery of war expenses	201	3,006	5,857
Total revenue	34,234	41,224	48,884

[13] Most of the information for this section is taken from Annual Reports of the Bank for International Settlements and scattered notes in financial and commercial publications.
[14] Bank for International Settlements, Thirteenth Annual Report, 1942–43, p. 189.

Spain [15]

The Spanish budget increased year by year. The budget for 1947 called for an estimated expenditure of 14 billion pesetas, slightly in excess of 1944, 1945, and 1946 which ran about 13 billion. Receipts closely corresponded to the so-called ordinary budget, while extraordinary items ran around 2 to 2½ billion pesetas. Large military and capital expenditures were characteristic. Direct taxes and indirect taxes each brought in about 40 percent of the total revenues, with the remaining 20 percent coming from monopolies and state properties.

During the 2¾ years of civil war, 1936–39, revenues of the National Government amounted to 3.7 billion pesetas against expenditures of 11.9 billion. Of the 8.3 billion deficit, 7.6 billion were covered by borrowing from the Bank of Spain.[16]

TAXATION

Summary

The tax system of Germany was an efficient one before Hitler. It remained so after Hitler. Italy's system was efficient neither before nor after Mussolini. The burden in both countries was severe. Both made some use of the tax system to accomplish the ends of fascism. Few additional taxes of importance were adopted by either country to finance war, although both raised rates.

Germany [17]

Summary.—Under Hitler, the efficient tax structure was centralized in the Reich, as distinguished from the Laender and local units. The system was coordinated with Nazi grand strategy and further centralized. Administration was considerably tightened. It was directed that the tax laws should be interpreted in accordance with the national-socialist Weltanschauung; this became a source of very broad discretionary power. The tax burden (which perhaps had reached its practical limits) was very heavy, especially the income tax which constituted the principal levy. Some use was made of the tax system for attaining economic objectives, but for the most part the ends desired could be and were attained by other and more direct means. Burdensome taxes and discriminations were imposed upon the Jews.

Types of taxes.—The principal taxes levied by the central government for decades were the income tax (individual and corporate), inheritance tax, property taxes, turnover tax, tobacco tax, and customs duties. In the Laender and local units, taxes on real estate and on gross receipts of business were most important. During the war heavy increases were made in some of the taxes in order to curb private spending for purposes not essential to the war effort.

For many years, the income tax was the most important Reich levy. It applied to individuals and corporations. Most of the tax on individuals was collected at the source. The amount of tax to be paid depended in considerable measure on the number of the taxpayer's children and on whether or not he was a Jew—as well as

[15] Most of the information for this section is taken from scattered notes in financial and commercial publications.

[16] Borrowing by the Republican Government amounted to 23 billion pesetas. Bank for International Settlements, Eleventh Annual Report, 1940/41, p. 146.

[17] Most of the information for this section is taken from the Treasury study cited in footnote 1 and the Nathan study cited in footnote 2.

on the amount of the income. The table below shows the effective rate of tax applicable to various income groups, 1942–43. It will be noticed how the effective rate declined with an increase in the number of children.

Effective individual income tax rates by income group in Germany 1942–43 [1]

Income RM's	Unmarried persons	Persons 5 years married having no children	Other persons having no children	Persons having children—number of children				
				1	2	3	4	5
	Percent	*Percent*	*Percent*	*Percent*	*Percent*	*Percent*	*Percent*	*Percent*
600	1.0							
700	2.4							
800	3.6	1.8						
900	4.9	2.9	1.2					
1,000	5.5	3.7	2.0					
1,200	6.7	4.8	3.1	.7				
1,500	8.2	6.1	4.1	2.2	.6			
2,000	11.3	8.2	5.1	3.4	2.2			
2,500	13.1	9.8	6.5	4.8	3.5	1.5		
3,000	17.4	13.2	9.0	6.6	4.9	2.8	0.9	
4,000	22.8	17.5	12.2	9.0	6.7	4.4	2.3	0.3
5,000	24.9	19.4	14.0	10.0	7.7	5.3	2.7	.6
6,000	27.8	21.5	15.6	11.8	9.1	6.0	3.2	.7
7,000	29.5	23.0	16.6	13.4	10.4	6.5	3.5	.8
8,000	31.0	24.2	17.4	14.6	11.5	6.9	3.8	.9
9,000	32.1	25.1	18.0	15.5	12.5	7.2	4.3	1.9
10,000	33.0	25.8	18.6	16.3	13.6	8.2	5.6	3.3
15,000	37.9	29.6	21.3	19.3	17.1	12.5	10.3	8.2
20,000	44.0	34.6	24.9	22.9	20.8	16.5	14.3	12.4
25,000	48.5	39.6	28.5	26.7	24.6	20.4	18.2	16.2
30,000	53.2	44.8	32.4	30.6	28.7	24.3	22.1	20.0
40,000	59.6	50.0	37.7	36.4	34.9	31.4	29.6	27.7
50,000	63.6	53.0	40.9	39.9	38.6	35.9	34.4	32.9
60,000	64.9	56.1	44.2	43.2	42.0	39.4	38.0	36.6
70,000	65.1	58.3	46.2	45.6	44.7	42.5	41.3	40.1
100,000	65.4	59.9	49.1	48.7	48.3	47.2	46.7	46.1
135,700	66.0	61	56	56	56	56	56	56

[1] Treasury study cited in footnote 1, pp. 202–203. The extensive definitions of the various classes of taxpayers which appear in the original source are omitted.

The corporation income tax levied after 1938 was (in most cases) imposed at the rate of 40 percent. Until 1936, the rate had been 20 percent, and for 1938 it was raised to 35 percent.

An excess-profits tax applicable to both individuals and corporations was imposed beginning in 1942, with respect to industrial profits declared to be excess according to any of five alternative bases. The rate was 25 percent for individuals and 30 percent for corporations.

Germany's death taxes (inheritance taxes) were low by most standards. A 1934 law gave considerable benefits to transfers between close relatives; their exemptions were also increased. Beneficiaries were classified in five groups with rates ranging as follows:

	Percent
Group 1, spouse and children	2–15
Group 2, descendants of persons in group 1	4–25
Group 3, brothers, sisters, parents, grandparents, and others of ascendant lineage	6–40
Group 4, parents-in-law, children-in-law, and direct descendants of brothers and sisters	8–50
Group 5, all other heirs and donees	14–60

Exemptions ranged from RM 500 for persons in group 5 to RM 30,000 for persons in group 1.

There were three property taxes in Germany. One was a general property tax levied by the Reich on all kinds of property. A second was imposed by the communes on land, while the third was a Reich tax on transfers, upon which the communes could add a surcharge. Under the Reich general property tax there was a credit of RM 10,000 for each person, plus an additional RM 10,000 for certain persons over 60 years of age. The rate was one-half of 1 percent. Under the land tax law the communes levied their own rates against land which was divided into three classes and assessed at values which were uniform throughout Germany. The Reich transfer tax was levied at the rate of 3 percent on the assessed value or sales price, whichever was higher.

The turnover tax was a tax based on gross receipts from the sale of goods and services. It applied to substantially all items of daily purchase or consumption. However, about one-fifth of all turnovers were exempt from the tax. About three-fourths of the taxed turnovers paid a 2 percent rate. The rate on wholesale transactions was one-half of 1 percent, and other rates applied on certain special kinds of sales.

Selective sales taxes were applied to certain products (usually at the manufacturing or processing level) such as tobacco and tobacco products, alcoholic beverages, salt, sugar, saccharine, mineral oils, illuminants, matches, and playing cards. Amusements were also subject to special taxes.

Economic and racial objectives.—Before the war, the German tax system was used to stimulate employment, to increase the population, and to facilitate rearmament. During the war, tax incentives were offered to citizens and entrepreneurs who cooperated in furthering other objectives. Jews were subjected to special taxes and denied certain benefits allowed under other taxes. On the whole, it was not necessary for Germany to use the tax system directly to attain economic objectives. The Nazis had such a firm control on the economy they were able to apply direct pressures without using the tax system.

Employment stimulation during the depression period was sought through special depreciation allowances for replacement machinery, building repairs and improvements, and capital equipment whose durability ordinarily did not exceed 5 years. Another measure, designed to encourage employment of female domestic servants, allowed such servants, not to exceed three, to be counted as an addition to the taxpayer's family.

Increased population was sought by raising tax deductions for dependents in computing income and inheritance taxes, and introducing them for the property and citizen taxes. Income tax increases made in 1939 applied only to single persons and childless couples.

Rearmament and self-sufficiency (especially in agriculture) were promoted by reducing the agricultural land tax in 1933, for 1 year, by about 25 percent, by reducing the turnover tax on agricultural commodities from 2 to 1 percent, by raising the tariff on various commodities, and by levying a tax of RM 50 per 100 kilograms on margarine, artificial fats, vegetable fats, and hardened blubber. To encourage production of automobiles, all new vehicles were exempted from the motor vehicle tax. Producers engaged in developing new production methods, and desirable ersatz commodities were encouraged by legislation in 1933 empowering the Treasury to exempt them from income, corporation, turnover, property, business, and land taxes. Import duties also encouraged synthetic production by taxing the natural product, such as raw rubber.

During the war, tax benefits were granted as incentives to Government contractors who accepted delayed payment, and to individual savers who facilitated the mopping up of excess income. For example, under the "new finance plan" introduced on March 20, 1939, tax credit certificates were issued to entrepreneurs which entitled the holders to additional depreciation allowances, the size of which increased the longer the certificates were held. Under a somewhat similar plan entrepreneurs were given further depreciation allowances for deposits of earnings which thus became blocked until after the war. And under the "iron savings plan" an automatic reduction was effected in the individual's taxes. The portion of income so saved enjoyed complete exemption from income tax and social insurance contributions.

Jews were subjected to special taxes and were denied exemptions and family considerations by other regulations. The flight tax bore almost exclusively on them.[18] In the assessment of income and property taxes, all exemptions and family considerations were removed for the Jews. In addition, a levy of 1 billion Reichsmarks (payable in installments) was imposed on Jewish property in 1938 in "atonement" for the "hostile attitude of Jewry toward the German nation and Reich * * *."

Italy [19]

Summary.—Italy had a tax system which—in contrast to that in Germany—was not very efficient either before or during the reign of Fascism.[20] There was a great variety of taxes at both the national and local levels. There were direct taxes, turnover, business, and transfer taxes, taxes on consumption, and then there were the revenues from monopolies. During the early 1940's, direct taxes were producing less than one-fourth of the total revenues, while the monopolies were yielding between one-seventh and one-fifth. The remainder came from the multitudinous other taxes, licenses, and fees. To only a relatively small degree was the tax system used to accomplish the purposes of Fascism.

Types of taxes.—The income tax in Italy was somewhat different from the system we know in the United States. In Italy, income was grouped according to the source from which it was derived, and then flat rates were applied within each particular group without reference to the total amount, except for small exemptions. Wages and salaries were taxed at the lowest rate, while business profits were taxed at the highest. A complementary tax was levied on the income of entire families at comparatively low graduated rates. There was also an excess-profits tax. Standard profits, for purposes of the excess-profits

---

[18] This was a tax on German nationals who abandoned their German domicile after March 31, 1931. The tax was at the rate of one-fourth of the aggregate assessed value of the property.

[19] The information for this section is taken from scattered notes in financial and commercial publications.

[20] A recent comment on Italy's tax system described it as one which in peacetime was archaic, unjust, and arbitrary. Levies on income were determined by bargaining between taxpayer and collector. The taxes on sales which produced most of the revenues were jeopardized by the extensive black market. In the spring of 1945, there were more than 200 different kinds of taxes in Allied territory. Yet there was an "aversion to financing the costs of the war by taxation and a penchant for complicated, often bewildering, forms of economic control." William D. Grampp, The Italian Lira, 1938–45, Journal of Political Economy (Chicago), August 1946, vol. 54, p. 325.

tax, were determined on the basis of average earnings of earlier years or on the ratio of profits to capital, at the option of the taxpayer.

Succession taxes in Italy were definitely geared into the Fascist policy of increasing the birth rate. Transfers between parents and two or more of their children were completely exempt. There were also special concessions when transfers were made to families with two or more children. There were five categories of tax rates which depended upon the relationship between the decedent and the beneficiaries. The rates ranged from 1 to 50 percent. The rates were also affected by the age, civil and family status of the decedent and his successors.

Among the many other national taxes levied in Italy were the land tax on "domanial" income (income which the soil was capable of producing whether used or not); building tax (based on the renting value of the building whether rented or not); property tax; a tax on bachelors; a tax on mortmain (actual or presumptive revenue of charitable and religious organizations); registration fees on deeds, leases, etc. (based on market value of real estate, securities, average price of personal property, etc.); stamp taxes on civil and commercial documents; annual taxes on stocks, bonds, capital of foreign companies; tax on issuance, renewal, or cancellation of mortgage; tax on governmental concessions; tax on motor vehicles; amusement tax; tax on insurance companies; tax on stock exchange contracts; tax on sale of commodities for use in business, except at retail; tax on manufacture of alcohol, beer, chicory and coffee substitutes, ascetic acid, explosives, beet sugar, gas, electricity, and lamps; monopolies (tobacco, salt, quinine, public lotteries, matches, automatic lighters, and cigarette papers).

Communal and provincial taxes were levied in great number. There were taxes on industrial and professional income, real estate, unearned increment following public improvements, hotel rooms, health resorts, numerous consumables, a great variety of license fees, taxes on animals and vehicles, domestic servants, pianos, billiard tables, advertisements, etc.

Economic and social objectives.—Italy used its tax system in some measure to effect Fascist policies. For example, in late 1937 the Government sought to stimulate foreign investments in Italy (thus providing foreign exchange) by granting important tax exemptions. In 1939, a special tax was imposed on profits from non-Government securities in order to discourage a "flight from Government bonds." To speed up the country's motorization as an "evidence of civil progress" and an "indispensable factor in the equipment of a nation for war," the license fee on automobiles was abolished in late 1938. Tax exemptions were used to stimulate building and allied trades. Other measures sought to curb stock speculation through heavy transfer taxes and taxes on capital gains.

Incentives to increase the birth rate were given through reduced inheritance taxes and a tax on bachelors. Under the inheritance tax, the rates varied according to the number of children born to the deceased or his beneficiaries, complete exemption being accorded to transfers to children, or between husband and wife. The bachelor's tax was imposed on all unmarried men between the ages of 25 and 65 at the following rates (as amended): 115 lire for men between 25 and

30 years, 155 lire for those between 30 and 55, 85 lire for those between
55 and 65.   To this tax was also added a special income tax.

Spain

There is little to suggest that Spanish taxation was influenced to
any great extent by fascist policies, although the system had been
largely centralized and provincial taxation abolished.   There were
several kinds of income taxes, a death tax, real property taxes, various
sales, use, and consumption taxes, and an extensive array of involved
and complicated indirect taxes.   In the years following the civil war
Spain derived about 40 percent of its revenues from direct taxes, 40
percent from indirect taxes, and the remainder from monopolies and
state properties.

BORROWING

Summary

A wide variety of types of borrowing was used in both Germany and
Italy.   Short-term obligations were the most common sort issued with
the advent of war.   Tremendous increases in total debt were incurred.
Perhaps a most striking phenomenon to Americans was the fact that
Germany had no bond drives like those in the United States and elsewhere.   Interest rates were continually being forced down in Germany (as in most of the rest of the world), but efforts in this direction
were unsuccessful in Italy.

Germany [21]

The Nazis used many types of borrowing.   Both long- and short-
term obligations were issued.   The short-term instruments were extremely varied.   An interesting feature of German war finance was
that during the whole period of the war the general public was never
asked to subscribe to a war loan.   The more usual practice was to
borrow from banks into which the people had placed their savings.
But special devices were used from time to time to divert funds into
Government bonds.   The extent of the Nazi borrowing is not fully
known because some operations were not made public.   By the end of
the war, the total debt was estimated to have reached RM 473,000,-
000,000 or even higher.[22]   It had grown, so far as disclosed, from RM
12,000,000,000 in 1934 to RM 34,000,000,000 in 1939, when Germany
entered upon a state of war.   Interest rates were gradually forced
down from the 6 percent paid when the National Socialist regime came
to power to about 3½ percent in the latter days before the war's end.
The average rates, however, were always higher than in the United
States and Great Britain.

Borrowing techniques used by Germany changed with changing
economic conditions.   Traditional considerations of what was "sound
finance" in borrowing gave way to questions of how much was needed.
The Government borrowed money wherever it was to be found.   But
this does not mean it accepted conditions as it found them.   The banks
and the financial sector, like the rest of the economy, were harnessed
to the needs of the military.   There were many stresses and strains

[21] Most of the information for this section is taken from the following sources: (1) Nathan work cited in
footnote 2; (2) Annual Reports of the Bank for International Settlements; (3) Richard W. Lindholm,
Germany's World War II Debt, Bulletin of the National Tax Association, vol. 31, May 1946, pp. 233-235,
and his German Finance in World War II, American Economic Review, vol. 37, March 1947, pp. 121-134.
[22] Lindholm (see footnote 21) estimates that a debt of RM 473,000,000,000 would be eight times any fore-
seeable national income in Germany.   Interest payments alone would be a fourth of national income.   The
present United States debt runs between 1½ and 2 times national income with interest payments being
slightly better than 3 percent of national income.

over the years. Both short-term and long-term obligations were issued, but by the second half of 1944 about four-fifths of all borrowing was short-term. Large sums were "borrowed" from the Reichsbank and the commercial banks.

In striking contrast to the practice in the United States, Great Britain, and Russia, the German Government did not conduct war loan drives. Government control of production and investment, rigid rationing, and heavy taxes, were enough apparently to convince the Government that the ways in which individuals and corporations could spend their income were adequately circumscribed. Whatever surplus income existed, it was felt, would find its way to the various credit institutions where the government could reach it easily—which it did. It relied largely on credit institutions other than commercial banks for long-term loans, and on commercial banks (with the re-discounting help of the Reichsbank) for short-term loans.[23] However, in 1941, special incentives were provided to wage earners to increase their savings. A scheme of savings (called "Iron savings") was developed under which amounts not exceeding 26 Reichsmarks (later 39 Reichsmarks) could be deducted directly from their earnings and transferred to local credit institutions. A tax reduction amounting generally to between 10 and 15 percent of tax liabilities was given. "Iron savings" could not be withdrawn until after the war, and then only on 1 year's notice. A somewhat similar scheme was worked out for entrepreneurs. Borrowing (in effect) from entrepreneurs, was also accomplished through partial payment for purchases, in delivery bills, tax credit certificates, and the like.

Italy [24]

Like most countries, Italy resorted to many varieties of financing, especially after its entry into the war. Compulsory lending had become an established practice that predated the Second World War. In early 1947, the debt exceeded a trillion lire. About four-fifths of the total was floating. It had grown from 134,000,000,000 lire in June 1938, when four-fifths of the total had been funded debt. Unlike most of the rest of the world, Italy was unable to reduce its interest rates; the effective yield approached 6 percent on long term issues.

Compulsory lending to the Italian Government was required by several pieces of legislation. In 1935, for example, each property owner had to subscribe to a loan in an amount equal to 5 percent of the taxable value of his property. An interesting feature of this was that a special tax was then imposed on the same property to retire the loan in 25 years. Other legislation required holders of certain foreign securities to exchange them for government bonds, and required banks to keep part of their assets in government securities. More for the purpose of control than for obtaining funds was a 1942 law which created a special 3-percent, 5-year treasury bond as a compulsory blocked investment for (1) war profits retained by the taxpayer; (2) 20 percent of new funds deriving from private issues of shares and other capital increases; and (3) funds equal in amount to those employed in the purchase of shares on the exchange.

---

[23] It is estimated that of the RM 81,000,000,000 increase in the German debt in 1940 and 1941, only about 13 percent was taken up·by private investors. The remaining 87 percent was acquired mostly by banks, insurance companies, etc. League of Nations, World Economic Survey 1941–42, p. 119.

[24] Most of the information for this section is taken from Grampp's article cited in footnote 20, and the Foa and Treves article cited in footnote 10.

Spain

The Bank of Spain during the civil war lent to the Spanish Treasury whatever funds it needed, in order "to meet the requirements of national defense and carry out the all-important services of national interest." [25] During the war, the bank turned over 10,000,000,000 pesetas to the state against non-interest-bearing Treasury notes. With the end of the war, special short- and long-term obligations were issued by the Treasury, principally to absorb the excess money in circulation. The National Government accepted no obligation for the debts of defeated Republican and Separatist Governments.[26] As of the first of 1944, the Spanish debt approximated 35,000,000,000 pesetas.[27]

CONCLUSION

Fascism to only a limited degree used fiscal policy as a primary instrument to effect its own peculiar aims. In Germany especially, other and more powerful weapons were at hand. Except perhaps in details, fascism was neither more nor less successful financially than other forms of government would have been in the same locale. Deficits plagued the fascist countries just as they did the democracies. Though perhaps traceable to military reverses rather than managerial ineptitudes, the financial vehicle of fascism was badly skidding as the war drew to a close, while that of Britain and the United States was still under control.

Few new sources of revenue were devised, though the Nazis did develop new methods for bleeding conquered areas with occupation levies. Agents of the great German banks also succeeded in drawing into their own vaults much of the wealth and control of the resources of the vanquished enemies. The Nazis also concocted diverse methods for discriminating against the Jews, and extracting from them additional and special tribute. Tax advantages to large non-Jewish families, and tax disadvantages to the unmarried and childless, were particular examples of fascism in action. The strict control of banking and the directing of investments into channels to suit the purposes of single party government, rather than the will of the investor, was characteristic of fascist control of business. In conclusion, perhaps the democracies worried more about their financial policies than did the fascists, because the latter had more or stronger strings to their bow.

---

[25] Report of the Bank of Spain, 1936–41, Federal Reserve Bulletin, vol. 29, May 1943, pp. 407–408.
[26] Bank for International Settlements, Twelfth Annual Report, 1941–42, p. 162.
[27] The Statesman's Yearbook, 1946, p. 1264.

CHAPTER V—FOREIGN TRADE

Statistical analyses along traditional lines fail to present a complete or meaningful picture of foreign trade under fascism where trade is the direct result of political and administrative decisions made as a prelude to military conquest. Control of foreign trade is only one means employed by fascist states to achieve nationalistic ambitions. Foreign trade thus becomes an active economic instrument of political policy.

Leadership in the economic foreign policy field, among the fascist states, rested largely with Nazi Germany. Other fascist states followed her example.

Economic foreign policy is important because it relates to the zone of impact between the home economy and the outside world. What any important country does, therefore, in the field of foreign trade has immediate impacts on other countries. Even a complete wall of self-containment, if constructed so as to sever a leading country from the rest of the world, would have important repercussions on the peoples of other countries in their day-to-day job of making a living.

GERMANY

It would be erroneous to credit the Nazis with having invented all of the devices that they used to force their weaker neighbors into economic submission to the design for a super-Reich. The control of foreign trade, primarily through manipulation of foreign exchange, was inaugurated in Germany several years before Hitler came to power and may, to a certain degree, be viewed as the culmination of an economic policy that was coterminous with the development of the German Empire itself.

Historically speaking, "protectionism" in Germany was aggressively national and directed toward the creation of a strong and self-sufficient State. Protectionism, as advocated by List[1] and followed by Imperial Germany, stresses the desirability of speeding up the economic development of a country so as to achieve, as quickly as possible, the goal of the fully developed and well integrated agricultural-manufacturing-trading state. In order to accomplish such an objective Germany inaugurated and maintained a system of tariffs designed to protect both agriculture and heavy industry. She consistently endeavored to protect her agriculture against wide price fluctuations in world markets and, largely through cartels, exercised considerable control over imports and exports of industrial products.

The chain of events that followed the First World War brought Germany to the brink of economic disaster. The characteristic economic nationalism of the German people, their propensity to follow strong leaders, and the dislocations that inevitably followed the

---

[1] Friedrich List, National System of Political Economy (1841). Pertinent passages are reprinted in F. W. Taussig, Selected Readings in International Trade and Tariff Problems, New York, Ginn & Co., 1921, pp. 277-299.

Kaiser's War, resulted in the imposition of rigid economic controls and, eventually Nazi dictatorship and national collapse.

The Nazi leaders took mechanisms of exchange control, refined them and used them as highly selective instruments for diverting imports and exports into well-known channels that were consistent with an over-all national plan. A study of foreign trade under the Nazi regime becomes, very largely, a study of their foreign exchange controls.

The Pre-Hitler period

Generally speaking, countries turn to control of foreign exchange when they find the debits in their international accounts running far ahead of their credits.[2] Under such circumstances the value of their own currency depreciates in terms of foreign currencies, and the acquisition of the latter becomes progressively more and more difficult. The normal corrective would be an increase of the country's commodity exports, or its equivalent. But when a country in question finds it extremely difficult, if not impossible, to generate exports, the depreciation of its currency in terms of foreign currencies ceases to be self-correcting and becomes self-aggravating.

Throughout the inter-war period Germany's international economic position was weak, being in large part a reflection of the economic changes occasioned by military defeat and world-wide economic depression. This condition did not show up immediately in Germany's international financial position. American and other foreign capital was flowing into the country and covered up what was essentially a lack of balance in her current international accounts. Imports of raw materials and foodstuffs gave the appearance of being paid for and some of Germany's key industries were enabled to modernize their equipment which had been heavily depleted by the speed-up of wartime operations. In some cases, however, the cost of such loans was high and heavy overhead charges were incurred.

Had the Great Depression not intervened it is possible that Germany might have been able to extricate herself from her international economic predicament. As it was, since Germany was not able to renew her maturing foreign loans, the artificial support that such loans had been giving to her essentially unhealthy international financial position was suddenly removed. By 1931 the situation became acute and there was a severe drain on her financial reserves. German nationals, as well as foreigners, rushed to convert their German properties into foreign assets before the values of such properties were completely swept away, and the resulting "flight of capital" made still less favorable the international position of the mark.

At this juncture the German authorities had to decide between devaluation of the mark and continuation of the process of deflation. The attractions of the former, and usually easier, policy were more than counterbalanced by the fact that the German people, remembering their dizzy experiences of the twenties, were still highly "inflation-conscious." The Bruening government, for this and other reasons, decided in favor of the latter alternative.

---

[2] Exchange control measures were adopted by Bulgaria in 1918, by Portugal in 1922, and by Iran and Turkey in 1930. There was also the control of German exchange under the Dawes plan of 1924 under which the Agent General for Reparation Payments was to see that remittances on reparations account should be made only to the extent that the mark was not depreciated. See E. M. Patterson, An Introduction to World Economics, The Macmillan Co., New York, 1947, pp. 494–495.

The foreign exchange situation became acute as the flight of capital continued, and in July 1931, exchange control was inaugurated as an emergency measure to halt the drain on the nation's gold and foreign exchange reserves.[3] The original exchange control decree provided that foreign credits obtained by German nationals could be sold only to the Reichsbank. Similarly, importers who had to make payments abroad in foreign currencies could obtain such currency only by purchase from the Reichsbank. All dealing in foreign exchange had to be conducted at the official rates which conformed to the gold parity of the Reichsmark. Gold and silver could not be imported or exported without permission of the exchange control authority.

The difficulty of maintaining the Reichsmark at its old parity was accentuated by depreciation of the British pound sterling and the currencies of several other countries, starting late in 1931. Had the German authorities allowed the mark to depreciate, or rather, found it possible to do so in view of the inflation-consciousness of the German people, it is likely that German domestic prices would have been brought into line with the external purchasing power of the mark without involving such intensified forms of foreign trade control as were soon to be promulgated, even before the advent of Hitler.

German exporters found it increasingly difficult to market German goods abroad, because of both the overvaluation of the mark by the German Government and by the imposition of heightened trade barriers by countries that had hitherto been important markets for German goods.

Starting in 1932, the German authorities conceived of means whereby exports and imports could be effected without the use of foreign exchange. These consisted of barter, or private compensation; exchange clearing, and the additional export procedure.[4]

Barter (or private compensation), a system whereby imports and exports were directly exchanged for each other by the same firm, was at first confined to trade with countries that practiced exchange control. Later on, a number of separate German importing and exporting houses began to cooperate with each other by clearing each other's balances. Eventually such arrangements were brought under central control by the exchange control authority.

Exchange clearing involved the "blocking" of foreign claims to German funds. Foreigners having claims against German nationals were restricted in the use to which they could put such funds; they could not be converted into the currency of other countries at the option of the claimant, but only in strict accordance with regulations of the exchange control authority.

Foreigners soon found themselves with substantial amounts tied up in "blocked marks." When it became evident that exchange control would continue for some time they were willing to sell their claims at substantial discounts. The German authorities capitalized on this situation by allowing German exporters, under certain conditions, to accept part of the proceeds from their sales abroad in this

[3] For a competent technical discussion of German exchange control from 1931 to 1939, see Howard S. Ellis, Exchange Control in Central Europe, Cambridge, Harvard University Press, 1941, ch. IV. In this chapter the author shows clearly how German exchange control, starting out in 1931 as an emergency measure, was soon transformed into an instrument of totalitarianism.

[4] This, and the following sections which discuss the technical side of German trade controls, are based largely on L. A. Morrison, Foreign Trade and Exchange Controls in Germany. Report No. 150, Second Series, U. S. Tariff Commission, Washington, D. C., 1942.

form. This, the so-called additional export procedure, made it possible for German exporters to sell abroad at lower prices than they
would have been able to do otherwise.

Around the middle of 1932, Germany entered into a number of
exchange-clearing agreements with other countries. Under the terms
of such agreements clearing accounts were established in the Reichsbank and in the central banks of the other contracting countries.
Payments for all goods passing between Germany and the other
countries were made through these clearing accounts on a bilateral
balancing basis.

The transition period, 1933–34

The period between January 1933, when Hitler became Chancellor,
and September 1934, when Dr. Schacht's "new plan" was instituted
might be called the transition period between *ad hoc* exchange and
foreign trade control, instituted to meet an intensifying financial
emergency, and the complete dominance of foreign trade by the state
as an active instrument of foreign policy.

During this period Germany's international financial position became even more precarious than before. The extreme nationalism
of the Nazis—including persecution of the Jews—among other things,
had the effect of stimulating new "flights of capital" and to scare away
new capital investment. On top of these internal difficulties was the
depreciation of the United States dollar which made it still more
difficult for Germans to export their wares.

The mark was clearly overvalued, in terms of other currencies, but
any serious attempt to correct the situation by devaluation of the
mark would have caused a diminution of Nazi prestige—at least in
their own eyes.

Instead, many German industries, previously producing for export,
were diverted to the production of goods deemed necessary for the
intensive rearmament program.

By the middle of 1933, these policies had resulted in a rise in many
German prices which, of course, had the effect of further aggravating
the discrepancy between the foreign-exchange value of the German
currency and its internal purchasing power, and in increasing the
demand for many foreign goods.

Within a few months the Nazis found it all but impossible to obtain
those foreign products—mostly raw materials—that were necessary
to carry out their program. They clamped down more severely than
ever before upon the release of exchange to pay for those goods that
they considered nonessential, and declared at first a limited, and
later on, a complete moratorium on the service of the German foreign
debt. To the extent that foreign countries retaliated against such
unilateral action on the part of Nazi Germany—and some did—the
international financial position of the latter became still more difficult.

Dr. Hjalmar Schacht repeated time and again that Germany could
not pay her foreign debt without a favorable balance of trade, and
assailed vigorously Germany's creditors for not importing more
heavily from Germany. What he scrupulously avoided saying was
that Germany's "active economic policy" being carried out under the
cover of exchange control was making it impossible to generate the

necessary exports which would have provided foreign exchange for servicing the debt.[5]

Germany's "New Plan"

Although established as an emergency measure, it was soon evident that the Nazis were making a "virtue of necessity, and were using the totalitarian control of foreign commerce transactions as an offensive as well as a defensive weapon."[6] By the middle of 1934 the announcements and actions of German officials foretold clearly (1) that there was no longer any hope that Germany would restore a free exchange market, and (2) that foreign-exchange control and aggressive bilateral bargaining were to be the principal bases of Germany's future international economic relations.

The so-called New Plan, credit for the authorship of which goes to Dr. Schacht, was initiated in September 1934, when, by a series of decrees, a number of commodity boards were established to control the importation and exportation of practically all commodities.[7] The new boards were subdivisions of the foreign-exchange-control administration, and each board was to have control over the release of foreign exchange for transactions in the goods under its jurisdiction. Strict regulation of exports, as well as of imports, was one of the important features of the new arrangements. Exports of certain products were stimulated either through the use of clearing-account marks or by direct subsidy.

Whereas prior to the New Plan imports were restricted by quotas bearing a percentage relationship to former average import needs, imports were now completely prohibited except under specific Government permit. Twenty-five import control offices were established and by 1935, according to Douglas Miller,[8] necessities were defined as goods of military significance. His on-the-spot description of import controls affords a graphic description of how fascist bureaucracy works:

In the beginning, the control offices attempted to apply rough-and-ready methods for rationing imported commodities as best they could. It proved rather difficult to put the economic life of a great people in a strait jacket so quickly, but the German people responded by restricting their consumption of foreign goods; and the new system got under way without too much friction or difficulty.

I called upon most of the control offices within a few days of their establishment and found that it was impossible to see the officials. There had been so many applications from business men that it was necessary to bar the doors and handle only written communications.

I could not even get in touch with the officials by telephone. In the case of the office handling food products, the number of employees increased from twelve or fifteen at the start to twelve hundred at the end of two weeks. It proved necessary to engage a Berlin theater in order to handle interviews with importers * * *. In a more leisurely way, this control was extended over nonperishable goods until everything was on a permit basis.

[5] Ellis, pp. 197-8. Also, on p. 210, he states: "The crucial determinant which fastened exchange control and bilateralism in trade upon the German economy was the 'active economic policy.' If it be said that this was a heroic program to lift Germany out of the slough of depression and unemployment, it must also be said that it delivered the *coup de grace* to Germany's reputation as the 'well-intentioned debtor' and to the prospect of Germany and most of her neighbors for resuming normal economic intercourse within the visible future."

[6] Douglas Miller, You Can't Do Business With Hitler, Boston, Little, Brown and Co., 1941. See especially pp. 63-92.

[7] Previously there had been such boards (Reichstellen) but they were limited to the control of imports and distribution of certain agricultural products. The first of the new decrees and orders, issued in September 1934, were R. G. Bl., 1934, pt. I, p. 816, 829; D. R. anz., 1934, No. 209; R. St. Bl., 1934, p. 1018; Reichszollblatt, 1934, p. 541.

[8] Douglas Miller, op. cit., pp. 65-68; Mr. Miller was American Assistant Commercial Attaché in Germany for 15 years, 5 of which were during the Nazi regime.

Lawyers in Germany have very largely ceased to function as interpreters of the law, because, as I said earlier, courts are instructed to render decisions according to "healthy public opinion." A knowledge of the written law is no longer of such importance as before. This gave an opportunity to Germany's lawyers to engage in the securing of permits. Since every transaction, foreign and later domestic, necessitated such documents, the legal profession quickly became permit procurers or fixers. The fast trains leading to Berlin from the provinces were labeled "permit trains" because they were principally occupied by legal gentlemen coming to government offices in search of these indispensable documents. Large sums of money changed hands in the course of these operations. One lawyer in Berlin's west end told me that as a result of such negotiations he had now become the largest owner of properties in the cloak, suit, and clothing business of the country.

Before long the foreign-trade permit system led to monopolies in imported articles and attendant price increases. To combat this the Government instituted price controls of all goods made from imported raw materials which was later expanded to a tight system of general price control of all products. This soon led to a system under which production itself was allocated among domestic firms.

Nazi foreign trade controls under the New Plan were pointed toward two unmistakable objectives; viz., maximizing the military strength of Germany and arranging for the importation, on the most favorable terms, of goods not produced at home in exchange for goods which could be exported with the least disadvantage to the national program. This change in orientation from an export (for pecuniary profit) to an import (for national need) psychology is one of the characteristics of a totalitarian regime, whether of the right or of the left.

The Nazis learned how to live on their own debts. Since international commercial transactions are not enforceable by any power superior to the state itself, there is no way whereby a nation can be forced to live up to its contractual arrangements. By getting itself into deeper and deeper debt, Nazi Germany was able for a considerable period to obtain foreign goods—mostly raw materials of military importance—without paying for them in currency. By shrewd and hard bargaining she was able to induce weaker supplying countries to accept in payment for such materials whatever merchandise she happened, at the moment, to be willing to spare. Sometimes she gave mere promises in payment.

Those were days of world-wide depression. Raw material producers were particularly hard hit and agricultural countries were unable on their own, to cope with the glut of agricultural products. Industrial countries, including Germany, were unable to sell their manufactured products and were thus lacking the foreign exchange with which to buy the raw materials so necessary to feed the armament machines.

Extension of the barter system seemed a simple and logical solution. Dr. Schacht and his associates offered to buy up entire crops of agricultural and other raw materials in exchange for unnamed products of German industry. What the Balkan, Latin American and other smaller countries did not realize was that the Nazi businessmen were, to all intents and purposes, agents of the Reich. Although technically the arrangements were "commercial" they amounted, on the German side, to state-trading. In the long run, as the merchants and governments of Rumania and other smaller countries who unwittingly fell into the economic trap of Nazi Germany found out, individual enterprise cannot stand up against the power of a sovereign state that is determined upon economic exploitation.[9]

As indicated earlier in this chapter, the Germans had, months before the Nazis acquired control, and mostly as an improvisation, hit upon the device of "blocking" marks and setting them aside for certain types of foreign transactions. Under the New Plan, the Nazis seized upon this device and by systematically depreciating the mark on a selective basis for various foreign transactions, made it a major instrument of foreign economic policy.[10] It was essentially a controlled system of multiple foreign exchange values where the rules were made administratively on a day to day basis, and in a way that made it all but impossible for foreigners to follow. No principles were laid down to which businessmen could refer, and what rules there were were changed without any advance warning.

The ASKI system

Some direct exchanges of German and foreign goods continued to be made until 1935. From then on, however, the direct barter system was replaced by the so-called ASKI [11] procedure under which it was necessary for every foreign trade transaction to be negotiated, or at least approved, by the Nazi foreign trade officials. Regulations establishing the ASKI procedure were first promulgated in December 1934. Under these, foreign firms selling goods to Germany agreed to accept ASKI marks which could be used only for financing German exports to the country of the holder of the marks. Usually the foreign holder could authorize disbursements from his account to pay for German goods to be delivered to others, but only in his own country.

Under this system the Nazi Government, since it retained absolute power to determine what goods could be exported, maintained a powerful bargaining position. The system was essentially one of bilateral balancing. The ASKI marks in any particular account could be used only to finance German exports to an importer in a country the imports from which gave rise to the account. Later on, the system was further refined so that distinctions were even made between ASKI credits arising from German imports of particular kinds of goods from the same country. Thus there were "cotton marks," "coffee marks," "copper marks," etc. "Each group of ASKI accounts that was differentiated from others formed a separate 'island of exchange' in which the German authorities could apply their control as the country's bargaining position in each case seemed to warrant." [12] There was thus no necessary connection between the values of ASKI marks to importers in different foreign countries, or, in fact, to all importers in the same country. The Nazis had at their command a versatile and powerful weapon which they could, and did, use to discriminate in favor of the imports that they wanted and against those that were not in accord with their national program.

---

[9] For an illuminating non-technical account of Nazi Germany's transition from World Trade to Trade Warfare, see Guenter Reimann, The Vampire Economy, New York, The Vanguard Press, 1939, especially ch. XIII.

[10] Cf. U. S. Tariff Commission, Report on Foreign Trade and Exchange Control in Germany, previously cited, pp. 10–14.

[11] Abbreviation for Auslaender Sonderkonten fuer Inlandszahlungen (foreigners' special accounts for inland payments). The ASKI marks were in the form of accounts in German banks which could be held in the name of the foreign exporter or a bank in the exporter's country.

[12] U. S. Tariff Commission, op. cit., p. 17.

ASKI marks were always kept depreciated in terms of the official gold value of the mark.   They could not be converted into foreign currency at the official rate of exchange and their degree of individual depreciation depended upon what German policy with regard to a certain country, or commodity happened to be at the moment. Always the objective was to balance the international accounts with particular countries on a bilateral basis, and to force the importation of those goods that the Nazis deemed necessary to their over-all national plan.

As time went on the Nazis induced a number of countries to enter into exchange clearing agreements with them, whereby Germany more or less regularized what she had already achieved through the discriminatory power of the ASKI system.   Those countries with whom exchange clearing agreements were not concluded continued under the ASKI system.   Regardless of the actual technique used, however, the purpose was always the same; viz., to acquire imports on the most favorable terms possible and to shift the burden of their financing to the supplying country.

Exchange clearing agreements

By the end of 1935, Germany had concluded exchange clearing agreements with Argentina, Chile, Uruguay, and all European countries except Albania, Great Britain, and the Soviet Union.   In actual operation these agreements varied widely in significance principally because of differences in Germany's bargaining position with the individual countries concerned.   The Balkans received inferior goods (or goods that they did not want) at high prices.   There were often large balances against which goods could not be obtained; banks often had to pay off the exporters; the governments were under pressure to buy German goods (rather than goods from other countries) in order to reduce the balances; and the governments, in turn, applied their own import and exchange controls in such a way as to stimulate their own importers to buy in Germany.

The weaker countries found themselves compelled to import in far larger quantities from Germany than they otherwise would have done. When Nazi officials contracted for their entire crop of raw materials it was with the understanding that the marks to which such purchases gave rise would be used to purchase German goods.   Frequently the German manufactured goods that importers in these countries wanted were not available because of their essentiality to the rearmament program.   Yet, the more of their raw material that Germany bought, the more their mark credits piled up and the greater was the pressure for them to take in payment goods that they did not really need or want.   If they failed to do so, their accounts in Germany grew, and, being noninterest bearing, the effect was a net loss.

As the process continued it became necessary for the foreign countries to import whatever they could from Germany, whether or not they were the goods that were actually wanted.   The alternative was to continue on an ever larger scale as Germany's involuntary banker.

There was no incentive for exporters in the supplying countries to refrain from selling their crops to Germany, since they received payment for them in their own currency and, in the absence of bulk sales, would have encountered great difficulty in finding markets.   The financial burden of such transactions was shifted to the Central Bank of the exporting country and only after considerable time could enough pressure be exerted to restrain the exporters from pursuing their own short-run interest.

As the system developed the Nazis did not confine their purchases of raw materials to the goods that they themselves intended using. By their pressure tactics they bought coffee, tobacco, and other world commodities and resold them on world markets for gold and foreign currency, much to the chagrin of the countries in which the materials originated.

On the export side the Nazis foisted on their weaker neighbors manufactured goods other than those that were really needed, such as typewriters, mouth organs, radio sets, and optical instruments. In fact, it was reported that so many German typewriters were sent to Rumania that that country's typewriter needs were satisfied for many years to come. And, when Rumania turned around and tried to sell the typewriters to other countries for whatever price they would bring, she was charged with "dumping"!

Efficiency of the Nazi system questioned

In the summer of 1945 a group of American investigators were sent to Germany under the auspices of the Historical Division of the United States War Department to investigate the economic preparations that Nazi Germany had made for war. These investigators were a part of the so-called Shuster Commission and they spent much time talking to Dr. Schacht and others who had been instrumental in effectuating Germany's economic foreign policy. Their findings, although they do not in the slightest cast any doubt as to the fundamental objectives of the Nazi regime in the economic foreign field, do show that the Nazis themselves were by no means as efficient as they might have been in achieving their objectives. The following quotation from their report is instructive in this connection:[13]

The Nazi economic foreign policy was established by Schacht in the early days of the regime, and there was no substantial later deviation from the procedures then developed. Schacht asserts that the two precepts on foreign trade that he communicated to Hitler were (1) to buy abroad no more than could be paid for and (2) to buy not necessarily in the cheapest market but where the seller would take in payment what Germany had to offer. The former of these precepts was scantly honored but the merely *provisional* payment for German imports, in mark credits in Berlin, transferred from the Germans to the exporting countries any embarrassment that the Germans might otherwise have felt at their inability to make final settlement on the excess of their imports over the German counterclaims against foreign countries.

Schacht was not greatly enamored of the system of international barter, which he sponsored as an ineluctable necessity for the restoration of the German economy and for "defensive" rearmament, and was no doubt astounded at its eventually proved efficacy in the service of Germany. There is little doubt that it could have been made even more efficacious in the German preparation for war if it had been employed more fully for political (that is to say *wehrwirtschaftliche*) rather than for traditionally economic ends.

The negotiation of trade treaties was, however, in the hands of the Foreign Ministry (with technical assistance from the Ministry of Economics), and the control of the Foreign Office lay at first with von Neurath, who was a traditional rather than resolutely war-minded diplomat, and then with von Ribbentrop who was not remarkable for clear-headedness. The result was that policy was determined by technical experts in the Foreign Office (Ritter had almost complete autonomy) in co-operation with their counterparts in the Ministry of Economics. These experts were apparently never instructed to proceed in other than the ways

[13] Frank D. Graham and J. J. Scanlon, Economic Preparation and Conduct of War Under the Nazi Regime, Manuscript of the Historical Division of the War Department Special Staff, April 10, 1946.

of presumptive peace and do not in fact appear to have shaped the German economic foreign policy to the requirements of prospective war. It so happened that a good deal of what they did served the Nazi war preparation (such as, for instance, the concentration of German trade relationships in the European zone) but this was the result of accident and of opportunistic action rather than of conscious preparation for war. It can at any rate be said that, *if* the trade negotiators were deliberately preparing for war, their practices, while issuing to the advantage of Germany in some cases, was full of errors of omission and commission.

The highest political authorities seemed to have intervened on only one occasion (when the Foreign Office was instructed to treat Hungary, no doubt for ulterior German ends, much more favorably than strict economic and business principles would have prescribed), and the military authorities, though occasionally represented in the discussions preliminary to trade treaty negotiations, were only interested in the imports they required for specific armaments and not at all in broad questions of *wehrwirtschaftliche* policy.

The negotiators from the Foreign Office in their dealings with the representatives of foreign countries drove the best bargain they could without resort to political or military pressure or even the threat of it, and otherwise operated on *business* rather than *wehrwirtschaftliche* principles. In fine it may be said that in the field of economic foreign policy as elsewhere the Nazis were very inept in their conscious preparation for war. They made some effort to tie the foreign suppliers within their military orbit to long-term contracts with Germany, but they showed no consistent concern for the foreign investment or disinvestment appropriate to war and, in general, were blind to their opportunities in the field.

Although, as indicated in the United States Army report, Germany's bilateral trade practices were inefficient and restricted her foreign trade,[14] they did succeed in large measure in accomplishing what the Nazi leaders set out to do. They effectuated a change in the distribution of Germany's trade by curtailing German exports to those countries with which she had had an active trade balance and by increasing imports from those countries with which she had previously had a passive balance. The fact that to accomplish this, it was necessary for her to subsidize exports in one way or another was of no serious concern to her since it was a price that had to be paid to achieve her over-all objectives.

Nazi policy was aimed at redistributing Germany's trade. Copper, petroleum, cotton, fruits, and lard, which had for a long time been supplied by the United States, now came, as a result of the policies outlined above, largely from Brazil, Belgian Congo, Chile, Yugoslavia, Denmark, and Rumania. South Africa replaced Australia and New Zealand as the source of wool, and Italian rice replaced that formerly imported from British India. German imports from, and exports to, the countries of southeastern Europe which in 1929, had accounted for 4.6 percent and 5.1 percent, respectively, of total German imports had increased to 10.5 percent and 13.1 percent, respectively, in 1938. Imports from, and exports to, South American countries in the same period, increased from 8.3 percent and 5.8 percent, respectively, to 11.1 percent and 8.0 percent. In the same period Germany's trade with what might be called "industrialized" countries had declined from 39.4 percent (imports) to 28.9 percent and from 49.3 percent (exports) to 36.7 percent.

The United States, because of its strong financial position and the comparative unimportance of its exports to Germany, was always able to maintain an independent course towards Germany's trade

[14] Bank for International Settlements. Sixteenth Annual Report, 1945-46, p. 9 (footnote). The Bank earlier had said: "In spite of these expedients, Germany signally failed to recover the volume of trade which it had enjoyed in 1929. Indeed, all through the thirties Germany's foreign trade was, in volume, some 30 to 40 percent below the 1929 level, while in other countries, which had not applied exchange control, the volume of trade was, by 1937, not far from the 1929 level." Fifteenth Annual Report, 1944-45, p. 106.

methods. In 1936 the United States invoked section 303 of the Tariff Act of 1930 and provided for the imposition of countervailing duties on imports of dutiable German merchandise "if the United States importer had paid for the German goods with depreciated aski marks which he had bought from a United States exporter who in turn had sold goods in Germany against aski credits." [15]

ITALY

Starting out, as did Germany, with an adverse balance of international payments and with a steady strain on her currency reserves, Italy resorted to the use of import quotas, import licenses, and various other restrictions to keep herself going economically. More and more her economy was tied to that of Nazi Germany until, when the Second World War broke out, her only important trade contacts were with Germany and southeastern Europe.

Italy, however, was even more dependent on foreign trade than was Germany. Most of the Italian industries depended on foreign raw materials and, in addition, on foreign coal. Italy's balance of payments was also determined to a significant extent by the tourist trade and emigrants' remittances. Even during the depression year of 1932, tourists' expenditures in Italy were estimated at a billion lire.

The adverse trade balance of Italy, which amounted in 1928 to 7 billion lire, was normally covered by the income from tourist expenditures, emigrants' remittances, and shipping services. With the decline in the invisible items, trade and exchange restrictions were applied to reduce the adverse trade balance, which declined to less than 1.5 billion lire, accompanied by a shrinkage in imports from 21.7 billion lire in 1929, to 7.4 billion in 1933, and a decline in exports during the same period from 15.2 billion lire to about 6 billion. One of the contributing factors in the cutting down of imports was the famous "Battle of Grain," which contributed to raising the cost of living and the difficulties of marketing Italian products at competitive prices. It was much more difficult to curtail the imports of raw materials and fuel, except in the case of the textile industry, where rayon and other artificial fibers gradually replaced cotton to a substantial extent.

Until 1934, Italy's foreign trade policy was comparatively liberal.[16] She depended primarily upon the tariff as a protective device and had not resorted to quantitative trade controls or other discriminatory devices. Certain important Italian industrial products, notably textiles, were highly competitive in world markets, even under normal conditions; but with the growth of trade barriers abroad and the competition from countries with devalued currencies, they were becoming more and more handicapped.

Authority to restrict dealings in foreign exchange was given to Italy's Minister of Finance in 1931.[17] It was not until 3 years later, however, that comprehensive decrees regulating foreign exchange were announced requiring all Italian exporters to sell to the National

[15] U. S. Tariff Commission, op. cit. pp. 158-160.
[16] Liberal, that is, in the sense that she relied on tariffs and not cn discriminatory quantitative trade controls. In fact, after 1929 Italy's tariff rates were successively raised, in part as retaliation against foreign tariffs on Italian goods, so that by 1935 the Italian tariff was one of the highest in the world. See Carl T. Schmidt, The Corporate State in Action, New York, Oxford University Press, 1939, pp. 125-127.
[17] Royal Decree Law of September 29, 1931, No. 1207.

Foreign Exchange Institute (Istcambi)[18] all foreign exchange received in payment for their exports. Subsequent decrees, in February and March 1935, placed a wide variety of commodities under license and quota restriction.[19]

The imposition of sanctions on Italy by the League of Nations in the Ethiopian War, with their implied threat to the imperialist ambitions of the Fascist regime, was largely responsible for the adoption of a policy of self-sufficiency in 1936. In view of the meager resources of the country and the long time required for carrying out the new policy, the effect on the import trade was not very great, especially in view of the increased demand for materials essential for the maintenance of the army of occupation in Africa and resettlement.

After the end of the Ethiopian campaign in the middle of 1936, Italian export trade was influenced very largely by colonial development. During 1936, 31 percent of Italian exports went to the colonies, and only an insignificant amount of imports was received in return. The excess of exports to the colonies increased from 166 million lire in 1934 to 1,538 million in 1936. Since the shipments were intended almost entirely for the maintenance of the army and the development of new settlements, this excess of exports did not result in the advantages in the way of returns derived from a real favorable trade balance, although the Italian foreign trade statistics did not make the distinction.

One of the significant results of the imposition of the sanctions and the growing foreign exchange difficulties was the increasing economic dependence of Fascist Italy on Nazi Germany, which was an important factor in shaping the political relations between the two regimes. In 1938, Germany contributed over 27 percent of all Italian imports and took nearly 25 percent of all Italian exports, with the balance against Italy amounting to over 1 billion lire. With the blockade at the outbreak of the war, Italy became entirely dependent on Germany for coal, which Germany undertook to ship by rail at the rate of nearly a million tons a month. Italy undertook to balance her trade with Germany partly by means of exporting manpower to work on German farms and in war plants. With the Italian entry into the war, her trade became restricted largely to Germany and southeastern Europe.

Clearing agreements were made and much of Italy's trade was carried on pursuant to such agreements. From the repeal of sanctions in July 1936 to May 1937, Italy negotiated over 30 trade and quota agreements.[20]

CONCLUSION

By their very nature fascist regimes tend to diminish the total foreign trade of a nation by diverting it into channels that are intended to be consistent with an over-all master plan. That master plan is usually pointed toward the goal of economic and military self-sufficiency. To the extent that the goal is not actually attainable and imports are necessary, they are stimulated and guided by the

---

[18] Ministerial Decree of May 26, 1934, No. 804, and Ministerial Decree of December 8, 1934. The Italian name of the Foreign Exchange Institute stands for the abbreviation of Istituto Nazionali per i Cambi con L'Estero (Istcambi).
[19] William G. Welk, Fascist Economic Policy, Cambridge, Harvard University Press, 1938, pp. 205-212.
[20] F. Guarneri, Italy's Commercial Policy, The Banker, London, September 1937, vol. 43 p. 235.

political authorities. Whatever instruments of control are at hand are utilized to achieve these ends. The criteria of success, therefore, of the foreign trade policy of a fascist state is not necessarily the magnitude of its trade. It is, rather, the degree to which actual imports and exports harmonize with the master plan.

Nazi Germany, determined to become as economically independent as possible in the event of a world war, seized upon barter schemes and exchange control devices that had been developed following the First World War and used them for political purposes with a consistency that the world had not seen before. Technically speaking, foreign trade was still conducted by individual traders. Actually, it was state trading in disguise. Every transaction was subject to license and control by the political authorities. Selective and arbitrary depreciation of the mark—a situation in which there were different kinds of marks for use in trade with different countries, each of which had its own value that bore no consistent relationship to the value of the others—made it possible for Nazi Germany to import what she needed at advantageous terms and to finance such imports by shifting the burden to her creditors.

In effect, Germany's smaller and weaker neighbors, principally countries in the Balkans and in Latin America, became her involuntary creditors. They were induced to sell their raw materials to Germany in exchange for promises of manufactured goods that either did not materialize or that materialized in forms that were of doubtful use to them. Nazi Germany had the advantage of being able to decide upon a unified economic foreign policy and to implement it logically and relentlessly without having to indulge in the luxury of open political debate. By the same token the individual German trader was denied the basic freedom of determining his own lines of action. All that he could do was to follow instructions and content himself with being a small cog in a big economic machine.

Notwithstanding the fact that the Nazi leaders were in a position to —and did—dictate the terms under which foreign trade could be carried on, recent researches, conducted under the auspices of the United States War Department, indicate that the Nazi leaders were not nearly as successful and astute as they at first appeared to be.

PART II—ECONOMIC

CHAPTER VI—ORGANIZATION OF THE ECONOMY: GERMANY

In Italy and Germany, respectively, the fascist economic organization meant the corporate state and the "new order." Businesses were organized like armies or navies, in successively higher echelons, with authority pyramiding in the office of a cabinet minister. Analogous to the company or battery as a unit in the army were the corporazioni in Italy, the Kartelle in Germany. Similar fascist organizations elsewhere were the groupements in Vichy-France, and the sindicatos in Spain.

In the beginning, fascism everywhere followed mercantilistic policies traditionally favored by business. It suppressed trade-unions, prohibited strikes, outlawed consumers' and workers' cooperatives, and lowered wage rates by government decree. Then followed reprivatization of industries governmentally or municipally owned, the substitution of sales taxes for business income taxes or the removal of taxes on capital issues, the creation of public financial institutions to take over the shares of bankrupt concerns until they could be restored to healthy condition, the imposition of high tariffs, the award of highly profitable contracts for greatly expanded public works or national defense, and the direct grant of subsidies and other financial aid to business.[1]

In general, fascism protected business from the rigors of competition. The cartels prevented price cutting or "chiseling," controlled the expansion of existing plants or the erection of new factories likely to cut monopolistic profits, and tried to stabilize production, markets, and international trade. In short, fascist regimes not only attempted to safeguard existing property rights,[2] but fostered further industrialization and concentration of business enterprise.[3]

This was in some ways the opposite of what had been promised. Before their advent to power, fascists appealed to the masses on anticapitalist platforms, exploiting among small businessmen and the lower middle classes not only the latter's fear of monopolistic capitalism and economic concentration, but especially their antagonism against communism. The Nazis, for example, prior to 1933, stressed · the economic planks of the 25-point party program of February 23,

---

[1] Maxine Y. Sweezy, The Structure of the Nazi Economy, Cambridge, Mass., 1941, pp. 231 ff.

[2] Sweezy, p. 235: "* * * the profit system is one of its integral parts; the inequality of distribution of wealth and income has increased, and wages have been kept at depression levels * * *." Also Guenter Reimann, p. 323, states categorically: "The Fascist totalitarian state of today is essentially a capitalist society with private enterprise and private property as the foundation of its economy." Also, pp. 311, 313.

[3] Reimann, p. 187: "In the totalitarian countries big corporations tend to become mere 'family trusts,' a trend which is especially typical of the large corporations [or Zaibatsu (Mitsui, Mitsubishi, Yashuda, Sumitomo)] in Japan. * * * In Germany, a few 'Aryan' families like Mannesmann, Friedrich Flick, Otto Wolff, and Graf von Ballestrem were able to acquire additional control of numerous plants and companies." In Italy, similar concentration was vested in such large entrepreneurs as Alberto Pinelli (the utility magnate), Guido Donegani (given a monopoly of chemicals in his Montecatini organization), Count Volpi, head of the Union of Italian Industrialists, Aguelli and Valletta of Fiat motor works, Marinotti of Snia Viscosa, etc. In Spain, the most favored industrialist was the fabulously wealthy Juan March, who engineered and financed Franco's seizure of power.

1920. Hitler even called Gottfried Feder's exposition of the Nazi economic program the catechism of the National Socialist movement. But Feder's ideas about the abolition of interest and rent, the complete confiscation of war profits, and the creation of estates and occupational chambers were forgotten after the Nazis attained power.[4] In short, whatever the early promises of liberal action may have been on behalf of laborers, consumers, and small business, fascist regimes later failed to keep them.

THE PRECARIOUS POSITION OF THE BUSINESSMAN

The predicament of business leaders under these circumstances was clearly demonstrated by the widely publicized case of Fritz Thyssen, head of the Vereinigte Stahlwerke.

Thyssen wrote in I Paid Hitler: "* * * Since 1923 I have supported the party."[5] At a time when Germany was suffering catastrophic inflation, he contributed about 100,000 gold marks to the party.[6] In December 1931, he not only became a member of the National Socialist Party,[7] but the coalowners' association, of which he was an influential member, pledged themselves to pay into the Nazi Party treasury 50 pfennigs for each ton of coal sold.[8]

On January 27, 1932, a full year before Hitler became Chancellor, Thyssen arranged the famous meeting before the Industry Club at Duesseldorf at which Hitler met with, and spoke to the entire body of German industrialists. " * * * in consequence of this, a number of large contributions flowed from the resources of heavy industry into the treasuries of the National Socialist party."[9] "In September 1932, Thyssen invited Adolf Kirdorf, Albert Voegler, and other great industrialists to his house in order to enable them to put their questions to Hitler.[10] Many industrialists identified themselves completely with the Nazi drive for conquest and war and occupied leading positions in the economic, political and administrative hierarchy which the Nazis built up.[11]

Thyssen wrote:

I [12] * * * was chosen by the National Socialist Party to found an institute [13] charged with the preparation of the introduction of the corporative order.[14]

Although he failed to create a corporative system (staendische Wirtschaftsordnung), Thyssen did work closely with von Papen to strength-

[4] Friedrich Naumann, Mitteleuropa, Berlin, 1916, pp. 228–229.
[5] Fritz Thyssen, I Paid Hitler, New York, 1941, p. 16.
[6] Thyssen, p. 82.
[7] Thyssen, p. 97.
[8] Hearings before a subcommittee of the Senate Committee on Military Affairs, published under the title "Elimination of German Resources for War," in 11 parts, 79th Cong., 1945 (hereinafter called, after its chairman, Senator Harley M. Kilgore, the Kilgore committee), pt. 5, p. 648.
[9] Thyssen, p. 101.
[10] Thyssen, p. 110.
[11] Kilgore, pt. 5, p. 649.
[12] "I have always imagined a state," Thyssen writes, "which recognizes the principle of private industrial profit, but which at the same time provides a corporative constitution for the regulation of industry and business." Thyssen, p. 122. This idea he attributed, on the one hand, to Prof. Othmar Spann, who developed a staendische or vocational economic system within the framework of his economic universalism, and on the other hand, to Dr. Klein, social welfare secretary in the I. G. Farbenindustrie (the great German Dye Trust). Thyssen, p. 124.
[13] " 'Just as the political movement originated in Munich,' [said Hitler,] 'so the economic reform shall originate in Duesseldorf' * * * The Nazis not only nominated me a Reichstag deputy, but Goering * * * made me Prussian state councilor for life." Thyssen, pp. 126, 127.
[14] Thyssen, p. 125.

en "the influence of the conservative elements [15] which he had brought into power [16] along with Hitler." [17]

On October 1, 1939, after the pact with Russia was signed, he broke with Hitler.[18] While on vacation in Switzerland, he publicly reprimanded Hitler for making friends with Russia and going to war. Thyssen's property was turned over by the Nazis to a trustee, Baron Kurt von Schroeder, a lieutenant general of the SS, head of the famous banking house that financed Nazi programs throughout the world. Thyssen later went to France and after VE-day was found in a detention camp in Italy.

His case is representative of the experience of the big business leaders under fascism. At first they guided and frequently dictated the economic policy and program of the state which they helped to create. In due course, however, the machinations of the party hierarchy and the requirements of military preparations shifted power away from them. They found themselves increasingly compelled to go along on policies they did not like and, ultimately, they too were no longer free to resist the regime without incurring political and even personal danger.

Only a few powerful business leaders, however, followed Thyssen into concentration camp. Most of them tolerated, if they did not welcome, the sharing of control over business with the party leaders. Thus it was that party members in increasing numbers began to emerge as heads of large business organizations.[19] The party label was important, and the majority of businessmen remained as leaders of their enterprises. Nowhere were they significant in resistance movements or the underground. The proportion in all totalitarian regimes that were removed from office or exiled was small (except for those who were in racial or national disfavor). Not a few became party leaders, such as those wearing the golden emblem representing the "first hundred" among the Nazis, contributed to party funds, carried out the program they devised or helped to devise, and exercised authority over labor and over other businessmen. Most of them, like the Prussian military official of old, however, not only gave orders—they had to take them.[20]

GOVERNMENT BUREAUCRACIES—THE OFFICIAL ECONOMIC STRUCTURE

According to the original blueprint, the state under fascism, far from attempting to take over financial, industrial, or distributive enterprises, was supposed to strengthen private initiative and control. Businessmen were admonished to be resourceful leaders and make as

[15] State Department Mission Interrogation Horace Greeley Hjalmar Schacht, Wiesbaden, Sept. 25, 1945.
[16] Thyssen, p. 132.
[17] When finally the different national vocational groups (Reichsstaende) were brought into being, the head of the National Industrialists Group was Herr Krupp von Bohlen und Halbach, called by Thyssen a "super-Nazi." Thyssen, pp. 108, 136.
[18] "I had always warned industrialists, as well as military circles, against a rapprochement with Communist Russia. For me, this regime was the enemy of Germany and of Europe as a whole. To deal with Russia seemed to me [a] great * * * crime * * * Hitler had preached the crusade against Bolshevik Russia as the enemy of the human race. And suddenly he had allied himself with the monster. He had the insolence to ask serious-minded people to support him in this adventure." Thyssen, pp. 41, 42. August Thyssen, the father of Fritz Thyssen, broke publicly with the Kaiser during the First World War and thereby ingratiated himself with the Allies.
[19] "The retention, in part, of a system of private ownership enables party members to build for themselves industrial empires * * *. The owning class still exercises one function—the receiving and accumulating of profits. But industrial concentration and the increasingly pervasive influences of the bureaucracy have given a new aspect to the 'capitalist' order. A new parasitic group—Nazi party members belonging for the most part to the old middle class—penetrates more and more into the realm of property." Sweezy, p. 239.
[20] Reimann, p. 123.

much profit as possible. Theoretically, fascism was designed to be the reverse of socialism or communism.

In practice, however, only a few months elapsed before some governmental body or other was organized with powers that cut across the managerial decisions of the private entrepreneur. An emergency of some sort—threat to stability of the currency in foreign exchange markets, considerations of national defense, or agricultural distress—led in all fascist countries to the creation of state agencies which shared control with business or were by themselves a dominant power over the economy.

Germany may be used as an example. There were similar bureaus in the other fascist countries, and for that matter in many other countries, especially during the war. The following is a select list of the agencies which, in 1938, most intimately affected private business operations in Germany.[21]

Ministry of Economics, and its subdivisions:
    Four-Year Plan Commission.
    Foreign Exchange Board.
    One or more of 25 Import Control Boards.
    Price Control Commissioner.
    Reich Administration for Economic Expansion.
    Reich Administration for Soil Exploration.
    Reich Administration for Usage of Scrap Materials
    Administration for Renovation.
    Administration Labor Service.
    Special Commissioners (Building Trade, Automobile Industry, Machine Industry, Power Industry).
Food Ministry and Reich Nutrition (Food) Estate, and subdivisions:
    Various Monopoly Marketing Boards.
    Various Compulsory Cartels of Processing Industries.
Labor Ministry, and its subdivisions:
    Labor Front.
    Labor Exchange.
    Regional Labor Trustees.
Reichsbank, and its subdivisions:
    Bank Control Board.
    Foreign Currency Department.
Reich Economic Chamber, and its subdivisions:
    Economic Groups.
    Occupational Groups.
    Regional Groups.
    Regional Economic Chambers.
Leaders of Defense Economy (War Economic Council).
Administration for Self-Help of German Industry (in connection with Export Subsidy Fund).

ACTUAL OR UNOFFICIAL GOVERNMENT STRUCTURE

The official economic structure just indicated, like blueprints of governmental organization everywhere in the world, did not in all respects represent the channels through which authority was exerted. The unofficial structure was considerably different [22] from the blueprint. Documents,[23] available since the defeat of Germany, make it possible for the first time to assess the economic structure correctly, and to discriminate between official Nazi propaganda, innocent mis-

[21] Reimann, pp. 94–95.
[22] Until recently, authentic information was virtually impossible to obtain. There were second-hand reports by foreign observers of varying competence. There were sincere and sometimes hysterical accounts by refugees and political opponents. There were official statements.
[23] Many of these documents are reprinted verbatim, together with interrogations of prominent German officials, industrialists, and bankers, and the findings of the War Department and other agencies in the hearings before the Kilgore subcommittee. See Kilgore, pt. 3, pp. 504–506.

understanding, and the actual facts. Administrator Crowley of the Foreign Economic Administration summarized the structure in operation as follows: [24]

The first impression resulting from such a study is one of terrific confusion of centers of authority, with much overlapping in fields of jurisdiction. The second impression is one of inexplicable gaps in the structure of economic control at most important points. For example, orders and decrees are numerous on textile fibers. On the other hand, there are almost none for the many branches of the chemical industry. * * * Again, there is nearly a complete blank in the laws on iron and steel production, but a multitude to govern the manufacture of ironwares of the kind that were, in general, made by relatively small firms.

A further fact becomes apparent in connection with the network of industrial and trade organizations (Gruppen) into which both rank and file were herded. In the branches of industry dominated by combines and controlled through well-established cartels, the Gruppen and similar bodies were of a perfunctory character, maintained to lend color to the fiction that all businesses were controlled by the state and subject to the same basic laws. In the branches of industry where combines were few and the producers small and numerous, the trade organizations served as control instruments operated by the bureaucracy. Decrees and orders placed onerous responsibilities on the members. * * *

Thus, the majority stockholders of the great combines, whose de facto authority in the government was equal to that of the military and political high commands, utilized the official bureaucratic structure, whose head was Hitler, for the control of the smaller sectors of industry. * . * * At the same time these men utilized the positions of their corporations as dominant members of the cartels to run the economy in its most critical sectors. There they would brook no interference. * * *

On this point, G. von Schnitzler, a member of the management committee of the I. G. Farben and director of numerous other large companies, answered an interrogation of the Allied investigators as follows:

Relations and negotiations with D. A. F. (Deutsche Arbeitsfront) and A. O. (Auslandsorganisation) remained and were always a most unpleasant chapter in I. G.'s activity. * * * Apart from these two main domains * * * the Gauleiter interfered * * * but seldom in direct business, mostly in personal questions and then generally in the favor of such employees who were being considered as "confidential men."

But up to the last, I. G. could retract from taking any typical party men on Vorstand or Aufsichtsrat, a fact which should not be overlooked, as pressure from the most different sides in this direction never has ceased. * * *[25]

Apologists for the position of German business in relation to the government have pointed out that business and finance have influence with government in nearly all parts of the world. This argument, however, ignores the legal position German big business has attained as ruler of all lesser business and the manner in which this position has been used to concentrate the power in a few great combines. * * *

Each major party leader also built up his own circle of industrialists and bankers.[26] While Thyssen and the I. G. group worked for the most part with Goering, there was also a Himmler-Circle to which belonged such men as Flick, the steel magnate; Rasche and Kranefuss, of the Desdner Bank; Buetefisch; Rostey; and others.

Despite the neat blueprints, the supreme economic power was not a monopoly of the big party leaders, top army officers and Junkers. It was shared by the big industrialists and bankers,[27] who were not

[24] The Foreign Economic Administration, the War Department, and the United States Treasury Department sent in intelligence teams immediately after VE-Day to secure these documents, to interrogate top Nazis, and to report their findings. The outlines of the true situation have been obscured by propaganda and struggles within the oligarchy; but a careful study of the German laws, decrees, and orders of the last 15 years makes the facts crystal clear.
[25] This paragraph from Kilgore, pt. 10, p. 1260. Also, see Reimann, p. 120.
[26] Kilgore, pt. 3, pp. 504–506.
[27] Sweezy, p. 23–27.

merely looked up to and consulted, but were obeyed by party leaders in local districts.[28]   Those party leaders that resisted such dominance by business interests and Rhineland industrialists [29] were either completely intimidated or ruthlessly eliminated by the famous purge of 1934.   "Thereafter Germany was ruled by the party, in partnership with the major owners of combines and the German General Staff." [30]

On the other hand, "of all businessmen the small shopkeeper is the one most under control and most at the mercy of the party." [31]   His status, like that of the small landed proprietor in the Middle Ages, who relied for protection on the local feudal lord, depended on the whim and strength of his overlord.   That is why in German legislation, and elsewhere under fascism, the rules and ordinances of government fell with crushing impact on small business; but was sometimes non-existent or merely pro forma, and usually considerably cushioned in operation, in the business run by strong combines.   In fact, the giant combines, as already noted, called the tune in the heavy and chemical industries.   These, in turn, dominated the national industry group, which organization constituted the hierarchy of Germany.

THE "NEW ORDER" [32]

Plans for the much publicized "New Order," mentioned in chapter V on "Foreign Trade," were started many years before Hitler came into power.   The Wehrmacht's 1926 comprehensive program of economic warfare depended upon the collaboration of German industrialists, Junkers, and the high command.   Both it and the "New Order",[33] called for the (a) freeing of Germany from war debts and reparations; (b) reorganization ("rationalization") [34] of industry; (c) development of domestic resources to a maximum, and of synthetic substitutes for critical materials not found in Germany or nearby in Europe; (d) legislating of stock piles; (e) rebuilding of the merchant marine and air fleets; (f) construction of strategic motor highways and railroads; and (g) institution of governmental economic and industrial controls well in advance of the outbreak of the war.

FIRST PRINCIPLE OF THE NEW ORDER: MONOPOLISTIC CARTELIZATION

The economy was reorganized.   The "prewar cartel program, as developed first by the General Staff and the big industrialists, and, after 1933, by the Nazis," [35] became an instrument of war and power politics.[36]   Cartels and economic groups were developed as "semi-

---

[28] Reimann, p. 29.
[29] "On the eve of the famous purge in June 1934, before ordering the execution of his own closest friends, Hitler consulted Krupp von Bohlen und Halbach at Villa Huegel, the latter's family residence near Essen." Reimann, p. 126.
[30] Testimony of U. S. Foreign Economic Administration, submitted by its administrator, Mr. Leo T. Crowley; Kilgore, pt. 3, p. 181.
[31] Reimann, pp. 31, 83.
[32] "Not long after 1918, the German General Staff set up schools to train German officers in military economics and industrial organization.   By the middle 1920's many German officers trained in those schools had been sent out to help and guide German industrialists to rearm Germany economically and industrially for World War II."   Kilgore, pt. 3, p. 153.
[33] See Lindley Fraser, Germany Between Two Wars, New York, 1945.   For elaborate documentation of this conspiracy to which Hitler was a latecomer, see British Basic Handbook: Germany, pt. I, Ministry of Economic Warfare, 1944.
[34] For an authoritative exposition of the fact that by "rationalization" was meant organization of cartels, supercartels, and monopolistic chicanery of all sorts, see Alfred M. Mond, Industry and Politics, London, 1927.
[35] See the following section, Cartels.
[36] For numerous volumes of hearings documenting to the hilt that the New Order was an instrument of aggression, see Kilgore, Senate Committee on Military Affairs, 78th Cong., Cartels and National Security.

autonomous public organs to aid in the administration of government procurement, allocation, price stabilization, and standardization and rationalization programs * * *." [37]

German industry and trade had for years been highly organized, by American standards overorganized. The Nazis found it more convenient to streamline the thousands of old organizations [38] and cartels [39] than to create new ones. The twofold division along territorial and functional lines was retained.

Cartels

The relation of a cartel to a group was in many respects like that of an infantry company to its regiment. It might operate individually but served the purposes and program of those topside. Thus, the old objectives of cartels to allocate and limit output, fix prices and terms of trade, and divide markets, [40] were transformed and coordinated with controls over the allocation of raw materials, foreign trade, wages, over the capital market and rates of interest, and over the direction of investment, in such a manner as to obtain maximum output of war materials and maximum self-sufficiency.

On July 15, 1933, cartel legislation went into effect enabling the government to invalidate cartel contracts without the intervention of the Cartel Court and authorizing the Minister of National Economy to compel cartelization in noncartelized industries, to force outside producers to join an existing cartel, and to prohibit the establishment of new plants or the expansion of existing ones. This power was greatly extended by the Community Works Law (Gemeinschaftswerke) of September 4, 1939, under which industrial plants could be combined by the Minister of National Economy, closed up, or compelled to change their product.

Gruppen

Further changes in the operation of cartels took place with the passage on February 27, 1934, of the fundamental law for the preparation of the Organic Structure of the German Economy. This authorized the Minister of National Economy to recognize trade organizations as the sole representatives of their branch, to organize, dissolve, or merge them, to change their charters, and to appoint and recall their leaders. By the executive decree of November 27, 1934, the top organization, the National Economic Chamber, was created, with the duty to coordinate the territorial and functional organizations. The decree of August 20, 1934, among other things, transferred the supervision of the chambers of industry and commerce to the Ministry of Economy.

The National Economic Chamber contained both vertical—i. e., functional divisions comprising all enterprises of a given trade—and regional divisions. The former were, of course, national in scope with about 43 so-called Economic Groups and 393 Functional Groups. [41]

---

[37] Testimony of William L. Clayton of the State Department; Kilgore, pt. 1, p. 58.

[38] The German Economic Ministry in 1930 listed 2,272 national, district and local associations affiliated with the Zentralausschuss der Unternehmerverbaende. See Jahrbuch der Berufsverbaende im Deutschen Reiche, 1930, p. 43.

[39] In 1930, according to one expert, there were 2,100 cartels in German manufacturing industry alone. See Horst Wagenfuehr, Kartelle in Deutschland, Nuremberg, 1931.

[40] An enormous amount of literature has sprung up from the extensive international debates on the numerous types of cartels. For an excellent bibliography, see Leisa Bronson's Bibliography on International Cartels, September 1944–January 1947, Library of Congress, Legislative Reference Service, Washington, D. C., 1947.

[41] Sweezy, pp. 39–44.

The latter lumped together into 23 Provincial Economic Chambers all groups, national trade, or local, resident in each of 14 provinces.

As a net result, the former trade associations became organs of economic and political policy. Membership was compulsory for every business, whether formerly members or not. Cartel policies, instead of being coordinated through the National Federation of German Industry, were coordinated through the National Industry Group. There were similar national groups for banking, commerce, insurance, handicrafts, power, and the tourist industry.

All business issues were centralized in the National Economic Chamber; all agriculture in the Reich Food Estate; all cultural activities in the National Chamber of Culture; all provincial government in the Reich; all local government in the Gemeindetag; all executive, legislative, and judicial authority in the Fuehrer.[42]

The fascist economy rested upon three basic principles: Leadership, authority, and the establishment of complete governmental control at the first appearance of any voluntarism. The leadership principle gave the employer play for personal initiative and venture, though, to be sure, limited by his duties as steward for the state, for his plant, and his employees.[43] He was the leader (Betriebsfuehrer); his laborers the followers. The stockholders were reduced to mere recipients of funds without the paper power to control management. The directorial and managerial ranks were filled by the practice of cooperative recruitment.[44] Dividend disbursements were limited to 6 percent. Competition was eliminated. All cartel price regulations, technically under the control of the National Price Commissioner, were made in accordance with the advice and proposals of the groups coordinated by the National Economic Chamber.[45] New plant capacity and investment were limited and directed; prices, quotas, and penalties were fixed, and markets and outlets were allocated by a process of "business self-government." [46]

The German economy in reality became one gigantic corporation, with the Fuehrer as chairman of a self-perpetuating board, with an executive hierarchy mutually selected by business and party leaders, each in his sphere with autocratic power and responsibility, economic, ideological, and political.

SECOND PRINCIPLE: MAXIMUM ECONOMIC WAR POTENTIAL

Not only in Germany but in all fascist regimes the overriding policy dominating the organization of the economy was that of developing maximum economic strength for war. This meant in practice an extraordinary emphasis on self-sufficiency, especially with regard to food and strategic materials. It also meant the imposition of price, priority, and other controls well in advance of the outbreak of a war to avoid hasty and bungling improvisation. It meant heroic programs of ersatz, Four-Year Plans, and the like.

German industry was remarkably well adapted to furnish the economic base for a modern war. The high development of the

---

[42] Sweezy, p. 40.
[43] For a full discussion of this relationship, at best a benevolent despotism, see Hans B. Brausse, Die Fuehrungsordnung des deutschen Volkes, Hamburg, 1940, pp. 163 ff.
[44] Sweezy, pp. 67–68.
[45] Naumann, pp. 307–309.
[46] For marked similarities, see Rudolf Callman in TNEC Hearings, pt. 25, Cartels, Washington, D. O., 1941, pp. 13347–13363.

metallurgical, mining, machinery, chemical, textile, optical and
scientific instrument industries; the high degree of concentration and
organization; the modern equipment acquired during the "rationalization" period in the late twenties; and the abundant supply of well-
disciplined, skilled labor and management made an ideal combination
for the building up of what the Nazis euphemistically called a defense
economy (Wehrwirtschaft),[47] but which was in reality a rearmament
economy being prepared for aggression.   There were, of course, some
serious gaps on the raw material front, such as the lack of domestic
supplies of cotton, rubber, tin, and insufficient supplies of iron ore,
copper, and some other nonferrous metals, wool, and fats.   Some of
the shortages were made good by the synthetic industries developed
under the Four-Year Plan; others, by an accumulation of stock piles;
still others, by establishing economic and, later on, military domination over certain sources of supply.   Considering the size and resources of the country, the degree of self-sufficiency attained for war
purposes was remarkable.   As one prominent Nazi writer on economic
subjects expressed it in October 1939: "The (present) economic
armament of Germany cannot be compared with that of the First
World War.   At that time our war economy had to be improvised;
now we have at our disposal an armed economy." [48]

Wanted: A self-sufficient agriculture

German war-making potential had always been limited by its lack
of agricultural self-sufficiency.[49]   Even in the 1890's the drive for
self-sufficiency, the new tariffs, and the extensive controversy concerning Agrar-Staat and Industrie-Staat was largely centered on
agriculture.   The German farmer was unable to maintain average
German living standards and compete with extensive methods of
cultivation overseas or even with those of eastern and southeastern
Europe.   Agrarian protection was, therefore, traditionally an integral
part of the German expansionist and armament policy.   With the
agricultural shortages of the First World War vividly before them and
also because the National Socialist movement received strong support
from the Junkers, the Nazis laid particular emphasis on the value of
the German peasant as a member of the national community.   Agriculture was given top priority.

The chief goal was to expand production through protection against
outside competition.   The German price level of agricultural products

---

[47] The following abstracted definition of "defense economy" is taken from an article in an authoritative
Nazi economic publication:
An approach to the national economy that recognizes the essential functions performed by the economy
during a modern war and that, therefore, endeavors to shape the economic policy with that essential purpose
constantly in mind.   This concept involves the following principles:
1. The economy is merely one of the national manifestations and is subject to the national will.
2. Security is essential for the nation.
3. The economy must serve the nation and assure its security and development.   It must supply armament in its broadest sense.   The armed forces must protect the nation and the economy.
4. No sharp line of demarcation between peace and war economy is recognized.   Economic warfare is
carried on in times of peace and merely becomes intensified when armed warfare begins.   Consequently
peace economy, to be a real national economy, must be a defense economy.   The liberal concept of economy
motivated by individual interest can no longer be tolerated.
It implies that the armed forces are productive and that defense expenditures are beneficial to the economy
as well as to the nation.
5. National defense has no responsibility to assure peace economy; the accumulation of war supplies does
not do violence to the normal economy.   Every step towards self-sufficiency enlarges the freedom of the
nation.   It therefore follows that there should not be too much dependence on world economy.   Heinrich
Hunke, Die Wehrhaftmachung der deutschen Wirtschaft, Deutsche Volkswirtschaft, n. 1, 1938, pp. 42–44.
[48] Josef Winschuh, Geruestete Wirtschaft, Berlin, 1939, p. xxiii.
[49] A detailed exposition of agriculture under fascism will be found in ch. 9, "Agriculture and the Farmer."
The discussion here merely assesses the spot assigned to agriculture in the general economic framework.

was isolated from the outside world.[50] The dairy industry was organized first. Under the law of July 20, 1933, the Food Minister was empowered to organize all phases of the industry, including distribution, and establish dairy associations and branches in the various parts of the country, with the alleged purpose of cutting down the cost of production and distribution.

In the case of the grain trade, fixed prices were established to counteract the pressure on the price level of the record crop in 1933. At the same time, a compulsory cartel was established for the flour mills so that they could be utilized in carrying out price policy. In the following year all phases of grain production and distribution were amalgamated into one association (Hauptvereinigung der deutschen Getreidewirtschaft).

The Food Estate (Reichsnaehrstand) established by the law of September 13, 1933, became the central agency with sweeping powers over the food industry. It was divided into bureaus and other subsidiary organizations, scattered over all parts of the country, dealing with all phases of agricultural policy: Marketing, farm technique, land utilization, cooperative purchasing of farm supplies, prices, production quotas, and even with social and educational questions and the qualifications of the farmer for the management of the hereditary farms. In certain cases, some of the functions of the Food Estate were turned over to compulsory cartels. This policy was adopted for the processing of milk, fruit, vegetables, fish, starch, oleomargarine, and potato flakes.

The Food Estate told the farmer how to utilize his land; how much of his output he could use for himself, and how much he was to turn over to the state purchasing agency at a fixed price, generally far above the world price; when he should fatten his hogs, and when he should market them; whether he was entitled to the privilege of a hereditary farmer; whether he could get a moratorium on his debts or not, and what interest he should pay for money; and, who should inherit his farm.

Owing to its widespread organization penetrating into every part of the country, the Food Estate was in a position to supervise not only the economic activity of the farmer, but also his political reliability and his devotion to the national socialist cause. Thus it eliminated a highly prominent Jewish element from the food distribution area. But its dominant purpose was to provide Germany with foodstuffs, especially bread grains, in the event of war. And that purpose it achieved, although the development of agriculture on an economic basis was impaired thereby and the costs to the German consumer were high.

Self-sufficiency in strategic materials

The increasing scarcity of natural raw materials, due to tightened exchange and import controls, stimulated the chemical industry as the chief source of substitutes; it also stimulated the rayon industry, and the production of aluminum both as a substitute for copper and as the material for the rapidly growing aviation industry. The self-sufficiency policy (Autarkie) brought about an intensification of the financial and managerial participation of the Government in industrial expansion. This applied not only to the aluminum industry, where

[50] Hans Merkel, Baeuerliche Marktordnung, Jahrbuch fuer nationalsozialistische Wirtschaft, 1935, p. 93,

Government financial control dated from the First World War, but also to the copper industry, and to the production of synthetic gasoline by the lignite industry. In the case of the latter industry, a special corporation (Braunkohlen-Benzin A. G.) was organized by the law of September 28, 1934, under which the lignite producers had to contribute a capital of RM 250,000,000 to finance the production of synthetic gasoline under the management of a state commissioner with very broad powers, responsible to the Minister of National Economy. The board of directors was appointed by the state commissioner. In another instance, weaving concerns were invited to form five companies for the manufacture of staple fiber, with the bulk of the capital provided by the banks under Government guarantee.

Self-sufficiency naturally served to intensify Germany's economic isolation. Thus, in the case of rubber, a very high import duty was imposed on the natural product to finance the development of the synthetic substitute. It also brought about a growing discrepancy between the rapid expansion of the capital goods industries and the much slower growth, or, in some cases, stagnation or curtailment of the consumer goods industries. Thus, for 1937, the index of production of capital goods had risen to 126 (1926=100) from 55.6 in 1933, while the index of production of consumption goods was 101.5 as compared with 84.1 in 1933. This discrepancy became intensified with the increase in the share of the national output devoted to rearmament.

Advance imposition of price and other war controls

At first the Nazis tried to ease Government controls over business. Hitler, for example, proclaimed an end to nationalization. Under the Weimar regime the state had, by purchase of capital stock, acquired a dominant interest in the Gelsenkirchen Steel Co., a 90 percent interest in the Dresdner Bank and Donat, 70 percent of the Commerz-und Privatbank, and 35 percent of the Deutsche Bank und Disconto-Gesellschaft. These banks were reprivatized, as were also the large steamship companies and shipyards. The liquidation of municipally owned enterprises was hastened by a special tax and a statute passed in 1935, repealing a 1919 law permitting public ownership and distribution of electric power.

In fact, during the first year of the Nazi regime, reemployment, stimulated by decontrol and other acts pleasing to business, was the determining factor in industrial revival. The iron and steel industry increased its output by 50 percent, largely to fill orders received from the Federal railways and also to meet the awakening demand for industrial and farm equipment, resulting from the Government policies of encouraging repairs and reequipment by means of tax concessions, and of guaranteeing higher prices for farm products. The textile industry was stimulated by advance production in anticipation of higher prices resulting from raw material restrictions, but also, to some extent, by the orders for uniforms for the reviving army.

But price control was not long in coming. Limited, prior to 1936, to the supervision of private price-fixing organizations, and to the fixing of prices on certain imported articles, the basic law for the 4-year plan promulgated on October 26 of that year, provided for the appointment of a Reich Commissioner with broader functions. These included not only supervision but participation in price formation, with the power to intervene at various stages before the final price to the consumer was determined.   This pertained not only to commodities but to services, such as transportation and communication, rents, interest rates, cultural facilities, medical services, insurance, and legal services.   Wages and salaries were exempted, as they came within the province of the Trustees of Labor, and were stabilized in 1933.

The Price Commissioner was to be appointed by the Chancelor (Hitler) and placed under the Administratior of the 4-year plan (Goering).   The penalties for violation of price-control regulations were made very drastic, including not only imprisonment in various forms but also unlimited fines, confiscation of the goods involved, and trial by the special courts established primarily for political offenses. The Commissioner also had the power to close the business and to exclude individuals from any branch of activity connected with the one in which the offense took place.

The new price control was inaugurated in the form of a decree (Preisstopverordnung), freezing prices and charges for services at the level of October 18, 1936.   The prices on imported goods were fixed in July 1937 at a maximum level covering the actual cost price, increased by economically justifiable expenses and profits instead of the customary mark-ups.   All price-fixing cartel agreements were made subject to the approval of the Price Commissioner.

Thus the German price-control system was so well established at the outbreak of the war that it did not require any drastic changes to meet war conditions.   The only important additional legislation was the War Economy Ordinance of September 4, 1939, which provided for the freezing of wages, salaries, and working conditions at prewar levels, and abolished extra pay for overtime, Sunday, holiday, or night work.   Freer use was made of other well-known price-control devices such as subsidies and freezing of price margins.[51]

Four-year plan

The 4-year plan, announced by·Hitler in his address at the Nuremberg Party Convention on September 9, 1936, and put into effect by the decree of October 18, 1936, was intended to make Germany industrially strong and independent, with particular emphasis on the production of synthetic raw materials and fuel.   Officially it was claimed that Germany was forced to adopt such an over-all economic plan because of the refusal of other countries to take German products in exchange for vital raw materials.

The appointment of Goering as Reich Commissioner charged with the execution of the 4-year plan, with enormous powers over the ministries and the whole German economy, emphasized the importance of the program.[52]   In his address on October 28, 1936, Goering made it plain that he was going to carry through the plan in the most aggressive manner, but took occasion to admonish private business to exercise free initiative.   In similar vein, in February 1937, Hitler told the so-called free business that it must prove that it could solve the problems of building up the synthetic industries assigned to them under the 4-year plan if it wanted to continue to exist as free business.

The opportunity given private business to exercise initiative under the 4-year plan was chiefly that of financing desired enterprises, the

[51] See Price Control in Germany—Policy and Technique, International Reference Service, U. S. Department of Commerce, April 1941.
[52] Nathan, p. 43; Annual Economic Review, Germany, 1936, p. 3, unpublished report of the American Commercial Attaché.

burden of which was shifted from the Reich Treasury to the private concerns with large reserves. Concerns like Krupp, I. G. Farben, Vereinigte Stahlwerke, and Mansfeld, formed special subsidiaries for the production of synthetics or for the expansion of the production of natural raw materials, and financed them directly or by the flotation of bond issues. Government assisted by being ready to purchase the entire output at the high prices necessitated by the high cost of production for a period of from 5 to 10 years. The length of the period was intended to facilitate reconversion. The most important products involved in the 4-year plan were: Synthetic gasoline, aluminum and magnesium, synthetic textile fibers, synthetic rubber (Buna), and various plastics.

Third principle of the new order: Encourage large combines

The establishment of numerous branch plants for the production of synthetic materials under the 4-year plan not only made large combines the chief beneficiaries of the financial support extended by the Government but encouraged interindustry supercombines, when needed or useful, to undertake joint production of synthetic materials or pooling collective research and experience.

Another factor favoring economic concentration under the Nazi regime was the so-called Aryanization of Jewish business. A few large German corporations acquired, in many cases at a low price, the properties of their former Jewish competitors. This was of particular importance in some of the consumption industries, like textiles, clothing, and leather. Many of the big concerns, with large war contracts, were in a highly liquid condition, largely as a result of the Government policy of granting financial advances and prompt payment for war work. Since they were not in a position to expand their inventories or invest their amortization funds in new equipment, and since the Government took only a part of their reserves through taxation, many of them used their free resources to acquire control of other business enterprises.

In the iron and steel industry, integration of the larger concerns was stimulated by the high cost of production and low profits in the primary stages of the industry, resulting partly from the compulsory use of poor domestic ores. Some of the combines tried to overcome the disadvantage by entering the more remunerative processing field, generally by acquiring financial control over plants turning out finished products.

The creation of the gigantic Hermann Goering-Werke, while presenting a striking example of industrial concentration, was a case by itself, in view of the political factors involved. Its heterogeneous structure had very little economic basis. Although the original purpose of the combine was to increase the self-sufficiency of the iron and steel industry by the utilization of low-grade domestic ore, it soon expanded into many branches of rearmament, automotive products, coal mining, shipping and machine tools, until it began to bear a close resemblance to the ephemeral Stinnes combine built up after the First World War.[53]

The occupation of certain European countries during the war and the annexation of Austria, Luxembourg, certain parts of Poland and Czechoslovakia, and Alsace-Lorraine, provided additional opportuni-

[53] For an excellent description including organization chart of this sprawling octopus, see Kilgore, pt. 3, pp. 232–49.

ties for the big German combines to expand their holdings by the acquisition of industrial properties in the subjugated and annexed countries.[54] This was particularly true of the iron and steel, coal and chemical industries. In some cases the German concerns managed to acquire the properties they had lost as a result of the territorial changes resulting from the First World War. Incidentally, small business shared in the distribution of the spoils. In Poland many small businesses were placed in the hands of German trustees to be held for the German war veterans.

Furthermore, those plants which had fallen into the hands of receivers or banks during the depression became, with the advent of rearmament prosperity, more attractive to the big combines.[55] Later the properties controlled by the banks taken over in Austria and Czechoslovakia were available. Reprivatization of the holdings of various German states and municipalities, together with restoration to private hands of the government's financial control of the big steel combine (Vereinigte Stahlwerke) likewise increased the already large concentration of economic power.

In an economic structure dominated by four large banks and shot through with industrial monopolies like that of Siemens-Halske or Deutsche Allgemeine Elektrizitaets-Gesellschaft, or Deutsche Metallgesellschaft, the two largest and most powerful combines were the Interessengemeinschaft Farbenindustrie, commonly known as I. G., and the Vereinigte Stahlwerke. The position they had reached before the war can be seen from the proportion of their output in the Reich total. These figures, which are approximate, have been arrived at in part from published figures on production and cartel sales quotas.[56]

Vereinigte Stahlwerke products	Percent of German total in 1938	I. G. Farbenindustrie products	Percent of German total in 1937
Pig iron	50. 8	Chemical nitrogen	70. 0+
Semifinished products	35. 3	Lithopone (for paints)	85. 7
Bar steel	27. 1	Synthetic camphor	60. 0
Hoops and strips	32. 8	Synthetic methanol	100. 0
Universal plate	41. 4	Aspirin	60. 0
Heavy plate	36. 0	Ether	50. 0
Medium plate	11. 6	Brown coal	20. 0
Sheets	26. 2	Explosives	60. 0
Fine sheet	31. 1	Magnesium	100. 0
Galvanized sheet	38. 5	Rayon filament	20. 0
Wire rods	27. 7	Rayon staple	30. 0
Wire	22. 1	Coal-tar dyes	100. 0
Pipe and tubes	45. 5		
Coal tar	33. 3		
Coal (bituminous)	15. 4		
Explosives (including output of subsidiaries)	1 35. 0		

1 Estimated.

Before 1932, the steel industry at one time or other even furnished arms to Hitler's followers.[57] In addition to Thyssen and Krupp, its

[54] For an authoritative account of the expansion of privately owned German concerns at the expense of Polish, Czech, Austrian, Dutch, French, etc., firms, see Kilgore, pt. 3, pp. 249–253; 269–275; 343–408. For a popular description of the techniques utilized, see Thomas Reveille, The Spoil of Europe, The Nazi Technique in Political and Economic Conquest, New York, 1941, pt. 3, pp. 151–318.
[55] Guenther Keiser, Der juengste Konzentrationsprozess, Die Wirtschaftskurve, Heft II, 1939, pp. 136–56.
[56] Kilgore, pt. 3, p. 507. Calcium Carbide at 52.0 and Insecticides at 50.0 might be added to the list.
[57] Senate Special Committee on Investigating the Munitions Industry, 73d Cong., 2d sess. hearings, pt. 5, pp. 1198–1199; pt. 12, pp. 2783, 2809, 2889.

great leaders provided some of the most ardent Nazi supporters in Germany, e. g., Wilhelm Zangen of Mannesmann, Hermann Roechling of Roechlingsche Werke, Poensgen and Voegler of Vereinigte Stahlwerke, and Friedrich Flick of Flick K. G.[58]

The special role of I. G. Farben

The table above likewise indicates that I. G. was far from being a mere dyestuffs concern. In fact, it actually manufactured hundreds of products and participated in or dominated 380 other German firms.[59] Its factories, power installations, and mines were scattered all over Germany.

I. G.'s foreign participations, both admitted and concealed, numbered over 500 firms * * *. Its holding companies and plants blanketed Europe; and its research firms, patent offices, and other agencies are clustered around every important commercial and industrial center in both hemispheres * * *. Its cartel agreements numbered over 2,000 and included agreements with such major industrial concerns as Standard Oil Co. (New Jersey), the Aluminum Co. of America, E. I. duPont de Nemours, Ethyl Export Corp., Imperial Chemical Industries (Great Britain), the Dow Chemical Co., Roehm und Haas, Etablissements Kuhlmann (France), and the Mitsui interests of Japan.[60]

The extent to which I. G. Farben control abroad was concealed only became evident after the war. Such camouflage (Tarnung) became, in the words of an I. G. memorandum, "more and more perfect * * * so that even a thorough investigation could not find any material that there was an indirect connection with I. G."[61]

The sales apparatus of I. G. abroad (which includes agent firms with their good will, mailing lists, connections, etc.) has, because of (1) tax laws, (2) national sales propaganda (buy in your own country), (3) the desire to avoid boycotts, (4) the desire to avoid special controls applicable to foreign companies, been organized, as a matter of principle, in such a fashion that I. G. or its several affiliated companies do not openly hold shares or other interests in these agent firms.[62]

It has been frequently alleged that military objectives,[63] such as the cloaking of economic warfare and commercial espionage activities,[64] played a no less prominent role.[65] The devices employed embraced every artifice known to the legal and extra-legal mind, including the use of bearer shares, nominees, option agreements, fictitious or intervening transfers, dividend and loan agreements, pool agreements, endorsements in blank, escrow deposits, pledges, collateral loans, rights of first refusal, management contracts, service contracts, patent agreements, cartels, and withholding know-how.

[58] These men held leading positions in the powerful quasi-governmental control agencies such as Reichsvereinigung Eisen and the Eisen-und Stahl-Gemeinschaft. Kilgore, pt. 3, p. 233.

[59] For a list showing extent of control, see Direct and Indirect Participation of I. G. Farbenindustrie A. G. in Germany, exhibit No. 2 as reprinted in Kilgore, pt. 10, pp. 1156-1164. The entire volume is composed of I. G. Farben exhibits.

[60] Testimony for War Department given by Col. Bernard Bernstein, head of Division of Investigation of Cartels and External Assets, Office of Military Government. Kilgore, pt. 8, pp. 1068-1069. For a discussion of the business practices and ethics involved, especially from the standpoint of American interests and security, see Wendell Berge, Cartels, Challenge to a Free World, Washington, D. C., 1944. For another point of view see the testimony of Ralph M. Gallagher, president of the Standard Oil Co. of New Jersey before the Senate Judiciary Committee on H. R. 3786, May 32, 1944 (quoted in Leisa G. Bronson, Cartels and International Patent Agreements, Washington, June 1944, p. 86).

[61] See Tarnung of German Agencies Abroad (translated by Dr. Knuepper) in Kilgore, pt. 10, ch. II, especially pp. 1203-1205.

[62] From confidential memorandum to the directors, June 8, 1939, of legal division of I. G. Farben as translated and reprinted in Kilgore, pt. 3, pp. 573-580. This quotation is on p. 574.

[63] This was the conclusion reached by the Senate Committee on Military Affairs after holding lengthy hearings on cartels and national security. (See rept. No. 4 from the Subcommittee on War Mobilization, November 16, 1944, pt. 2, pp. 73-85.)

[64] The same, p. 75.

[65] For systematic exposition and further illustration of numerous cloaking devices used by I. G. Farben and other German firms, see the testimony of Assistant Attorney General Herbert Wechsler and Alien Property Custodian James E. Markham in Kilgore, pt. 3, pp. 564-614.

FOURTH PRINCIPLE OF THE NEW ORDER: ECONOMIC CONQUEST

German leaders conceived and carried out the plans for a new order for Europe, with active foreign assistance and collaboration.[66] Said von Schnitzler: "In preparing the 'Neuordnung', we were following the lines of the 'Gross-Raum-Politik' ".[67] The basic principle was one of giving carte blanche to industry to proceed as it saw fit through established cartels. In the words of a now famous document:[68]

The entire European industry is to be organized on a voluntary basis in such planned cartels. This organization would be able to regulate production and sales under German supervision and according to German interests. Relations between these cartels and those in non-European countries would be handled by special syndicates which are attached to the cartels.

Among the many documents describing what the new order would mean for Norway, Belgium, Denmark, Holland, and other countries under Nazi domination, that for France provides an illuminating and representative illustration.[69] In addition to the compulsory organization of French industry into groups (groupements), the new order required a preferential tariff system favoring Germany, the abolition of discriminatory measures as to certificates of origin, compulsory declarations and registration; the granting to German nationals of resident and work permits without restrictions; the establishment of "fair" regulations of foreign exchange and currency; the taxation of German branch establishments and agencies on the basis of assets, profits, and volume of turnover, which the German parent enterprise would certify to be involved; the granting of "sufficiently large quotas" for German imports; the provision of protection for German patent trade-marks and know-how; the limitation of French production to French domestic and colonial markets; and the requirement of government licenses for the construction of new plants and for the expansion of existing facilities. "* * * a number of small and unimportant laboratories, most of which are of local importance only should be closed." [70] "Cooperation between German and French industry * * * can best be achieved—while continuing already existing agreements—by the creation of *long-term international syndicate agreements*, which would have to be preceded by the creation of French national syndicates." [71] [Italics in original.]

Foreign collaborators

The plans for the new order also named the firms in other countries that were to be dominant, and after each conquest there came to the fore a group of native citizens ready to put the new order into practice. Again the case of France is illustrative. There fascism was not imposed from without, but grew out of internal forces, which found the war an opportune moment to seize control of the government.[72]

[66] For a reprint of numerous original documents dealing wholly with I. G. Farben's new order, see Kilgore, pt. 10, ch. VI, pp. 1413-1527.
[67] See letters of von Schnitzler to I. G. Farben's business committee, June 24, 1940, as reprinted in Kilgore, pt. 10, pp. 1413, 1524.
[68] Highly confidential memorandum Planning for the Peace, Berlin NW 7, Unter den Linden 82, August 7, 1940, as produced in Kilgore, pt. 10, pp. 1517-1520. Berlin NW 7, Unter den Linden 82, is the famous · address through which I. G. Farben carried on world-wide commercial, industrial, political and even military espionage. See ch. III, Foreign Policy.
[69] For the document as a whole entitled "Neuordnung (New Order) for France," see Kilgore, pt. 10, pp. 1422-1445.
[70] Kilgore, pt. 10, p. 1442.
[71] Kilgore, pt. 10, p. 1434. On succeeding pages is given a detailed list, commodity by commodity, of precise percentage tariffs to be allowed on imports from Germany and elsewhere, of export limitations or prohibitions, of exact division of markets, and of production and plant limitations.
[72] See Charles Micaud, the French Right and Nazi Germany 1933-39, Durham, N. C., 1943.

To trace in detail the labor strife, the political maneuvers, of the right-wing parties and the increasing centralization of economic power into the hands of the famous "Two Hundred Families" of prewar France is unnecessary here. That has been so well done in a series of books [73] that mere mention of their conclusions is sufficient. Said prewar Minister of Aviation in France, Pierre Cot, in his book, Triumph of Treason:

Through hate of the popular front, good Frenchmen, or men who considered themselves such, served Hitler gratuitously by doing work to which they would never have consented had they been offered payment. Why? Because they detested the Republic and democracy more than they loved France. They accepted defeat as a necessary evil which permitted them to rid France of the democratic system and to keep in power in the neighboring countries the Fascist dictators whom they considered solely capable of maintaining order in Europe. They afterward became unconscious collaborationists of these dictators.

In similar vein Charles Micaud, in his authoritative analysis of newspaper propaganda (with a list of pro-fascist, moderate, and leftist newspapers in France from 1933 to 1939), comes to the conclusion:

Undoubtedly the anti-Marxist outcry of the conservatives expressed their hatred of the popular front, their aversion to social reforms and to the rule of the majority. * * * Victory * * * even over Germany meant to them a victory of the working classes in France and of Soviet Russia in Europe, and this victory had to be opposed whatever the effect on national security.[74]

Pertinax is in some ways even more outspoken:

Between 1931 and 1936 the financial community, an oligarchy of officials, bankers, money dealers, company directors, most of them having risen to eminent positions less by their own merit than by biased cooptation, inheritance, or, in the case of stockbrokers, by purchase of their offices, have cast France upon the rocks. * * * The Bank of France, the membership of the stock exchange, big business—all deserve to have their names written on this roll. Among others, one might single out the metallurgist and coal-owner committees (Comité des Forges and Comité des Houillieres), the general confederation of producers, with crews of academic camp followers, devotedly in their pay. * * * We must conclude that France was betrayed by its supposedly conservative classes * * *.[75]

According to Hermann Rauschning,[76] this was planned that way. Internationally, he characterized fascism as a conservative revolution.

In the sit-down strikes of 1937, the Comité des Forges, the top iron and steel association in France, absolutely refused to deal with the union of the workers, the Confédération Générale du Travail, led by Léon Johaux. Instead, it openly charged the union with "becoming totalitarian under the influence of communist elements."[77] It demanded that "the employer, the ranks of authority and the independent trade unions (non-CGT and company unions) united and fight against labor dictatorship, attacks on liberty of labor and thought, and injuries to the principle of ownership." "You," said the organization that later welcomed Hitler into France, "are the leaders."[78]

Needless to say, fascism in action in France meant the immediate dissolution of all French labor unions, the reorganization of the old

<hr/>

[73] See, for example, Micaud; Pierre Cot, Triumph of Treason, Chicago, 1944; and Pertinax (pseudonym of a famous columnist, André Gerand, in the most important conservative daily newspaper of prewar France, Le Temps) The Grave Diggers of France, New York, 1944.
[74] Micaud, p. 226–227.
[75] Pertinax, pp. 364–366, 578.
[76] See Hermann Rauschning, The Conservative Revolution, New York, 1941.
[77] In its publication, Syndicats, April 15, 1937.
[78] C. J. Gignoux, president of the Comité in his Patrons, Soyez des Patrons, Paris, 1937.

employer's associations into groups or "occupational families" and the appointment of directors general or corporative commissioners with a plenary power to handle wages, hours, hiring and firing, etc. The Germans found French industrialists eager to serve.[79] Thus von Schnitzler of I. G. Farben testified:

In the chemical domain it was only Péchiney * * * which showed a more refractory attitude. All the other companies did cooperate in full * * * As another example I may cite the name of M. Marcel Boussac, the greatest industrialist in the textile field * * * The same applies * * * to the iron and steel industry, and the work done by Schneider-Creusot for the Wehrmacht is publicly known.[80]

In similar fashion, Robert Carmichael, a leader of the French jute industry, became director general of the Comité Générale d'Organisation de l'Industrie Textile.[81]

I am sure [said von Schnitzler on another occasion] that all these people having worked with I. G. in Spain and France, in Norway and Finland, in the Southeast as well as in Italy have not had the feeling of being pressed or looted. On the contrary, they nearly all had personal profits of this collaboration and were after us to intensify our help. Dozens of files will and can prove that.[82]

SUMMARY

The German example of what happened to industry under fascism has been explained in considerable detail because it illustrates virtually every type of political and military use to which industry can be molded when economic power and political power are fused together in a monolithic authoritarian regime unhampered by the operation of checks and balances between industry and government. The main features are clear: compulsory cartellization, abolition of free markets and freedom of trade, totalitarian control of prices and wages, apportionment of labor supply and raw materials by edicts and quota arrangements rather than in response to the stimuli of flexible prices and profits, drastic limitation of managerial functions and discretion by party functionaries wielding absolute power, under-cover manipulation of normal contractual operations of business to the achievement of military objectives, proliferation of mercantilistic restrictions and trade barriers of all kinds, including tariffs, barter deals, currency manipulation, general financial legerdemain and arbitrary administrative discrimination.

The four basic principles of the new order also stand out in clear relief: Organize business like an army into cartels and higher associations; develop maximum industrial and economic power for war even if it means costly self-sufficiency programs and over-all control and economic planning; foster large combines as spearheads of economic warfare; and absorb the enterprises of neighboring countries with the aid of collaborators.

---

[79] For a Who's Who of important Dutch, Belgian and other companies and individuals that collaborated, as well as of prominent German industrialists who brought about the new order in Europe, see Kilgore, pt. 5, pp. 662–687, 838–885.

[80] Statement at Frankfurt, August 30, 1945. Exibit 37–A, Kilgore, pt. 10, p. 1389.

[81] For representative case histories of the manner in which French industrialists and family proprietors took over controls under the Nazis, see exhibits of Foreign Economic Administration, e. g., The Textile Industry of France, or The Coal Economy of France in Kilgore.

[82] Kilgore, pt. 10, exhibit No. 13, p. 1258.

CHAPTER VII—ORGANIZATION OF THE ECONOMY: ITALY, SPAIN, JAPAN

ITALY

From an industrial standpoint, Italy was poorly equipped to work out a Fascist economy. She depended almost entirely on outside sources for coal, oils, wood pulp, raw cotton and wool, metals and (in decreasing measure) cereals. In fact, nearly every raw material for heavy industry was lacking with the exception of bauxite, mercury, and sulfur. While water power was highly developed, coal imports of 1,000,000 tons a month were needed for running the railroads, industries, and public utilities. Not only was self-sufficiency impossible, but even the production of substitutes had to be limited to such items as synthetic textile fibers.

The economic reorganization of Fascist Italy was characterized by (1) the abolition of free private enterprise, (2) the establishment of industry-wide corporations with compulsory membership for individual businesses, (3) the abolition of trade unions and free collective bargaining, (4) the state subsidization and encouragement of large-scale enterprise, and (5) the state control of prices, wages, foreign trade, and capital markets. In short, it was economic protectionism.

The first years of Fascist economics

Fascism began by pleasing business, disciplined labor, suppressed independent trade unions, prohibited strikes, and checked consumer cooperatives. Mussolini announced early in 1923, that "we must put an end to state railways, state postal service, and state insurance." The match monopoly was turned over to a consortium of match manufacturers. The 1912 legislation, that would have made life insurance a state monopoly, was abolished. Two years later, the telephone system was reprivatized, and municipal ownership of public utilities was brought to a halt. As a result, services were improved.

The first 5 years under Fascism, 1922–26, "might aptly be termed 'the dictatorship of big business'." [1] It produced mild currency inflation and cheap money, a tax policy favorable to property accumulation, the protection of a high tariff wall, the abolition of a commission of inquiry into illicit war-profiteering, the refloating by direct gifts of such banks as the Banco di Roma, Banco di Napoli, and Banco di Sicilia. A subsidy of 400 million lire was granted to the powerful Ansaldo Metal Trust and large imports of foreign capital, including a $100,000,000 loan from American financiers in 1925,[2] were sought. These, plus world-wide prosperity, caused Italian iron and steel production in 1926, to be double that of 1913, and hydroelectric power to be quadruple that of prewar levels. Italy became the principal European producer and the world's leading exporter of rayon. Its major exports, however, continued to be agricultural products, fruits,

[1] Schmidt, pp. 117, also pp. 51, 158.
[2] For numerous other examples, see Daniel Guérin, Fascism and Big Business, New York, 1939, pp. 218 ff.

vegetables, wine, and cheese. Foreign trade in 1926, went up 90 percent over 1922. Other indicia of prosperity, such as rising security prices and feverish speculative activity, were likewise at hand.

With the stabilization of the lira in 1927, the era of easy profits was brought to an end. Production and exports fell.

In order to readjust domestic prices, pressure was exerted by the Government to force down wages, living costs and interest rates. The impotence of the workers made drastic wage cuts relatively easy to impose.[3]

But industrial production contracted still more and national income fell by perhaps one-third from 1928–31.[4]

After 1931 conditions grew steadily worse. The life-blood of purchasing power in the domestic markets was drained by wage cuts and by the imposition of higher trade barriers. Though (as will be explained in detail) the Government set up a liquidating corporation to bail out weak banks; though it established enlarged credit agencies to finance public utilities, agricultural reclamation, shipping and shipbuilding; though it ordered all foreign credits and securities held by Italians to be exchanged for state bonds in order to support the lira; though tariffs were successively raised until in 1935 they were 274 percent higher than in 1914 and the highest in the world;[5] though rigid quota controls, import licenses, export subsidies and bounties, and lower-interest-bearing loans were tried; and though more taxes were shifted to consumers in the form of sales taxes, the economy remained prostrate until revived by huge armament expenditures.

The corporate state

The full development of the corporative state was delayed for more than 12 years after the Fascisti seized power, even though the corporative idea had an ancient and eminent Italian background going back to the medieval church [6] and subsequently to the famous merchant guilds of the flourishing sixteenth century city-states of Genoa, Venice, and Florence. The merchant guilds, it will be remembered, included all master craftsmen who fixed prices, quality, production quotas, exports, and terms of trade. Its philosophy of protectionism flowered, during the seventeenth and eighteenth centuries, in the mercantilist school of Mun, Petty, and Colbert.

Four basic actions were required to construct the corporate state: (1) all persons of similar occupation or trade must be included in a syndicate;[7] (2) these syndicates, some 13,464 in Fascist Italy, needed to be centralized into provincial unions, 882 in Italy, and these needed to be further centralized into national category federations, 150 in Italy; (3) there must be all-inclusive parallel employer and employee organizations; (4) and all then had to be arranged like a military hierarchy under national federations, confederations of federations, and finally the national council of corporations.

[3] Schmidt, p. 119.
[4] Schmidt, p. 120.
[5] Schmidt, p. 126.
[6] See C. Gide and C. Rist's famous Histoire des Doctrines Économiques, especially the chapter on Doctrines Inspired by Christianity. Likewise, the Papal Encyclicals de Rerum Novarum of 1891, and Quadragesimo Anno of 1931, which specifically hark back to the ideal of medieval scholasticism of one body corporate, including both capital and labor, within whose bosom strife would be eliminated by common allegiance to higher spiritual values.
For an account of the basic organization of the corporate state, see ch. I, Government and Political Parties.
[7] The term syndicalism is usually associated with George Sorel, the French philosopher, who had developed the concept of revolutionary syndicalism as a mechanism for achieving worker control of economic life. Mussolini capitalized on workers' fondness for the idea and used it to achieve the opposite. See Gaetano Salvemini's chapter on Sorel and Mussolini in Under the Axe of Fascism, New York, 1936, pp. 405–12.

A beginning was made in 1926, when the syndical associations of employers and workers were designated by the Law of April 3 as the only bodies authorized to negotiate collective labor agreements and to represent employers' and workers' organizations in Parliament, in corporations, and in the labor courts. While membership in the syndical organizations was not compulsory, none other could be used by those who refused to join. In addition, nonmembers were subject to the payment of dues and to the working conditions fixed by the contracts. The officers of the organizations were selected by co-optation: that is, the nomination and selection of "safe" men, friends of the ruling oligarchy.

The final step in the construction of the Italian corporate state was the Law of February 5, 1934, which established the category corporations.[8]

Heading up this corporate structure were the Ministry of Corporations, the Central Corporate Committee, and the National Council of Corporations. The Ministry of Corporations had charge of the administration, drafted social security and labor legislation, and supervised the activities of the corporations so as to harmonize them with the general political and economic program of the regime. The Central Corporate Committee included all the ministers and undersecretaries of state and the higher officials of the Fascist Party. It determined the broad economic policies of the corporate system and also passed on the rules and regulations of the corporations. The National Council of Corporations consisted of all the members of the Central Corporate Committee, with the addition of delegates from the corporations. This was the supreme corporate body.

Attempts to increase economic war potential

Despite the speeches of Il Duce,[9] Italy became dependent on Germany. In addition to the "Battle of Grain," Mussolini proclaimed battles against unemployment, tuberculosis, and malaria,[10] designed to strengthen the labor force and the war industry.[11]

On the eve of the Second World War, Italy was occupied with placing banking and industries on their feet. Most important in the quest for self-sufficiency was the Institute for Industrial Reconstruction (Istituto per la Ricostruzione Industriale—I. R. I.). It was established under the decree of January 23, 1933, with two sections: the Financing Section and the Industrial Demobilization Section. The first (amalgamated with the second on May 25, 1936), had for its function the granting of loans to private Italian concerns for the purpose of technical improvement and better financial and economic organization.

The second, the Industrial Demobilization Section, which took over the assets and liabilities of the former Liquidation Institute established in 1926, started with a combined annual state subsidy of 285 million lire and became the state agency for the financial control of the Italian economy. At the end of 1938, the Institute controlled financially many of the principal Italian industries, investment banks, and ship-

[8] Just what part was played by Gabriele d'Annunzio's spectacularly publicized Fiume programs, known as "Carta del Quarnaro," is hard to assess. He proposed 10 compulsory but self-governed corporations or guilds, of producers grouped by major occupational interests.

[9] On March 23, 1936, Mussolini proclaimed that "the dominant problem in this new phase (after November 18, 1935—the date of the inauguration of the sanctions) will be that of securing in the shortest possible time the maximum degree of economic independence for the nation."

[10] For details see ch. IX; Agriculture and the Farmer.

[11] For a brilliant description of these "Battles," see Salvemini, pt. II, ch. XIII, XIV, XX, and XXII.

ping companies, with a direct and indirect financial liability of 20 billion lire. Reorganized in 1937, it was given a capital of 1 billion lire, and was assigned tasks of a permanent nature consisting of: (1) the management for the state of the shares, which the State took over; (2) the liquidation of such stock as the state actually owned but was not interested in; and (3) the financing of business which it thought proper to foster within the framework of a policy of national economic self-sufficiency or to the end of exploiting the Italian Empire in Africa. It proved to be "a very efficient instrument for carrying out the economic policies of the Fascist Government".[12] Examples of its operations may be found in its supplying capital in equal shares with Pirelli (the rubber trust for the setting up of a synthetic rubber company), and in its ownership of half the capital of Finmare (the holding company that controlled Italian shipping) and Finsider (the steel and iron trust).[13]

So closely was the I. R. I. tied to the Government that it was authorized to issue tax-free obligations with a term of not less than 20 years, guaranteed by state subsidies, admitted on the stock exchange, eligible for trust investment and as collateral on loans by the Bank of Italy. The president and vice president of the Institute were nominated by the head of the Government, and the board of directors was made up of representatives of the Government departments.

Strengthening of monopoly

The most important long-run consequence of Fascism economically was the sweeping movement toward big business combination. All through the twenties—

to escape the rigors of intensive competition, agreements were made for price-fixing, production control, sharing of markets, establishment of sales syndicates. The concentration movement also took the form of outright consolidation of concerns in holding companies and in mergers and amalgamations.[14]

Cartels were formed in the iron and steel, shipbuilding, railway equipment, chemical, rayon, cement, and electric lamp industries.

Whereas in the 10 years prior to 1927, there had been only 160 business mergers and amalgamations, during the 5 years after 1927, there were 465 mergers, which caused 1,240 firms to disappear. Directors of the four leading commercial banks in 1929, held 149 seats on the boards of other banks, and 1,510 directorates in 839 industrial companies, which comprised two-thirds of all Italian stock companies. Only 118 firms, or one-half of 1 percent of all private corporations, held 48 percent of total stock company capital.[15]

The step from such voluntary concentration of economic power to compulsory cartelization is small. In June 1932, a decree forced the small recalcitrant businesses to join Consorzioni and made the installation of new factories subject to Government license. In 1934, as has been seen, came full state control.

Several authoritative analyses [16] reached the same conclusion as did the eminent Italian scholar, Gaetano Salvemini:

[12] This paragraph is based on Bianchini's article cited in ch. IV, footnote 6, pp. 227-228, 231-232, and the Fascist Era, year XVII, cited in ch. IV, footnote 8, p. 71.
[13] Miller, Work cited in ch. V, footnote 6, p. 559. At the end of 1938, the I. R. I. had assets of 20 billion lire as follows: (a) 9 billion in fixed and working capital of industries controlled by it, (b) 9 billion lire either in I. R. T. or I. R. I.-controlled banks, and (c) 2 billion lire in Government securities, Bruno G. Foa and P. G. Trevas. Italian Finance and Investment. Economica, London, August 1939, v. 6, p. 273.
[14] Schmidt, p. 121.
[15] Schmidt, pp. 121-123.
[16] See, e. g., Angelo Rossi, the Rise of Italian Fascism, London, 1938; William Ebenstein, Fascist Italy, New York, 1939; Schmidt, pp. 49-53, 130-134; and Louis R. Franck, Les tapes de l'Economie Fasciste Italienne, Paris, 1939, pp. 43-45.

The oligarchy of which Mussolini is the supreme chieftain, * * * would not be able to survive in Italy if the masses of the middle, lower middle, and working classes were not kept in obedience by no less than three bureaucracies: the officers of the regular army, the civil service, and the officials of the Fascist Party.[17]

Ex-Minister Signor Belluzzo said:

It is the confederations and not the state who control the national economic system, and who have created a state within the state to serve private interests which are not always in harmony with the general interestes of the nation.[18]

The groups which gave Fascism an hierarchical character were: (1) the General Confederation of Agriculture, consisting mostly of absentee landowners of the large estates (latifondi) in the south, and large commercial farms in the Po Valley and elsewhere; (2) the general confederation of Italian industry dominated by Montecatini (chemicals), Snia Viscosa (rayon), Ercole Morelli, and Pirelli (electrical manufacturing), Breda (railroad equipment); (3) the upper ranks of the army and navy that were intermarried with leaders of industry and commerce, and often retired to hold responsible positions in these fields; (4) the civil service; and (5) the Black Shirts.[19]

On the other hand, industry never became sufficiently integrated with the state, nor sufficiently powerful, despite the wide ramifications of Pirelli and Montecatini to be useful to any considerable extent for achievement of military or political objectives abroad.   Montecatini (I. G.'s Italian chemical partner), the Consorzio Obbligatorio per l'Industria Solfifera, the mercury cartel, and minor industrial monopolies, became members of international cartels and acted in a few instances through such cartels to wage economic warfare.   But such action was relatively weak and of minor importance.

Summary

Fascist Italy reorganized her economy along mercantilistic lines. Most businesses were grouped into corporations and compulsory consortia; competition of small business was controlled; and large monopolistic business was strengthened.   Free trade unions and free collective bargaining were suppressed.   Governmentally owned enterprises were put back into private hands.   The government "socialized the losses" of large concerns in heavy industry and banking.   The basic industries, such as steel, cement, and construction, operating at low capacity were put to work first on large public works programs, such as electrification of railroads, port improvements, luxury liners like the *Rex*, magnificent motor highways, and "embellishments of the Eternal City," but ultimately on "defense" orders.   High tariffs, embargoes, exchange and foreign trade controls, were imposed to give the nation a self-sufficient fortress economy.

SPAIN

The fascist new order in Spain was conditioned by several facts. First, Spain, in April 1947, still had a predominantly agrarian economy, characterized by poverty for the million or more small peasants and

[17] Salvemini, p. 419.   The entire chapter entitled "Fascism, Capitalism, and Democracy" is worth most careful reading, pp. 419–429.
[18] Quoted by Liberta, September 21, 1933 also quoted in Salvemini, p. 421, footnote 1.
[19] Guérin, ch. 1.

by opulence for a handful of feudal grandees.   Second, a most destructive civil war, while leaving industrial equipment as good as ever (since the people valued their property too highly to carry out a "scorched earth" policy), not only killed off hundreds of thousands of industrial workers, but exhausted the energies of the survivors. Third, Spain lost 61 percent of her passenger cars, 22 percent of her freight cars, and 27 percent of her locomotives in the civil war.   The iron and steel industry was unable to provide the necessary replacements, and the outbreak of the Second World War made it impossible for Franco to obtain necessary materials from abroad.   Fourth, the shortage of labor was further intensified by the imprisonment of Spanish refugees who returned from France when it was overrun by Germany.   Fifth, the shortage of raw materials and of goods generally was extreme.   Sixth, the civil war brought an aftermath of inflation which was aggravated during the Second World War by the preemptive purchasing operations of both Germany and the Allies.

Thus the economy of Spain was practically prostrate.   As late as April 1943, the industrial and economic reorganization of Spain had not progressed beyond chaotic improvisation and wishful blueprints.

The sindicatos

It was authoritatively announced in 1937, that the economy would be reorganized into syndicates to—

provide for the modernizing of implements; attend to the fusion and coordination of factories, suppression of unproductive establishments, etc.[20]

Some 18 trade and regional councils were projected.

Actually,[21] however, it was not until the decree of June 23, 1941, that a beginning was made.   The Minister of Labor was placed in charge of the organization of vertical syndicates under the direction of the Falange.   The groupings were as follows: Cereals, fruits and horticultural products, olives, wine, beer and beverages, sugar, wood, cattle, fish, leather, textiles, confectionary, metal trades, chemical industries, fuel, water and electricity, paper and printing and the graphic arts, transportation and communications, hotel keeping and catering, insurance, banks and markets, entertainments, colonial products.[22]

Economic antarchy

Spain was too limited in natural resources to achieve economic self-sufficiency.   In addition, she was handicapped by lack of friends, incompetently administered government regulations,[23] and by the constriction of foreign trade [24] in the early thirties.[25]

Strengthening monopolistic combines

The domestically dominated industry began to be organized into cartels and combines long before the advent of Franco.   As early as 1919, the Spanish paper industry, for example, formed a Nation-wide

[20] Diego Abad de Santillan, After the Revolution, New York, 1937, pp. 50, 51.

[21] On the changes in government made by Franco on acquiring power, see ch. I, Government and Political Parties.

[22] Thomas J. Hamilton, Appeasement's Child, New York, 1943, p. 103.

[23] Hamilton, p. 139.

[24] If real wages in Great Britain in 1930 are taken as a standard of comparison equal to 100, those in the United States were 191, in Australia 145, in Sweden 101, in Ireland 85, in Spain 45, in Estonia 41, and in Portugal 32.

[25] A. Ramos Oliveira, Politics, Economics and Men of Modern Spain, 1808–1946. London, 1946, p. 242.

cartel (Sociedad Cooperativa de Fabricantes de Papel de España), which not only determined prices, production quotas and market territories, but closed down so-called "surplus" plants and bought up newspaper such as El Sol, and publishing houses such as Espasa-Calpe with its internationally famous Enciclopedía Espasa. It was still operating in 1947.

The Spanish historian, A. Ramos Oliveira, states that:

> As if high tariffs are not enough, the capitalists have united in cartels and combines so that neither from outside nor in the internal development of industry and finance can the breath of competition enter.

Four banks (Urquijo, Bilbao, Viscaya, and Herrero) controlled the industry and commerce of the nation. Sixteen directors of these banks were also directors of 400 companies of all kinds: Railway, electrical, chemical, mining, oil, and sulfur.[26] The control of commercial enterprises and of land was concentrated in a few hands. A surprising amount was held by religious orders, such as the Jesuits, who therefore had considerable influence over banks, public services, and commercial undertakings.[27] In Spain, the powers behind the dictator were not only the Monarchists, Carlists, the Army, the right-wing groups, but also bankers like Cambó and the powerful Juan March.

The latter personally controlled a great many Spanish banks, newspapers, and steamship companies, negotiated the deal whereby, in exchange for Spanish minerals and mercury, Germany sent tanks and other military equipment to the aid of the insurrectionary forces under Franco. As a partial reward he was given a monopoly of all Spanish trade with England,[28] an enterprise which, unlike his highly profitable smuggling of supplies to German submarines in the course of both wars, proved to be unsuccessful, due in part to the ingenuity of "estraperlistas," or black-market operators. In short, "the new solidarity" merged into one supreme reactionary nucleus, the great landowners and the bankers.[29]

> As on previous occasions, the oligarchs found a useful ally in the Army. They had recovered their fortune and their lands with the triumph of the counter-revolution.[30]

Foreign industries in Spain

Spanish fascism, unlike that of Germany and Italy was aided from abroad. Ramos Oliveira says:

> The asphyxiation of the second republic was the work also of the international trusts with ramifications in the peninsula.[31]

Some idea of the extensiveness of this foreign interest may be noted in that up to 1940, British capital controlled almost all the copper output of Spain,[32] a large fraction of the manufactures of Spanish cork,[33] with lesser holdings of suriferous quartz, iron ore mines of Vizcaya, sulfur, municipal water works, and railways. French

---

[26] Ramos Oliveira, p. 254.
[27] Ilsa and Arturo Barea, Spain in the Postwar World, London, 1945, p. 14.
[28] Hamilton, p. 136.
[29] Ramos Oliveira, p. 253.
[30] Ramos Oliveira, p. 678.
[31] Ramos Oliveira, p. 255.
[32] Compañía de Río Tinto (150 million pesetas) and Thersis Sulphur Copper Mines, Ltd. (60 million pesetas).
[33] Manufacturo de Corcho Armstrong, S. A. (35 million pesetas)

capital, in addition to owning various important mines,[34] was invested in the profitable Unión Española de Explosivos (60 million pesetas), in fertilizers and in the textile industry. Canadian capital controlled 50 percent of the hydroelectric industry of Catalonia through a holding company called La Canadiense of 600 million pesetas capital. Belgian holdings were likewise in excess of a half billion pesetas, largely concentrated in tramways, railways, timber and potash industries.[35]

JAPAN

The economic program of fascism in Japan was in every vital respect like those already discussed.

Following the ancient idea of the state being a body corporate (Kokutai), modern Japan was molded into an efficient totalitarian community. Its trade and industry were patterned after those of other highly industrialized states.[36]

In the thirties, the old political parties [37] were supplanted by the Imperial Rule Assistance Association which, in effect, was the Supreme Economic Council. By 1936, a labor front had been organized, taking the name All-Japan Convention of Patriotic Trade Unions. It not only opposed and later supplanted the regular Japan Trade Union Council (and with it even the shadow of collective bargaining that had developed), but it adopted a platform calling for "propagation of Japanese spirit," for "control over labor," and denouncing "social and democratic thought as contrary to Japan's national constitution."[38]

Compulsory cartelization in Japan

As early as 1897 a law was passed making it compulsory for the manufacturers in each branch of industry to form associations for the "purpose of jointly abolishing deficiencies." This was supplemented by a series of legislative enactments for special industries, such as silk, rice, and steel.

This law was considerably amplified by the Major Industries Control Law of 1931, and set up a Bureau of Rationalization in the Ministry of Commerce and Industry, and provided that, on application from more than two-thirds of the participants in a cartel agreement (adopted by a simple majority of the entire number in the industry), the minister would declare such agreement binding on all, including nonmembers. The Bureau was also empowered to foster cartels. As a result, "cooperation and control (was) established in almost all leading industries," [39] including cotton yarn, spun silk, paper, sugar, canned foods, coal, copper, cement, pig iron, steel bars, plates and angles, heavy chemicals, etc.

[34] Minero Metalúrgica de Peñarroya (309 million francs); Miñas del Castillo de las Guardas (12 million pesetas.)
[35] Ramos Oliveira, p. 260, reports that 80 percent of the shares were bought at a cost of £14,250,000, £12,500,000 in State bonds, the remainder in cash
[36] Wendell Berge, Cartels, Challenge to a Free World. Washington, 1944; pp. 132–36.
[37] For the Government of Japan see the famous volume by Dr. Inazo Nitobe, Bushido, the Soul of Japan. Philadelphia, 1900.
[38] Foreign Affairs Association of Japan, Japan Year Book. Tokyo, 1938–39, p. 773.
[39] Mitsubishi Economic Research Bureau, Japanese Trade and Industry Present and Future, London, 1936, p. 133.

These cartels enforced restrictions on total output,[40] established individual output quotas, fixed selling prices, terms, allotment of orders, division of markets, arranged joint purchases of raw materials, and joint storage of manufactured goods, limited installation and extension of equipment, etc.[41] A particularly interesting feature in many of these cartel agreements was the provision preventing "an evil practice of offering inducements to good workers to leave their employment," by enforcing a regulation that "no worker can be taken on while he or she is in the service of another employer, without the permission of that employer." [42]

In contradistinction to the large cartels just mentioned, there were in 1935 some 662 industrial associations or guilds covering small scale enterprises in about 70 industries.[43] These were controlled by the provisions of the Industrial Association Law. Government supervision here was considerably more strict and covered detailed managerial assistance, standardization, simplification, and the like, in addition to the usual cartel restrictions. Whereas control over the large cartels "rested merely on mutual consent",[44] small enterprise had to toe the mark.

Increasing economic war potential

From the day that Admiral Perry's guns shocked Japan into a realization of her military weakness, almost the sole purpose of the nation became that of developing military strength.

The state utilized every form of tariff, subsidy, or other mercantilistic device known, trying to hasten industrialization especially of its armament industries. Government subsidies to shipping amounted to more than 10,000,000 yen a year. It remitted a goodly proportion of regular income and other taxes for iron and steel plants and colonial enterprises.

It was the state which gradually made "capitalists" out of a small, heterogeneous, inefficient, and not very wealthy group of merchants, feudal lords, and unemployed officers, who were instructed to accumulate investment capital and to develop industrial initiative. The state-built model factories, banks, and railways.[45]

In 1926, it employed 20 percent of the workers in manufacturing, mining, and transport, and commanded 30 percent of total investment. Even as recently as 1931, it owned 66.5 percent of total investments in transport, 51 percent of total investments in iron and steel, 13 percent in machine building.[46] In addition, there were state monopolies of tobacco, salt, opium, naphthalene, camphor, and phosphorus in the mandated islands, alcoholic liquors in Formosa, and most minerals including the large coal and iron works in Manchuria. It likewise bailed out bankrupt concerns such as the Kawasaki [47] and Fudzinagata shipyards, and the Toyo Seitetsu Steel Co. It awarded unusually profitable (gift) contracts to other concerns such as the Oriental Nitrate Co. The state was one of industry's most important cus-

---

[40] Thus, for example, in 1935 official production curtailment percentages were 33.8 in cotton spinning, 40.6 in spun silk, 55 in cement, 45 in bleaching powder, 43.7 in foreign style paper, 25 in sulphuric acid, and 20 in rayon. See United States Department of Commerce, Expansion of Japan's Foreign Trade and Industry, Trade Information Bulletin No. 836 (Washington, D. C., 1937) p. 16.
[41] For an excellent account and lists, industry by industry, of the control organs and agreements in operation, see Japanese Trade and Industry, ch. VIII, The Organization of Industry, especially pp. 116–127.
[42] Ibid., p. 247.
[43] Ibid., p. 125.
[44] Ibid., p. 116.
[45] Stein, Made in Japan. London, 1935, p. 120.
[46] Japanese Trade and Industry, Ch. VIII, The Organization of Industry, pp. 118–129.
[47] Ibid., p. 305.

tomers, taking 14 to 16 percent of total output, while orders from abroad took 22 percent and private home consumption about 62 to 64 percent.[48]

The industrialization and modernization of Japan that took place was extraordinarily rapid, particularly in the 30-year period preceding the attack on Pearl Harbor. In the two decades between 1914 and 1934, national production, exports and imports of Japan increased about fourfold.[49] In that same period industrial output increased from 45 percent to 72 percent of total national production, while that of primary and agricultural products decreased from 41 percent to 27 percent.[50]

But Japan never developed self-sufficiency. It became an island empire geared to international trade. In 1933 Japan exported 78.5 percent of the raw silk it produced, 12.7 percent of its rayon tissues, 41.8 percent of its output of pottery and porcelain, with lesser amounts of other things. Exports as a whole average 20.5 percent of national production.[51] Its most important imports consisted of such vitally essential and strategic items as raw cotton, iron, and steel, wool, mineral oil, legumes, timber, pulp, wheat, crude rubber, and various minor fibers, ores, and raw materials.[52]

Encouragement of large combines

Industry in Japan comprised virtually every type of organization, from myriads of small household enterprises and small or medium-sized handicraft units to large factories feudally organized under paternalistic family management, equipped with latest mass-production techniques and apparatus. In 1933, one-half of Japan's production was manufactured in workshops employing less than 75 workers, the other half in larger units. At the center of the system, however, were less than a dozen family enterprises.

The best known were Mitsui, Mitsubishi, Sumitomo, and Yasuda "money cliques," or Zaibatsu. Perhaps as much as 60 percent of all investments in Japanese joint stock companies was controlled by these four family enterprises.[53] They controlled easily half the production of coal, copper, merchant shipping, paper, flour, sugar, chemicals, aircraft, glass, and foreign trade. A description of the Mitsui combine reveals a pyramidical hierarchy similar in all respects to I. G. Farben,[54] with a founder's constitution which reads like the charter of a modern patriarchal holding company.

It was around these giants that were clustered the horde of small, satellite plants and industries.[55] The latter at times caused a measure of "instability" despite the Government sanction of cartel controls. Consequently, just 3 months prior to Pearl Harbor, there was formed a new economic structure of supercartels or "control associations," embracing all firms, trade associations, and cartels. The president of each had absolute power to appoint or dismiss all officials and directors not only of the association, but of the member companies or

---

[48] Stein, p. 126.
[49] Japanese Trade and Industry, p. 488.
[50] *Ibid.*, p. 15.
[51] *Ibid.*, p. 494.
[52] *Ibid.*, chs. XXVIII–XXXI, inclusive.
[53] Neil Skene Smith, Japan's Business Families, The Economist, June 18, 1938, 651–656.
[54] Oland D. Russell, The House of Mitsui, Boston, 1939.
[55] I. Otsuka, Characteristic Features of Japanese Small Industries and Policies for their Development, Kyoto University Economic Review, October 1939, pp. 22–23.

cartels. The head selected for the iron and steel association was Hachisaburo Hirao of the Mitsubishi interests, former president of the Iron and Steel Manufacturers Association. Mitsui's Kenjiro Matsumoto, president of the old trade association, became president of the Coal Control Association, and Noboru Ohtani, head of Mitsubishi's N. Y. K. Line, became president of the Central Marine Transportation Association.[56]

Japan's industrial offensive

Japanese industry and trade were designed from the beginning to serve as an implement of economic warfare and economic conquest.[57] That was one of the compelling reasons why the state, without protest from Japanese industrialists or businessmen, owned outright, or dominated, the big Japanese colonial development companies so extensively used as agencies of economic conquest on the mainland of Asia, notably the South Manchurian Railroad Co., the Oriental Development Co. in Korea, the Chosen Bank, the Bank of Formosa, the East Asiatic Industrial Co., the Japanese steamship companies in China, and the large China exporting combine, known as Nikka Dzichugio Kyokai.

Similarly, in order to promote exports, an Exporters' Association Act was passed in 1925, which not only enabled the Government to supervise the assortment, quality, quantity, prices, and destination of goods exported, but guaranteed the exporters 50 percent of any loss they might suffer, gave them export subsidies, bounties, and rebates, and enabled them through the Japanese consulates to carry on economic espionage in foreign markets.[58]   From the very start a hothouse system of subsidies, direct and indirect, tariffs, import quotas, export bounties, foreign exchange controls, and other mercantilistic procedures [59] were used.   In short, long before 1931 or 1941, Japan was creating a "Greater East Asia Co-Prosperity Sphere," i. e., a fortress economy in which the Zaibatsu, as acknowledged leaders, constituted the hierarchy of graduated economic power.[60]

Finally, in Japan, as in Germany, Italy, and Spain, the groups exercizing state control of industry consisted of an oligarchy from the upper strata adhering to the same kind of medieval mercantilism. Gunther Stein writes:

Leadership within the state gradually changed.   First the Army and the Navy came of age, then finance and industry.   The fighting services and industry, originally creations of the bureaucracy which—with Imperial authority in the background—had created the new State, gradually became its partners.   Both the fighting Services and industrialists gained influence and power, and neither dominated.[61]

Again one finds the same reactionary quadrumvirate—the militarists and Samurai, the nobility and top Government hierarchy, the large landlords, and the heads of Zaibatsu—cooperating to suppress economic liberty in Japan and build a self-sufficient "Greater East Asia Co-Prosperity Sphere."

[56] For a detailed outline of the organization of Japanese cartels, see Japanese Trade and Industry, ch. VIII.
[57] Kalijarvi, p. 639.
[58] Ibid, pp. 409–415.
[59] Eijiro Kawai, Neue politische Kraefte des wirtschaftlichen Aufbaues, Weltwirtschaftliches Archiv, vol. XLVI, July 1937, pp. 62–78.
[60] Kalijarvi, pp. 646–650.
[61] Stein, p. 120.

INTERNATIONAL CARTELS AND CONCLUSION

The ramifications of the cartels has been particularly noted in connection with the German economy. One analyst has asserted that:

It was the monopolists in nation after nation who fostered the Nazi-Fascist movements; helped to give them state power; fed them the victories to make them strong; (and) prevented the democratic peoples from uniting aganist them; * * *.[62]

In Italy, Japan, Germany, Austria, France, and Spain stable, cartellized, monopolistic new orders not only aided in winning fifth column support for fascism in democratic countries[63] but constituted a formidable obstacle to the preservation of peace and the organization of a free world.[64] A flood of evidence[65] has come to light in recent years proving that international industrial monopolies or monopoloid enterprises have set up elaborate international economic governments that have fixed prices, divided world markets, enforced quantitative and qualitative allocations of output, controlled technological progress, carved out exclusive territories internationally by myriad devices such as patent cross-licensing, made and unmade tariffs, foreign policy, and even governments.[66]

Each such international cartel, when fully developed as, for example, the famous electric lamp or Phoebus cartel,[67] had an international executive body with power to act, an assembly made up of representatives from the leading firms in each country with vote proportional to size of operations, and an arbitration court or committee to settle all disputes within the family.

It was at these meetings that top executives in each industry got to know each other until, to cite but one example, de Wendel of the French Comité des Forges ultimately felt that he had more in common with Ernest Poensgen of the German Vereinigte Stahlwerkverband than he did with the Communist Léon Jouhaux, the vigorous leader of organized labor in his plants. The businessmen of Europe became a like-minded community with more or less identical right-wing beliefs, who felt, as did Dr. Carl Duisberg of I. G. Farben, that—

The narrowness of the national economic territory must be overcome by transnational economic territories. For the final settlement of the problem of Europe

---

[62] David Lasser, Private Monopoly, the Enemy at Home. New York and London, 1945, p. 4.
[63] See for example, Joseph A. Borkin and Charles S. Welsh, Germany's Master Plan, the Story of Industrial Offensive.
[64] See Berge.
[65] The literature is extensive. See: (1) U. S. Senate Committee on Patents, Bone Committee, Hearings, 9 vols., Washington, D. C., 1942, popularized in Guenter Reimann's Patents for Hitler. New York, 1943. (2) U. S. Senate Committee on Military Affairs, Subcommittee on War Mobilization, Hearings, 16 vols., and especially Monograph No. 1, Economic and Political Aspects of International Cartels by Corwin D. Edwards, Washington, 1944. (3) George W. Stocking and Myron W. Watkins, Cartels in Action, Twentieth Century Fund, 1947. (4) For a summary of cases, with names of hundreds of German, French, British, Italian, Japanese, Swedish, Dutch, and other concerns, involving more than 100 commodities, see, together with the individual court records and briefs and files of the Department of Justice, the extensive hearings on Cartels and National Security by the Kilgore committee, describing the operations of cartels covering aircraft instruments, carburetors, dyestuffs, electric lamps, aluminum, synthetic rubber, alkalies, nitrates, vitamins, electrical equipment, magnesium, plastics, newsprint, optical instruments, quebracho, titanium, and tungsten carbide.
[66] The most recent example is the violent overturn of the Villaroel regime in Bolivia, engineered by the tin cartellists Patiño and Hochschild.
[67] For a brief exposition of its prewar organization and operation (together with charts and verbatim reproduction of agreements governing the prewar potash, rubber, dyestuffs, and other industries), see testimony of Theodore J. Kreps in Hearings before the Temporary National Economic Committee, pt. 25, Cartels, Washington, 1940.

* * * a close economic combine must be formed from Bordeaux to Odessa as the backbone of Europe.[68]

Economic totalitarianism in the interwar period set up a series of supranational economic states, commodity by commodity, each with its own government divisions and private trade barriers, often implemented by tariffs and other discriminatory measures, imposed and superimposed over one another with increasing complexity. Agreement among these economic great powers (such as the Loucheur-Stinnes agreement in 1924 preceding withdrawal of French troops from the Kuhr) was often the prerequisite to agreement between their respective governments.

It was from the ranks of the owners, managers, and bureaucracies of the business membership of these international combines and cartels that embryonically fascist right-wing movements throughout the world derived the hard core of enduring financial support. Wherever totalitarian economic regimes were advanced they were associated with such men as F. H. Fentener van Vlissingen of the Dutch rayon cartel, and, from 1933 to 1937, the president of the International Chamber of Commerce; [69] with Fritz Mandel, the munitions magnate in Austria; or with Ferdinand de Brinon of the French Comité des Forges recently convicted of treason. They have been spearheaded, in the famous phrase of Pertinax, by the elite, that is, by the upper hierarchy of landowners, industrialists, and financiers, the nobility, and the topmost echelons of army and navy.

All such totalitarian movements similarly attracted as followers those with consuming hatred against labor, against Jews or other racial minorities; the timid that wanted to be sure to be on the winning side; the opportunistic and indeed lawless elements; the confused; the small that imitated and envied the powerful; those ready to sacrifice a considerable amount of conviction or principle in order to escape getting hurt; the unemployed and others who felt that they might gain while having little to lose save theoretical freedoms.

[68] Speech delivered in Munich 1931 from Helmut Wicked, I. G. Deutschland, Berlin, 1931.
[69] See a description of his activities among those of less illustrious Dutch collaborationists in Kilgore, pt. 3, exhibit No. 5, especially pp. 697–698.

CHAPTER VIII—LABOR

The role of labor in the fascist economic and political system is one of subservience. All labor activities are reorganized, guided, and controlled in conformity with the interests of the state. One of the most important changes fascism brings about is the abolition of free collective bargaining and of self-governing labor organizations. Labor policy under fascism first of all takes away from the worker all means of self-defense. It renders all militant labor action impossible. Furthermore, the state regulates all significant employment relationships and terms of the wage contract. By way of compensation, extensive programs of labor education and reorientation are established to lead the "misguided" labor masses away from materialistic goals, such as higher wages and shorter hours, to spiritual and cultural appreciation [1] of their status, their trusteeship, and the harmony of their interests with that of employers, the army, and the state.

BEFORE THE DICTATORS

Before the advent of fascism, the workers of Italy, Germany, and Spain enjoyed substantial freedom, individually as well as collectively. In addition, they were protected by social legislation and administration.

Individual rights

Individually, persons could accept or refuse work, select or change careers, select or change jobs, migrate in search of work, and wrest from employers as high wages and as favorable terms of employment as possible.

In all three countries under review, workers could join a labor union of their own choosing, a right generally held to include the right of not joining a union. Freedom of association was generally well enforced in Germany, but was curtailed to some extent in Italy and Spain. The closed shop and the other union security clauses, and the check-off, were foreign to the collective agreements of Germany, as they also were to those of Spain and Italy. However, social pressure was often equally effective.

Union structure

Many kinds of unions could be found in the pre-fascist states. For the most part they were organized: (1) along plant, employer, craft, occupational, or industrial lines; (2) along local, regional, and national lines; and (3) along philosophical and political lines. In some cases, unions included the majority of eligible workers; in other cases they included only minorities. In Germany the occupational or industrial nation-wide centralized highly or fairly representative

---

[1] Robert Ley, Fuehrer of the Arbeitsfront, in New Forms of Community Work (in English) Reichsarbeits- und Reichswirtschaftsrat, Berlin, 1935.

union of manual workers was predominant. There were also unions of broadly amalgamated crafts, of pure crafts, and of salaried employees (white-collar workers). Most manual workers were organized into unions with a Socialist tendency, although one encountered important national and regional organizations of employees representing the Roman Catholic and the liberal-democratic school of thought. There were small Communist unions and Nazi labor organizations— the latter purely political. In Italy, labor organization was not as highly developed as in Germany. The majority of workers belonged to Socialist unions and an important minority to Roman Catholic unions. There were also independent organizations; and in 1921, Mussolini established a Fascist labor organization of his own. Spain possessed anarcho-syndicalist unions' which competed with both Socialist unions and with very weak Roman Catholic ones.

Labor unions were free to form national federations and confederations. Thus, the Socialist unions of Germany belonged to the General Federation of Labor Unions (Allgemeiner Deutscher Gewerkschaftsbund), those of Italy to the General Confederation of Labor (Confederazione Generale del Lavoro), and those of Spain to the General Federation of Spanish Workers (Unión General de Trabajadores de España). The manual workers of the Roman Catholic unions of Germany formed the Federation of Christian Labor Unions (Gesamtverband der Christlichen Gewerkschaften), the Roman Catholic unions of Italy organized the Confederation of Italian Workers (Confederazione Italiana dei Lavoratori); and the anarcho-syndicalist unions of Spain united into the General Confederation of Labor (Confederación Nacional del Trabajo.)

The Catholic and Socialist national confederations and federations, as well as many of their unions severally, joined with similar groups in other countries to form such organizations as the International Federation of Trade Unions and the International Federation of Christian Trade Unions.

Union operations

Labor unions were essentially free in their activities, with one significant exception in the case of Germany.

(1) In Germany, collective bargaining was engaged in on all levels. Elaborate contracts fixed the terms of employment in all reasonably well-organized trades and industries. In Italy labor organization was less developed, and collective bargaining was not as far advanced. In Spain, except for some highly industrialized regions, collective bargaining had only just begun.

Dispute cases in Germany were handled by a nation-wide network of mediation boards and mediation officers. If mediation failed, unions—except in specified public utilities—were free to strike, and employers were free to lock out the workers. But the right to strike and to lock out ceased at the pleasure of the German Government. The Minister of Labor, or an official serving under him, had authority to declare the findings of the mediation authorities to be binding on both parties; that is, to arbitrate the dispute. This power was often used. It was very effective since the arbitration award was as binding on the parties as a collective agreement freely arrived at. The funds of the union were liable for breach of award or agreement alike. Moreover, the Minister of Labor had authority to extend collective agreements and arbitration awards to cover an entire trade or industry, locally, regionally, or nationally, as the case might be. This power was also often used. Unorganized employers and workers were thus effectively brought within the reach of a collective arrangement which became, in effect, the law of the industry and region in which it operated.

Thus it can be seen that, even before Hitler, dictating and standardizing conditions of employment by the German Government had become a matter of routine and had reached a high degree of technical perfection.

(2) The unions engaged freely in a wide range of welfare and educational activities. They would pay benefits in case of sickness, accident, unemployment, and death; would provide legal assistance; but they also established savings and banking facilities, conducted cooperative enterprises, and organized recreational clubs and associations. They published trade weeklies and monthlies, ran evening classes, set up research bureaus, and schooled their members in whatever political, philosophical, or economic doctrines seemed to offer desirable answers.

(3) Unions in their corporative capacity engaged in politics. They used their organized power to bring pressure upon the national, state, and local governments, and upon political parties. The German General Federation influenced strongly, and in many instances actually controlled, the German Social-Democratic Party. The General Confederation (Confederazione Generale) of Italy had a somewhat less powerful hold on the Italian Socialist Party. The German and Italian Catholic workers' organizations carried weight respectively with the Center and the Popolare Parties. The unions were given official representation in various councils and authorities of the state in all three countries under review.

Protective legislation

Workers in Germany were cared for under an extensive system of social insurance, covering old age, disability, accidents, sickness, and unemployment. There was also extensive protective legislation, for example a statute of 1920 provided for the free election by the workers of a steward or a committee in every plant to take care of grievances, unjustified discharges, and other matters arising out of plant relationships. Legal contests arising out of individual or collective labor relationships were brought into and speedily decided by special courts. Protective measures were less effectively developed in Italy than in Germany, and very little in Spain.

As will be seen, many of these protective measures were continued and expanded by the fascist governments.

UNDER THE DICTATORS

The labor policy of the fascist countries can only be understood if it is recalled that every worker is regarded as a minute part of the productive and fighting capacity of the state. Labor becomes a part of the economic and political might and activities of the state. An organized, led, and unquestioning labor is represented as a public service. Labor ranks march side by side with military forces. The shovel replaces the rifle, the labor battalion is blood brother to the military battalion.

Mussolini, Hitler, and Franco destroyed the freedom of labor that had existed before they came to power in their respective countries; by subjecting the worker to control by his government. The techniques used and the degree and speed of subjection differed with each country and with each activity involved. The result, however, was always the same—regimentation by the government. Loss of freedom was accompanied by an increase in protective measures—legislative and administrative.

The regimentation of labor began in all instances with the destruction of freedom of association.[2] But it should not be assumed that the dictators disposed of workers organizations. Rather, they organized workers more thoroughly than they had ever been organized before.

General structure of new labor organizations

The general structure of the new labor organizations differed widely in the three countries under review. Mussolini proceeded along conventional lines. In 1925, the Confederation of Italian Industries recognized the Confederation of Fascist "Corporations" as the sole representative of Italian labor. Following this development, a law of April 3, 1926, provided for the organization of Italian labor under fascist control along the familiar lines of occupations and industries. For every specified occupation or industry, an association of workers (sindacato) was set up, with authority to represent all the workers of the occupation or industry involved—locally, regionally, and nationally. Closely related associations were joined together in local, regional, and national federations; and the several federations were lined up in national confederations representing broad branches of the economy. As finally constituted, there was one confederation for industry, one for agriculture, one for commerce, one for credit and insurance, and one for the liberal professions. Employers were organized into separate groupings broadly on the pattern of those set up for the workers. The employers' federations were more numerous than the workers'. During the 1930's this structure was consolidated and centralized in favor of the federations and confederations.[3]

In contrast to Mussolini, Hitler evolved an entirely new and unprecedented structure of labor organization. For some time he toyed with the Italian corporative idea, but finally decided upon the German Labor Front. First, it included employers and employees alike. Therefore it has been argued that it was not a labor organization. Second, it organized both employers and workers in a personal way rather than because of any specific economic capacity. The units of subdivision chosen were regions, localities, plants or firms, and fractions of the latter. Regionally and locally, the labor front followed the pattern laid out for the Nazi Party to which it was linked on all levels by close personal ties. In each firm or plant the employer and the workers formed one big grouping which was taken care of by a Nazi Party shop steward, while large firms or plants were split into "cells" or "blocks," with minor stewards in charge of each. There was no line-up of workers as members of any craft, trade, occupation, or industry. This wiping out of the traditional lines, dividing the German working class, was designed to make it impossible for any

---

[2] See Salvemini, especially ch. VII.
[3] Anselmo Anselmi, Trade associations and corporations in Italy after recent reforms, *International Labor Review*, vol. 31, January 1935, pp. 6ff.

section of workers to advance its own specific economic interests. It was an ideal device to achieve regimentation of all workers under the control of an overpowering government.

Franco combined the more conventional ideas of Mussolini with the revolutionary ones of Hitler. He set up separate organizations, national syndicates (sindicatos nacionales) along broad industrial lines, but they all included employers.[4]

Labor organizations in the three countries (1) were industry-wide; (2) covered each worker (and employer to the extent here indicated); (3) excluded all organizations except those of the state; and (4) were placed under the complete control of the government. Let us examine each of these characteristics in greater detail.

Inclusiveness and privileges of the new organizations

(1) All industry was covered. In addition to the traditionally well-organized fields, the new groups covered the trades, occupations, and industries that previously had not been organized, or inadequately organized as in the case of agriculture, household industries, domestic services, and office employment. It should, however, be noted that in contrast to the Italian and Spanish groups, the Nazi Labor Front did not organize agriculture, but left that to a special agency, the Reich Agricultural Corporation, which, as a whole, was affiliated with the Labor Front.

(2) The personal coverage was total. The new organizations included all workers—manual, white collar, men, and women—who were employed in the trades and industries covered. In Italy, membership was automatic. Every employee (and employer) was compelled to pay dues and was represented and supervised by the proper association or federation.[5] In the case of Germany and Spain, membership was compulsory rather than automatic; an act of joining was required. While legally there was freedom of choice, in fact the official organizations compelled the employees to join and to pay the dues. The German Labor Front quite openly boasted about the pressure it exercised. However, little direct pressure was necessary because both in Germany and in Spain membership in the official organization was a prerequisite for any job. This continued to be true in Spain in 1947.

Automatic or compulsory organization brought about the following three results: (a) All shops were, in effect, "closed." (b) The check-off arose and became a general institution. The paying of dues to the official organizations was as inescapable a duty as contributing to the statutory social-security funds, or paying the wage tax. The dues assumed in fact the nature of a professional head tax, deducted by the employer, who in Germany turned them over to the Labor Front, and in Italy to the tax collector who, in turn, split them up and transferred them to the proper Fascist bodies. (c) The official organizations enjoyed a flow of income broader and steadier than that ever enjoyed by the free organizations of labor. The financial position of the German Labor Front was always brilliant.

[4] For details see Antonio Annós, La Ley Sindical Española, Edicione de la Revista de Trabajo, Madrid 1943, pp. 81ff.; and Pedro Miguel Quijano, Legislacion Sindical, Madrid 1943, pp. 124ff.
[5] A fine line of distinction, however, was drawn between plain dues-paying members, officially not named members at all, and members technically speaking who could be admitted on application and had to pay an additional fee to the organization. See Schmidt, ch. IV, Workers of Field and Factory.

In Germany and in Spain alike, the official organizations could refuse or cancel membership on a number of grounds or pretexts. In Spain, with unemployment chronic and widespread, the national syndicates have steadily used this weapon to starve out actual or suspected political opponents to the Franco regime.

(3) The position of the official labor organizations was exclusive. In Italy, under the law of April 3, 1926, and under the so-called Labor Charter of 1927, union organization was "free." However, only the Fascist associations of workers and employers received "legal recognition." All other organizations of workers were permitted to exist de facto but were, in fact, deprived of all privileges, including the right to levy dues; they were progressively squeezed out of existence. Toward the end of 1926, groups of Fascists ransacked several Socialist union headquarters, and in January 1927, the General Confederation "dissolved itself." Similarly, the Christian confederation of labor "ceased to exist."

In contrast to Mussolini, Hitler and Franco proceeded "lawfully." As early as December 1933, the German Government formally dissolved all existing non-Nazi workers organizations which until then had lived a precarious existence. In Spain, under an act of January 26, 1940, all associations designed to protect or represent economic or class interests, all trade-unions and employers associations were "incorporated in the trade-union organization of the [Falange] movement." The funds and assets of, and the institutions controlled by the defunct organizations were turned over to the new official ones. Any attempt to establish new labor organizations to operate in addition to, or to compete with, the official ones was either made impracticable or unlawful. It was, however, creditably reported as late as summer 1947, that the free Spanish labor unions had maintained a nucleus of organization within Spain, and that many of these centers were publishing periodicals with a certain degree of regularity.

(4) The new labor organizations were completely controlled by their respective governments. This was achieved by applying simultaneously two different devices:

(a) The organizations were tied in with the state. In the case of the German Labor Front and the Spanish national syndicates, the link with the state was an indirect one, achieved primarily through the Nazi Party and the Falange, respectively. The Labor Front, while technically distinct from the Nazi Party, was led by the latter, and the high Front officials were also high party officials. Similarly, the Spanish national syndicates were headed and controlled by the National Trade Union Office (Delegación Nacional de Sindicatos) which, in turn, seemed to be an outgrowth of the Falange Party. In the case of Italy, the relationship of the organizations to the state appears to have been more direct, namely (1) through constant supervision of their structure and operations exercised by the Ministry of Corporations and by the local and regional representatives of the national government, and (2) through their participation in the corporate organization of the state.

(b) The organizations were administered according to the leadership principle. The rank and file had no active voice. Their views might be sounded out, and in the three countries under review, they were given infrequent opportunities of accepting or rejecting candidates for minor offices named by the bosses.[6] But they could neither develop nor formulate policies, nor elect officers. Policies were developed by the leaders only, and officers were appointed from above all along the line down to the smallest jobs. In each country under review, the regime took great care to appoint only party members or persons of proven loyalty.[7] It was the job of these office holders to run every branch of the labor organizations in such a way as to give support, application, and expression to the labor policies of the government.

As exclusive instruments of national policy and because they were directed by their governments, the fascist labor organizations soon seceded from the international federations of labor mentioned above.

The end of collective bargaining

In addition to destroying the freedom of labor organization the dictators also destroyed the operations of free labor unions and substituted government action for the latter. Collective bargaining was ended. Individual bargaining was not restored. Government took over all functions of wage rate setting and basic conditions of employment.[8]

In *Spain*, the Falange government, apparently from the very outset and without hesitation, worked out and imposed all essential conditions of employment under the Ministry of Labor in Madrid. It issued orders to regulate the conditions of employment in a steadily increasing number of industries. Action seemed to be even more highly centralized than it had been either in Italy or in Germany. As a rule, the regulations were nation-wide, though not uniform for all regions of the country, nor for all branches of each industry regulated. They included elaborate wage schedules and detailed provisions relating to a great variety of terms of employment.

The Nazi government assumed complete control of basic conditions of employment as a result of a drawn out process. It at first relinquished control to the owners or to the managers of capital who, as a class, had contributed heavily to Hitler's rise to power. Indeed, a—supposedly basic—law issued as early as January 1934, seemed to make the German employer master in his own house.[9] As a "leader of his establishment" he was free to issue unilaterally "provisions respecting the amount of remuneration and other conditions of employment" which, together with other items to be included in the shop rules, were legally binding on his employees.

But this was changed as the supply of available labor shrank. Wage rates were stabilized and standardized. They were raised only to the extent deemed compatible with official price stabilization and employment policies. For each employer to control wages and other conditions of employment was inconsistent with the over-all control required. The Nazis therefore nationalized the regulation of wages and of other essential conditions of employment. The Labor Trustees,

[6] "Elections are only * * * means that enable the masses to affirm their loyalty to the government by voting for men who are persona grata." From Lavoro Fascista, Rome, February 21, 1931.
[7] The syndical officers are in no way dependent upon the worker members for their positions—no more than generals owe their posts to the common soldiers of their armies. Ignazio Silone, Der Fascismus, Zuerich, 1934, p. 202 ff.
[8] This without prejudice to the question of whether or not capitalists as a class received a larger share of the national income under fascist than under democratic governments.
[9] The manager has been promoted to the rank of leader by the racial state order which has equipped him with a power previously attributed only to state institutions. See Walter E. Kinkel, Unternehmer und Betriebsfuehrer in der gewerblichen Wirtschaft, Munich and Berlin, 1938, p. 58.

successors to the Republican mediation officers referred to above, issued wage schedules and other provisions to regulate the conditions of employment in each industry on a regional or national scale. Under the 1934 statute individual shop rules had to square with the Trustee's regulations. This ended in effect the control by the employers of the conditions of employment. In this as in all other essential phases of the operation of his business, the German employer was demoted from the position of a master in his own house to that of a servant of the government.[10]

In *Italy*, it seemed at first as if collective bargaining was to continue and the regime made it appear, especially abroad, that collective bargaining had never been as widespread and as flourishing as it was under fascism. Two devices contributed toward that impression:

(1) The set-up of the Fascist labor organizations was not ostensibly inconsistent with the structural requirements of collective bargaining, for it divided workers and employers along separate fairly parallel occupational or industrial lines.

(2) Far from outlawing or merely ignoring the processes of collective bargaining, the Fascist government enacted a very bulky body of legislation, painstakingly regulating all its essential phases. It laid down requirements for the form, the content, and the duration of the collective contract; specified its reach, formulated its relationship to the individual labor contract, and provided for adequate enforcement. In addition, it created machinery for the bargaining parties to resort to in the event that they failed to come to terms. Within each of the 16 courts of appeal of the kingdom, the government set up a special section to act as a tribunal for labor matters (magistratura del lavoro). These Labor Courts were designed to mediate and, if necessary, to arbitrate collective disputes arising out of the demand for new conditions of employment (in addition to deciding appeals on regular individual or collective lawsuits relating to labor). Essential items such as the constitution of the courts, actions and jurisdiction, procedure, awards, and appeals were well provided for.

This legislation was not only highly elaborate, totaling about 100 sections in the law of April 3, 1926, the royal decree No. 1130 of July 1, 1926, and the so-called Labor Charter of 1927; it was also technically modern, codifying some of the best results of labor-relations experience in progressive countries. Together with the equally elaborate regulations on the structure of the Fascist organizations for workers and for employers, and for the corporations, it formed a truly ideal hunting ground for the analysts of labor relations in Italy and abroad—the partisan, the prejudiced, the idle, and the unwitting ones alike.

Fascist legislation on collective bargaining was a masquerade. There never had been any collective bargaining worthy of the name in Fascist Italy. To the end, the Fascist government controlled the conditions of employment in the majority, if not in all, of the industries. In so doing, it differed from the Nazi and the Falange governments merely in the instruments and techniques of control. While the Nazi and the Falange governments openly operated through the specific offices and officials, the Italian Government operated deviously through the two parallel networks of organizations of employers and workers. While the Nazi and the Falange governments dictated

---

[10] Ludwig Hamburger, How Nazi Germany Has Controlled Business, Washington, D. C., 1943, pp. 98 ff.

regulations, the Italian used the formality of collective agreements supposedly negotiated between the organization of employers and employees.

Mussolini and the Ministry of Corporations evolved the basic national policies relating to wages and other essential conditions of employment. In succession, the confederation, the federations, and the associations of employers and of employees translated broad instructions received into more specific wage schedules and other provisions, and handed them down the line to the various industries, branches of industries, regions, localities, and business units. Presumably because it involved a certain amount of mutual consultation between the parallel organizations, this process was called "collective bargaining", and the resulting rules and regulations were styled "collective agreements".

There is ample evidence to show that the Fascist government controlled the conditions of employment in the major, if not all, Italian industries. (1) At repeated intervals in the 1930's it cut wage rates on a nation-wide scale, which cuts the organizations of employers and employees were required to carry out. (2) Such disagreements as seemed to arise from time to time between the organizations were not bargained on; but they were eliminated by outright dictation of the final rules. (3) The Labor Courts were frustrated in mediating and arbitrating disputes. It is reported that in the decade from 1926 to 1936, they handled about forty cases, actually deciding fourteen.[11]

It can thus be seen that the dictators withheld from their organizations of labor the economic functions that had been essential to the free labor unions. How, then, did the new organizations operate?

The operations of the new organizations

(1) They created extensive top-heavy administrative services indulging in an enormous amount of paper work. Their income secure, they staffed themselves lavishly. Jobs were often distributed as a matter of political patronage or graft. Thus in Spain we are creditably informed that jobs often went to regular army officers who, poorly paid and not fully occupied in their military capacity, were thus given a financial lift as well as a stake in the Franco regime.

(2) They engaged in broad welfare and vocational education activities similar to those of the free labor unions. In Germany, this was primarily a matter of expanding services or institutions that had been taken over rather than of creating entirely new ones. Thus the Labor Front organized nation-wide contests to develop the skills of young German workers belonging to practically every industrial craft (Reichsberufswettkampf). It improved, as did the Italian and apparently also the Spanish organizations, legal aid for workers in individual disputes with their employers. It enlarged the banking and insurance facilities that had been established by the free unions, until the Bank of German Labor became one of the four largest banks of Germany. In time the Labor Front formed a major unit in that sector of German economy that was owned and operated by or on

---

[11] Schmidt, p. 93. In October 1933 Signore Anselmo Anselmi, then Chief of the Bureau of Labor Relations in the Ministry of Corporations, told the writer that formal mediation and arbitration procedures were not needed. Divergence of views arising from time to time between the organizations of workers and employers in the process of establishing wage schedules and other conditions of employment were settled administratively—within or by the federations, the confederations, or the Ministry of Corporations. For the record, he added, a few minor cases had been turned over for settlement to the Labor Courts.

behalf of the German Government. During the war the Labor Front took over the important assets and facilities of the German consumers' cooperatives.

In Italy, a number of new welfare activities were added to the old program, and in Spain the Falange government claimed to have created a great variety of welfare services and institutions through the medium of the national syndicates.[12] All fascist labor organizations laid major emphasis on the recreation and leisure phase of workers' welfare.[13]

(3) The fascist labor organizations acted as compliance divisions of their respective governments. Like the free unions, the new organizations were pressure groups, but the direction of pressure was changed: While the free unions exerted pressure on government, the new organizations brought the full pressure of government on the workers.

It was the duty of the organizations to see that workers supported, or at least did not resist, government; that they accepted the changed structure of society and the new position of the individual; that they supported their dictators in war; and, that they put up with the stabilization and standardization of wage rates, the restrictions on free mobility of labor, the wage cuts imposed in Italy, the undue lengthening or shortening of hours, and with other measures calculated to arouse feeling and opposition. In a sensational reversal of policies of the free unions, it became the duty of the new organizations to prevent and to suppress strikes, and, in the case of Germany, to suggest and to promote labor-saving devices.

In enforcing compliance with official policies the new organizations worked on the minds and emotions as well as on the fears of the workers. They both educated and policed labor.

The major operations of Dopolavoro and of Strength Through Joy were accompanied by propaganda imbuing the workers with the basic philosophy and explaining to them the broad political objectives of their respective regimes. In addition, Strength Through Joy ran specific courses on Nazi philosophy, national history, current political problems ("race science"), and related topics. The labor organizations published a variety of journals and of trade weeklies, semimonthlies, and monthlies, which, in the case of Germany at least reached the bulk of the workers. These publications, as well as the general daily press, constantly dinned the political objectives of the Government into the ears of the workers. This was also done in the factories and offices through frequent assemblies or roll calls.

In policing labor, the new organizations, because of their inclusiveness and their power, were able to reach down to the last worker in the land and to keep a close eye on his every move. The techniques of policing were especially well developed in Germany, where the elaborate splitting up of all major plants into blocks and cells was followed by the creation of plant troops (Werkscharen) and political shock troops (Politische Stosstruppen) to impress and to intimidate the rank and file.

The new organizations were not equally effective in enforcing compliance with official policies. Nuclei of labor unions have maintained

[12] See Giron (Spanish Minister of Labor), Social Policy of the Spanish State, Madrid 1945.
[13] See Ch. XII, Use of Leisure Time.

a measure of resistance against the Falange regime. Strikes—minor ones, to be sure—were said to have occurred in Italy during the height of Mussolini's power. The German Labor Front, on the other hand, seems to have successfully regimented the workers under the control of the Government. In contrast to Mussolini, Hitler never went to the trouble of enacting legislation or of issuing executive orders to outlaw strikes. The Nazis had full confidence that they could out-educate, out-police, out-organize collective labor disputes, and in fact eradicate all resistance of labor to Nazi policies.

The regimentation described did not erase the rights of labor in their entirety in any of the three countries under review. Theoretically a person was still free to accept or to refuse to work for wages or a salary; to select and to change his career, and to select and to change his job. In varying degrees both Fascism and Falangism interfered with these liberties; but Naziism crushed them completely and replaced them by mobilization and allocation of labor under the government. The house of the German Labor Front was finished, roofed, and painted as early as 1934. However, the mobilization and allocation of labor emerged only as a long, drawn-out, complicated, and at times erratic process of trial and error which can here be sketched but in its barest outlines.[14]

Mobilization and allocation of labor by the Nazi Government

In mobilizing and allocating labor, the Nazis used the so-called Employment Book and the National Employment Service Agency, the latter of which they inherited from the Weimar Republic. In November 1935, the Agency, with a nation-wide network of regional and local offices, was granted full monopoly of employment service, vocational guidance, and the placing of apprentices. Similarly, Italy in 1928, and Spain in 1943, established official, monopolistic employment services, and compelled both employers and employees to utilize their facilities. The Employment Book, inaugurated in February 1935 (after an Italian enactment in January, and followed by similar Spanish action in 1943), was a record to show the particulars of the worker's vocational career. By the fall of 1936, a copy of the prescribed Book had been made out for every German worker. In April 1939, operation of the Book was extended to cover independent business.

It became the duty of every person to accept work for a wage or a salary. The Employment Service struck first at the self-employed. Beginning in January 1938, many peddlers and itinerant salesmen were refused licenses necessary for their work if they refused jobs offered. In 1939, artisans and craftsmen were similarly dealt with. Thousands were struck off the artisans' rolls, and "joined the ranks of the industrial working class." In March 1939, the shops of tens of thousands of retailers were closed to force the owners to take employment for wages. Simultaneously, pressure was brought to bear upon married and single women to accept jobs on farms, in offices, or in factories. The working age was extended at both extremes. Beginning in July 1938, labor conscription was extended to everybody—men and women, schoolboy and aged, employer and worker, civil servant and businessman. An ever-growing number of persons was inducted into industrial service.

---

[14] For full treatment, see Ludwig Hamburger, How Nazi Germany Has Mobilized and Controlled Labor. Washington, D. C., 1940.

No longer could the worker select or change his career; he was obliged to accept employment in such crafts, occupations, and industries as the Government decided. To some extent, this duty was a mere phase in the enforcing of labor conscription; the employment authorities, of course, assigned draftees to such occupations or industries as they, rather than the draftees, held "essential." But, in using their monopoly over vocational guidance fully, employment authorities also directed that young people be apprenticed only in "essential occupations." A decree of September 1939, made all apprenticeship subject to their approval. In addition, persons who had chosen to work in crafts, trades, or industries now held nonessential, were forced to change to essential ones. The employment authorities took the view that the individual worker was productive above all in the field he had been trained for and redistributed labor accordingly. Beginning at the end of 1936, with a few selected occupations, this policy was extended gradually to all occupations and industries.

The worker was tied to his job like a serf to the estate of his lord under conditions of feudalism. If he moved, it was only by leave or by order of the employment authorities. In tying workers to their jobs, the Nazis began by controlling the hiring of workers who wished to move. An employer could not engage a worker without permission from the proper employment office. Originally this requirement applied to the employers of nonagricultural labor who wished to employ farm hands; gradually it was extended to all employers wishing to employ any type of worker.

While control of hiring was a check on mobility, it did not tie up the workers fully. In due course, therefore, control of release was added to control of hiring. The release of workers without permission from the proper employment office was prohibited. At first this requirement applied to selected occupations and industries, but finally it was extended to all employers and to all classifications of workers. By the beginning of the war free mobility of labor had practically ended. Workers' emigration was subjected to severe controls, since 1935. Later on, workers were imported.

CONCLUSION

Fascist countries, as evidenced by Germany, Italy, and Spain, supplant all free labor organizations by state-controlled, monopolistic organizations prescribed in structure and inclusive in scope. In each of the three countries under review it was the government which controlled or actually took over the function of setting wage rates and prescribing other basic conditions of employment for practically all categories of employees. Collective bargaining was brought to an end.

CHAPTER IX—AGRICULTURE AND THE FARMER

Agriculture and the farmer occupied an important place, perhaps the most favored, in the prewar policies and programs of fascism. Unsolved agricultural problems and growing unrest among farmers resulted in crises which aided and assisted the fascists in their rise to power. Problems of the rural section, as of other sectors of the economy, were regarded through the tinted glasses of a nationalistic, and in the case of Germany at least, a racialistic ideology. But in that ideology agriculture and the farmer held a favored spot. The farm provided food, much needed in any case, and, if imports should be cut off in case of war, essential to physical survival. So too, the peasant was considered a paragon of virtues—racially and culturally; from his loins were to come the regenerated population and culture of the future.

But promises were easier than fulfillment; philosophy less complicated than programs. Even programs not infrequently were modified, redirected, submerged or abandoned in line with new goals of the party, stated or unstated. Even so, the rural economy fared better than other sectors under fascism, both at intermediate stages, and at the final debacle.

THE AGRICULTURAL FRAME OF REFERENCE

The agriculture of Germany, Italy, Japan, and Spain is best described as intensive, mixed, general farming with most of the types prevailing in the United States. Climate, soil types, and topography vary widely within the four countries and among them. Complex and widely different types of farming have been developed over the years, dependent in part on special aspects of the natural environment and in part upon the skill of the agriculturist and availability of domestic or foreign markets. Such types include intensive dairying, vegetable gardening, sugar beets, citrus fruits and vineyards, as well as wheat, rice, potatoes, and rye. Agricultural techniques range from the most specialized and highly scientific to the very primitive; it is said that at least one-fourth of Spain's cereals are still reaped and threshed by man-power and woman-power alone.

Compared to the United States these are very densely populated countries, the approximate number of inhabitants per square mile being: [1] United States 41; Spain 147.4; Italy 360.7; Germany 349.1.

The abundant population density might suggest that these are rich areas. But such is hardly the case; these countries are not particularly blessed naturally with agricultural resources. Even after centuries of trial, considerable areas have proven to be so refractory, agriculturally speaking, that they have continued in forest or waste land even under the economic compulsions of mounting population pressure and hard-pushed government programs aimed at food self-suffi-

[1] World Almanac, 1936, New York, pp. 529 and 717–720

131

ciency. Of the Spanish Plateau and the sandy soils of the North German plain it might be said, as it has been of Italy:

> Few European countries have so large a proportion of their territory irredeemably unsuited to agriculture or reclaimable only at a heavy capital outlay. The agricultural wealth which Italy can claim is not so much due to the bounty of nature as to the diligence of her farmers.[2]

As might be expected from such close settlement, these European areas are more largely cultivated, the percent of total area under cultivation being approximately as follows:[3] United States 17.8 percent; Spain 31.2 percent; Italy 41.1 percent; Germany 41.2 percent·

In these countries, especially Germany, as in the United States, there has been a trend toward industrialization, with agriculture employing a smaller and smaller percent of the total population; yet the rural population makes up a very sizable fraction of the total; nearly half in the case of Italy, whereas Spain is predominantly rural.

By and large, the agricultural economy is based on relatively small owner-operated farms with the farmers living in villages, and in some areas the land used by any one farmer lying in several separate tracts. Large holdings have, however, been sufficiently numerous in some areas, particularly in the East Baltic plain of Germany, the Po River Basin of Italy, and the plateau of Central and Southern Spain to stimulate demand for land-subdivision and tenure reform.

Number and area of agricultural land holdings in 1930 (Classified on basis of total area of holdings)[1]

Size of holdings [2]	Germany	Italy	United States
Up to 2 hectares:[3]			
Number	[3] 849, 218	2, 763. 671	[4] 358, 504
Area	[3] 950, 720	3, 043, 792	[4] 772, 298
2–20 hectares:[3]			
Number	1, 870. 405	1, 278. 995	2, 000, 005
Area	13, 275, 219	9, 110, 271	21, 869, 842
20–100 hectares:			
Number	321, 882	132, 536	2, 717, 892
Area	11, 579, 459	4, 970, 718	112, 867, 425
Over 100 hectares:			
Number	33. 949	21, 064	1, 212, 247
Area	15, 761, 387	9, 126, 963	263, 826, 797
Totals:			
Number	[3] 3. 075, 454	4, 196, 266	6, 288, 648
Area	[3] 103, 916, 962	65, 629, 360	998, 340, 905

[1] U. S. figures shown above based on these area divisions: Up to 4 hectares (10 acres); 4–20 hectares (10–50 acres); 20.2–80.9 hectares (5–200 acres); over 100 hectares (200 acres and up).
[2] Only units 0.51 hectare upwards are included; in addition 5,378,463 units of up to 0.50 ha. and having a total area of 556,606 ha. have not been included because many of them are more residential than agricultural.
[3] 1 to 3 hectares.
[4] Conversion figure 2.5 used in calculation of total acreage.

Source: Arranged from International Yearbook of Agricultural Statistics, 1939–40, Rome, 1940, pp. 266–267 and pp. 270–271, table 72.

Tenancy in general has not assumed the proportions it has in the better land areas of the United States.

AGRICULTURAL CRISES—A SEEDBED FOR FASCISM

The primary subject of inquiry is that of how the farmers and farms fared under fascism. It is not, however, beside the point to

[2] Asher Hobson, Agricultural Survey of Europe: Italy, U. S. Department of Agriculture, Washington, 1925, p. 9, quoted by Carl T. Schmidt, The Plough and the Sword, New York, 1938, p. 4.
[3] Annuaire International de Statistique Agricole, Rome, 1935–37, Institut International D'Agriculture, Rome, 1937, p. xiii.

inquire briefly into the matter of what part the rural economy played in the rise of fascism.

As in the United States, the period following the first World War was a period of serious economic and social readjustment with consequent stress and strain on the agriculture sector of the economy. In Italy the reaction against the hardships and disorganization following the First World War was expressed in strikes both urban and rural, and in attacks on private property, particularly by seizure of latifondists' estates; such seizures are estimated as high as 200,000 hectares in 1919–20. Not only the resentments aroused by the privations, suffering, and controls during the war, but promises made, which were not kept, were part of the pertinent background of later events.

Italy will give land and everything that goes with it to the peasants, so that every hero who has fought bravely in the trenches can become economically independent.[4]

Rural unemployment followed the War, partly because machines had been installed during the wartime scarcity of labor. Land reforms, as to ownership and conditions of tenure, were among the demands to which the response was certainly less than adequate considering the temper of the times.

Prices, credit, and taxes were also major problems that served as a base for growing unrest, a potent force which, in the case of Germany, at least, was to provide the ladder to power used by the fascists.

German industry and commerce began to feel the depression in 1928. At the same time the prices for grains began their downward sweep and in Schleswig-Holstein, East Prussia, and in southern or Upper Bavaria the livestock and meat markets suffered some severe seasonal price depressions which led in the case of Schleswig-Holstein to the sabotage of foreclosures and legal administration and to bomb throwing, in short, to a farmer revolt.[5]

The following tribute paid by Adolf Hitler is not without its political aspects, yet contains much more than the flattery of a recently arrived leader:

Our revolution would not have been possible at all if a certain part of the nation had not lived on the land. If we review the revolution soberly we must admit that it would not have been possible to accomplish this revolution from the cities. In the urban communities we could not have reached a position which gave to our policies the weight of legality.[6]

The successful rise of national socialism is held by Holt not to be assignable to any one economic group, but the National Socialist Party published its agrarian program in March 1930 and in the election of the following September increased its seats in the Reichstag from 12 to 107, gaining particularly in northern and northwestern Germany.[7] This was the fuel that fed the flame leading to full victory in July 1932.

Holt further says:

A study of the growth of National Socialism shows it to have been to a significant extent an agricultural revolt. The appointment of Darré to head a National Socialist agrarian political propaganda organization, the Party's 1930 program of absolute protection of the farmer against all the depression threats which might culminate and were culminating in the eviction of the "yeoman" from his soil and

[4] Schmidt, p. 27, quoting Prime Minister Salandra.
[5] John B. Holt, German Agricultural Policy 1918–34, Chapel Hill, N. C., 1936, p. 179.
[6] A. Gerschenkron. Bread and Democracy in Germany, Berkeley and Los Angeles, 1943, p. 3, quoting Voelkischer Beobachter, April 6, 1933.
[7] Holt, pp. 179–181.

home, and the farmer's loss of faith in the former regime prepared the rise of National Socialism in Agriculture.[8]

In the earlier case of Italy and the more recent case of Spain, the farm population is less clearly involved en masse as direct supporters of the incoming fascists. In the case of Italy, reaction of landowners against the rising tide of rural labor demands for land reforms and the growing strength in bargaining of rural labor unions seems to have been a most potent factor in the rise of the Fascists, regardless of the promises of reforms that were being made at that time.

In Spain, the Franco regime in 1940 set aside the land reform law enacted in 1932 by the liberal predecessor. Substituted instead was a National Institute of Colonization, emphasizing not the division of large estates but irrigation, rural electrification, and other rural programs.

THE FARMER AND THE PHILOSOPHY OF FASCISM

As might be expected of political parties bent on winning friends, the philosophy of the fascists in each case has had a rural slant. Of the several more or less integrated facets of fascist philosophy, within the over-all framework of which divergent group interests were reconciled by subordinating them to a higher national goal, three dealt especially with the farmer and agriculture.

Ruralization

An agrarian mysticism with its praise of rural life was primary. The rural sector of the economy, the rural family, and the rural village were considered to have virtues and strength, tangible and intangible, superior to other parts of the economy, hence to be strengthened, cherished, and protected.

Italy must be ruralized, even if it costs billions and takes half a century.[9]

The Government looks on the peasants, in war and in peace, as the fundamental forces on which the country relies for its success * * *. The people who abandon the land are condemned to decadence * * *. I have willed that agriculture take first place in the Italian economy.[10]

By being able to take fast root in his inherited soil, the yeoman should be enabled once more to become the instrument of the racial regeneration of the German People.[11]

Blood and soil

The second major rural facet of the philosophy was biological and social with emphasis on an elite of blood and culture. The "Blood and soil" ideology was to find its major expression under the German brand of fascism. The second item of "Bread, motherland, and justice," the motto of Franco, might be interpreted to have the same roots, though without equivalent emphasis on the biological.[12] Essentially, the ideology is that the Volk, or racial unit, bound by language, blood and cultural heritage, is the most fundamental unit in the social-economic and political evolution of mankind. A rupture of its cohesion through class warfare, foreign cultural influence, or blood mixture leads to its disintegration.

The greatest disintegrating threat to the German folk lies in the materialization of its standards through the growth of capitalistic society with its emphasis on the

[9] Holt, p. 215.
[9] Schmidt, p. 43, quoting Mussolini, L'agricolture e i rurali, p. 87.
[10] Schmidt, p. 42, quoting Mussolini. L'agricolture e i rurali, pp. 109-110.
[11] Holt, p. 204, quoting Darré, Im Kampf um die Seele des deutschen Bauern, p. 42.
[12] I. e. Franco's motto, Bread, Motherland, and Justice, in Hamilton, p. 177.

individual, its division of the folk into warring classes bound to one another by no higher moral ties or mutual obligations * * *." [13]

In Italy the elite seems to have been a less complex and less mystic concept, depending rather on economic success. For example, the large landowners were held to have "not only the right but also the Fascist duty to remain in their superior positions as leaders." [14]

Food

Food self-sufficiency, autarchy, as a preparation for defensive or aggressive warfare, was based on a rationale of hunger during the First World War and continued vulnerability and insecurity. In terms of resources or economics, there is no adequate base. The battle for bread (paraphrasing the Italian Battaglia del Grano, meaning "battle of grain") while represented in the ideology of all three countries, assumed dominant position in the case of Italy. This apparently grew out of a shrewd appraisal by the newly established Fascist regime of the political value of the acute food situation. [15] Heavy imports, particularly of wheat, to feed a growing population, plus harvest reverses in 1924, carried unmistakable meaning to those who might later risk war. Hence the struggle to become self-sufficient, at least in food.

In the case of Germany, though the struggle for food self-sufficiency through protectionism had been a part of national agricultural policy since Bismarck, this aspect of the fascist philosophy never assumed full dominance, but it was a part of most programs affecting agriculture.

Spain, normally an exporter of special foodstuffs, such as wines, citrus fruits, and winter vegetables but an importer of grains, was hungry after the destruction and disorganization of prolonged civil war, hence bread, more bread, was needed.

POLICIES AND PROGRAMS

Philosophy and the promises of politicians are ethereal without policies and programs to back them up. Without examining either the theory or the organization and functioning of the corporate state, or its agricultural subsidiaries, for example the Food Estate of the Nazis, which are dealt with elsewhere, it is nevertheless pertinent to examine the major agricultural programs attempted.

Reclamation and settlement

Settlement of additional people on the land and the expansion by "reclamation" of the farm area of the economy were important aspects of the fascist programs. Psychologically and socially they operated to tie the land hunger of the peasants to the ideological emphasis of the Party on rural virtues and racial theories, and the primary efforts toward the much-desired national food self-sufficiency. Settlement and reclamation were interrelated programs, yet after the initial stages, settlement tended to be less emphasized, particularly so far as it involved the breaking up of larger estates.

These were not new programs but only new emphases. Even more than in the United States, reclamation and settlement had gone on

---

[13] Holt, p. 183.
[14] Schmidt, p. 41, quoting G. Pesce, Contadini d'Italia, Bologna, 1926, p. 87.
[15] Walter J. Roth, in Journal of Farm Economics, vol. 16, No. 2, 1934, pp. 342–343, reviewing Mussolinis Getreideschlacht; Italienische Landwirtschaft im Zeichen der Diktatur, Regensburg, 1933, by Emil Mueller-Einhart.

slowly for centuries in these old farming areas.   In the case of Italy, the Fascist Minister of Finance estimated that expenditures during the period 1860–1924 were 1,162,000,000 lire authorized and 666,000,-000 actually spent, with the result that by the end of 1922, 597,000 hectares had been drained and reclamation was progressing on more than 600,000 hectares additional.[16]

In Germany, between World War I and the advent of fascism, a settlement program had been operating in a modest fashion.   Some 57,000 new farms of 600,000 total hectares had been "settled" plus additions of 144,000 hectares to 97,000 Anlieger farms.[17]

But the advent of fascism in each case initially carried emphasis on subdivision of large estates.   In Italy during the First World War and very soon thereafter some 700,000 to 800,000 hectares had passed to about half a million peasants, mostly by purchase from large estates.   The Visocchi decree of September 1919, interpreted by many peasants as being the first step in a general expropriation program—

authorized provincial prefects to requisition "uncultivated or insufficiently cultivated" land and to cede it for at least 4 years to "responsible" cooperatives.[18]

Mussolini in his early statements said:

We demand expropriation of the land   *   *   *.

And later:

Within a few months all Italy will be in our power, and then we shall complete the agrarian revolution, which must give—in various ways suggested by the different regional conditions—the land to those that work on it.

And still later a more restricted proposal:

The diffusion of small holdings in all districts where agricultural and other conditions render them suitable and likely to be productive.[19]

But within a few months after the March on Rome in October 1922, the Party found it expedient to withdraw support from agrarian revolution or reform and eventually emphasize reclamation.

The problems of settlement by expropriation and by reclamation have interlaced the recent history of Spain.   In 1932, a law providing for the expropriation of the estates of certain revolting grandees, and the settling of peasants thereon, had hardly been passed when a change in political power slowed up the program.   By early 1936, only 17,000 peasants had been settled on 410,000 acres.   But in the 6 months after the Popular Front Government came to power in early 1936, 2,000,000 acres were opened to "temporary occupancy" by the peasants, followed in the next year and a half by expropriation of more than 7,000,000 acres.[20]   But the Franco regime was just around the corner.

The reclamation story is different.   In Italy in 1923 and shortly thereafter basic laws were passed providing for the undertaking of reclamation projects, especially those with a substantial social interest. The Government was directly or indirectly involved in such projects, mostly through the channel of state supported consortia of landowners, which could be formed under compulsion and might expro-

---

[16] A. De Stefani, L'azione dello Stato italiano per le opere pubbliche, 1862-1924, Rome, 1925, p. 120, as quoted by Schmidt, p. 77.
[17] Statistisches Jahrbuch fuer das Deutsche Reich, 1933, quoted by Holt, p. 160. The "Anlieger" were too small units, made self-supporting by additions from larger adjacent estates.
[18] Schmidt, p. 31.
[19] Schmidt, p. 40, quoting Mussolini, L'agricoltura e i rurali, p. 18.
[20] Geoffrey Brereton, Spanish Peasants at War, Current History, vol. 27, April 1938, pp. 38-40.

priate the holdings of unwilling owners. The improved property remained in private hands.

Even so, it was not until late 1926, with deepening agricultural depression, that large-scale reclamation began. That phase ended in 1935 with the beginning of the "imperial" phase of Fascism. By that time "reclamation" of some sort was either "completed" or "under way" on approximately one-sixth of the area of the country. The best known of the projects was the Agro Pontino, a marsh and dune area of some 75,000 hectares not far from Rome.[21]

Reclamation seems to have been pushed less by the Nazis than by the Italian Fascists, though some 58,000 hectares of land reclaimed from swamp and unused land became a part of new German settlement between 1919 and 1937.

The hereditary farm

The hereditary farm became a basic cornerstone of the German phase of fascism, the fundamental unit of the blood and land philosophy. Farming is not a business or a means of getting wealthy; it is a way of life. It is a way of service, to the nation and to the family; food, children, morals, and culture are its prized products. Hence it is desirable and necessary to provide security of tenure and satisfying social position for the farmer.

The hereditary farm (Erbhofe), created by the new federal hereditary farm law, effective October 1, 1933, could be held only by German citizens of Aryan descent. It had to be of such a size as to fully maintain and support a peasant (Bauer) and his family; size varied with soil and climatic conditions from a minimum of about 20 to more than 300 acres.

The farm, for all practical purposes, could not be mortgaged, sold, or divided. Only one principal heir might inherit; other heirs could take only property other than the farm, its buildings or equipment. Thus uneconomic parcellization and overindebtedness were done away with.

The following priority of inheritance was provided for:
1. The sons of the farmer, and their sons and grandsons.
2. The father of the farmer.
3. The brothers of the farmer and their sons and grandsons.
4. The daughters of the farmer and their sons and grandsons.
5. The sisters of the farmer and their sons and grandsons.
6. The female descendants of the farmer and their descendants insofar as they do not come under the fourth category above.[22]

But further, in order to qualify for the inheritance and as Bauer, the farmer had to be approved as to his marriage and as to his ability as a farmer.

Economic controls

Economic controls were even more implicit in the fascist approach to the agricultural economy than were such semisocial programs as settlement, a rural elite, or reclamation. Attempts were made to strengthen the rural economy and to attain food self-sufficiency, at least as regards certain major items, by whatever economic means seemed likely to be effective.

---

[21] Schmidt, pp. 92–93.
[22] Summarized from D. F. Christy and G. P. Boals, Germany Adopts New Land Ownership Law, Journal of Farm Economics, vol. 16, No. 2, April 1934, pp. 326–329.

In Italy, where the overwhelming emphasis of the battle for bread was on wheat, with the program in charge of a committee of 24 members, primarily top-flight Government officials including Mussolini, production was stimulated and consumption checked by the old stand-by, the tariff. A tariff of 7.5 gold lire per quintal of wheat which had been suspended in 1915, was restored in 1925. From time to time this was increased, to approximately the equivalent of 19 gold lire by 1931, but was lowered in 1936, because of the poor crop that year. Even so, other measures were found to be necessary as world prices of wheat declined sharply in the late 1920's—quotas were established which required mixing of Italian wheat with imports. Also higher tariffs on imported competing cereals were established.[23] All of this led, practically, to fixed wheat prices at a high level.

The Germans used not only the flexible high tariff, but also direct price control. Primary was the import monopoly of grain, the purpose of which was to separate the domestic market from world price movements and manipulate prices to a level which would guarantee the profitability of a majority of the farms.[24] The human consumption of rye was stimulated by elaborate bread laws. Open market purchases and operation of public granaries were other methods used. Feed grains, the sugar beet, and the potato as well as fats and oils all received attention in the increasingly complex program. Price was no longer the determining factor in the origin of imports; the rigid control of foreign exchange and foreign trade led to bilateral trade agreements, including barter, especially with the surplus food nations of the Danube Basin. Food autarchy after 1932 was the propelling force.

Production stimulation

Subsidies, research, and propaganda all played a part in the efforts toward food self-sufficiency. In Italy subsidies on gasoline used in farming, lower freight rates, and lower cost chemical fertilizers were provided by the Government. Indirect subsidies in the form of debt-lightening measures, loans at low interest rates to wheat growers and agriculturists of special merit and other financial favors were prevalent. Research efforts took the form of developing farm machinery suited to Italian conditions and to improving seeds and farm management practices. Propaganda had a bit of Barnum in it but basically was tied to competition for highest yields among growers.

Research and farm management were already highly developed in Germany. Higher prices for farm products plus lower prices for fertilizers and electricity were utilized as a stimulus as were some forms of credit and tax relief. Competition and an increased sense of social value were utilized.

STATE CONTROL OF THE FARMER

Theoretically, state control over the farmer and the farm was complete. The National Corporation of Agriculture or National Food Estate, established in September 1933, was "authorized to regulate production, marketing, prices, and profits" of German landowners, tenants, cultivators, agricultural workers, wholesale and retail traders

---

[23] Schmidt, p. 51.
[24] Karl Brandt, German Agricultural Policy—Some Selected Lessons, Journal of Farm Economics, vol. 19, February 1937, pp. 287–299.

in agricultural products and foodstuffs, agricultural cooperative societies and marketing associations.[25] "Farm management" cards were held for each farm in Germany showing data on acreage and yields of crops, livestock population, and farming methods.

Practically, it has been said that the regulations did not directly penetrate deeply into the agricultural activities of the individual farmer. The Reich Food Estate directives seem to have manipulated prices to the point of increasing or decreasing the production of certain commodities; import controls, especially tariffs, were made so excessive on some commodities as to eliminate the possibility of competition. Subsidies were provided—on fertilizer, for example. Overall production goals were set, but production quotas were not dictated to individual farmers as such, though the Government requisitioned stated percentages of crops and livestock and kept marketing in channels.[26]

The general price and production policy of Italian Fascism seems to have been one of government price support through import limitations, protective tariffs on selected commodities, straight subsidy payments, and in some cases restrictive marketing standards and quotas, and production controls. Specifically, imported wheat and sugar had heavy duties placed on them; output of sugar and tobacco were curtailed to maintain domestic prices; Government bounties were paid to silk and rice producers.[27]

RESULTS

Evaluation of the degree to which the agricultural programs of the fascists succeeded or failed is difficult. For the most part these programs did not have time to prove or disprove themselves fully before reorientation for war or other reasons ended or suspended the experiment.

New farm settlements in Germany in the period 1933–35 were made at little more than half the rate of the years 1931–32, certainly not at a rapid enough rate to take care of population desirous of such units. Yet this comparison with the deep depression years is probably valid only as an indication that the Nazis did not emphasize this aspect of rural resettlement; certainly there is no evidence that they pushed the breaking up of the large estates of the east Baltic plain. Additions to small units, however, were expanded, probably to make units eligible as hereditary farms.

In Italy the emphasis on reclamation bore significant results but whether the land so gained was worth the cost is another matter.[28] The cost of the reclamation works of all sorts actually executed in the Fascist era in Italy before the Imperial phase was nearly 8 billion lire.[29] Nearly 5 million hectares or almost one-sixth of the total area of the country appears to have been more or less included in projects, but substantial progress appears to have been made on about 2 million hectares, including one project of about half a million acres in the lower Po River Basin. The 75,000 acres of the Agro Pontino,

[25] Heinz Soffner, Food for Freedom versus Nazi Food Estate, Survey Graphic, vol. 31, May 1942, p. 249.
[26] Sweezy, pp. 187–188.
[27] Schmidt, pp. 52, 53, 144, 145, 147, 148.
[28] Schmidt, p. 97, quotes Arrigo Serpieri, the first Undersecretary for Land Reclamation: "Too many works have been carried out with insufficient consideration of their economic aspect, resulting in heavy burdens on the land which today (1931) are very hard to carry."
[29] Schmidt, p. 86.

reclaimed at a cost of about 1 billion lire, exclusive of future maintenance costs, served as a much-acclaimed official demonstration
area. But by the end of 1935, 2,215 new units (19,048 individuals)
had been settled as against an announced goal of 40,000 to 50,000.[30]

Information is not at hand as to what, if anything, has been accomplished by the relatively new Spanish reclamation organization.

As regards the creation of a new rural elite, it appears that some
650,000 to 700,000 German farm units actually were accepted as
heridatary farms and their owners declared Bauern—this out of a goal
of something like 1,000,000. Brandt holds this to have had most
important psychological results, reversing the former social structure
and creating a new sense of social worth among a considerable fraction
of the agriculturalists.[31]

The Italian Battle for Grain seems to have been won at a cost of
deterioration in other parts of the rural production. Schmidt says:

> The immediate goal of the Battle—virtual self-sufficiency in wheat—has been
> closely approached.[32]

Even this was accomplished by increasing the unbalance of other
sectors of the agricultural economy. Sullam points out that the
increase of some food crops conflicted with over-all self-sufficiency
goals by eliminating the wheat-bean rotation in the South and by
requiring increased amounts of fertilizer and coal.[33] Apparently the
increase in wheat self-sufficiency had been accomplished in considerable part by an increase in yield, acreage standing at 4.7 millions
of hectares in 1923 and at 5.03 millions of hectares in 1935, whereas
yields were up at least two quintals per hectare.

As to Germany, several students of the problem have concluded
that the self-sufficiency program had not brought about any significant
increase in the degree of agricultural self-sufficiency.[34] Brandt says:
"In spite of all the efforts, at the end of 1936 food autarchy is not yet
attained. In fact it is no nearer than it was in 1932." [35]

That the farmer did get higher prices for what he produced is clear
enough; prices were juggled to favor the farmer as against the urban
laborer and exporting industrialist.

> To sum up the latest experience of the German farmer with the authoritarian
> agricultural policy, we have to state that the disparity between farm prices and
> industrial prices has disappeared, that the gross returns for agriculture rose from
> the depths in 1932–33 till 1935–36 by approximately 38 percent, while the total
> income of labor and the white-collar class rose during the same period by only
> 23.3 percent * * * agricultural policy is responsible for the disproportional
> gain in purchasing power of the farmer in comparison with the rest of the popula-
> tion.[36]

In Italy wheat prices were definitely higher than in the world
market. Such increased income, of course, went largely to producers
of surplus wheat, not to all farmers.

Economic controls appear to have been more effective than the
efforts at stimulating production. However, national financial ex-

[30] Schmidt, pp. 93–94.
[31] Karl Brandt, The German Back-to-the-Land Movement, Journal of Land and Public Utility Economics, vol. 11, No. 2, May 1935, pp. 123–132.
[32] Schmidt, p. 53.
[33] Victor B. Sullam, Fundamentals of Italian Agriculture, Foreign Agriculture, vol. 7, December 1943,
p. 286.
[34] Benjamin Higgins, Germany's Bid for Agricultural Self-Sufficiency, Journal of Farm Economics, vol.
21, May 1939, pp. 456–57. See also: K. T. Wasley, German Agriculture: The Drive for Self-Sufficiency
Contemporary Review, vol. 157, No. 891, March 1940, pp. 334–340.
[35] Karl Brandt, German Agricultural Policy—Some Selected Lessons, Journal of Farm Economics, vol.
19, February 1937, p. 289.
[36] Brandt, German Agricultural Policy * * * , p. 298.

igencies in the case of Germany forced sharp compromise with the promised low long-term interest rate of 2 percent—agricultural credit at 4 percent appears to be the level achieved. Taxes, too, remained high but were based on quality of property. Some resistance was encountered to delivering farm products. Wholesalers and retailers were squeezed in the process of obtaining higher prices for farm products.

In regard to agricultural labor (discussed in the Labor chapter) there was apparent an increasing scarcity under the Nazis—counteracted in part not only by forbidding by law that agriculturists take other positions but also by propaganda regarding rural nobility, by the construction of low-rent agricultural workers' dwellings, and by requiring a year of agricultural labor by many of the youth.

In essence, it appears that the farm and the farmer under fascism were regimented and propagandized, but compared to the other sectors of the economy, his lot was not worsened. In part this was a matter of philosophical ideology; more largely an attempt to build food autarchy for war. Landowners found their status improved. So too, the farm was reclaimed, conserved, and more heavily fertilized. The land was worked harder; management perhaps improved.

It seems probable that the agricultural sector of these fascist economies proved to be a tower of strength in war; these countries were not starved out of the war this time. Through no credit of its own, the early postwar period finds the rural parts of these blasted economies much less damaged and much nearer to prewar production than is true of other parts. This is a tribute not to fascism and its favored treatment of agriculture, but to the virtual and comparative indestructibility of the basic rural economy.

CHAPTER X—TRANSPORTATION

The difference between transportation in fascist and in other countries lies less in the facilities available than in the objectives for which the facilities are used. Some fascist and democratic objectives are alike, especially those which call for increase in speed and extent of facilities, decrease in cost of services, and use of construction of roads as a means for combatting unemployment. But while democratic transportation is governed largely by economic demand and costs, fascist transportation, in addition to moving persons and things, is also used to enhance the power of the state, facilitate territorial expansion, and increase the prestige of the nation and rulers. It is governed by political considerations and characterized by regimentation.

This chapter is devoted to Germany and Italy principally. Japan is not included because of space limitations and peculiar elements in the Japanese economy. Transportation in both Germany and Italy experienced a pronounced break between the fascist governments and their predecessors. The development in Japan appears to have been more gradual. Transportation developments in Spain early in 1947 had not advanced as far as in other fascist countries. The Spanish emphasis appears to have been placed on the improvment of shipping.

The railroads were the backbone of the transportation systems of both Italy and Germany, but highways and shipping, especially inland shipping in the case of Germany and coastwise shipping in the case of Italy, increased during the Fascist rule.

German (including Austrian) railroads in 1937 covered 40,706 miles, and thus represented about 17 percent of the mileage of the United States or 350 percent of that of Italy. Each mile of railroad track in Germany served an average of 1,955 persons, as compared with 552 persons in the United States and 3,865 persons in Italy.[1] Similar relationships prevailed in railroad equipment. Until 1937, all three countries failed to replace locomotives, freight cars, and passenger cars when they were discarded. In almost all cases, however, when replacements were made, the new locomotives were more powerful and the new freight and passenger cars were greater in capacity. The increase in rolling stock in Germany in 1938 was due less to new construction than to the acquisition of railroad stock from Austria and the Sudetenland. It was not until the beginning of the Second World War that an intensive campaign to increase rolling stock for war purposes was initiated—then too late to prevent severe transportation crises from occurring.

Germany

During the years of Nazi growth (1933–38) German freight loadings grew from 26,232 million ton-miles in 1933 to 49,962 million ton-miles

---

[1] Economic Almanac of 1945–46, New York, 1946; computations from pp. 25 and 253.

in 1938; in Italy the increase was smaller, rising from 5,661 to 6,907 million ton-miles during the same period; while in the United States 226,885 million ton-miles were registered for 1933 and 257,000 million for 1938.[2] The pronounced rise in Germany may be accounted for by (1) rearmament and other public-works programs; and (2) by the fact that the railroads were not subject to the same degree of competition as they were in a number of countries from other forms of transportation, notably trucking.

In spite of the emphasis and dependence on railways, the Nazi government did not permit the National Railway (Reichsbahn) to make the best economic use of its facilities and income. Hitler ordered the construction of new superhighways and new canals. He directed the Reichsbahn instead of buying more vehicles to pay out hundreds of millions of Reichsmarks to move railroad facilities into cities which were then being reconstructed for purely aesthetic reasons, and also to expand routes which were important militarily or for the war economy.[3]

Most Nazi railway legislation had the purpose of integrating the Reichsbahn with other forms of transportation and of making it serve the purpose of the Nazi leadership. As expressed by two officials of the Ministry of Transportation in 1943:

> The primary goal of the Reichsbahn policy is the infusion of national socialist ideology into the entire personnel of the Reichsbahn * * * Besides placing well-planned orders and furthering the national economy by low rates, the railroads must further the objectives of the national socialist movement in political, cultural, and "folk" matters * * * The railroads will take the lead in turning as far as possible to the exclusive use of German products and in the thrifty use of new raw materials.[4]

On January 30, 1937, Hitler repudiated the reparations obligations of the Reichsbahn under the Treaty of Versailles. The Director of the Reichsbahn, Dr. Julius Dorpmueller, was given the cabinet post of Minister of Transportation while at the same time he was permitted to retain his post as the head of the Reichsbahn. This, of course, meant that the railroads had a powerful spokesman in the Government. It may account for the fact that the Reichsbahn was able to compel common-carrier trucking to adopt the Reichsbahn freight tariff.[5] The repudiation of Versailles also meant the integration of supervision and operation which had been separated under the Dawes plan of 1924.

The law of February 10, 1937, dissolved the Government railroad corporation (Reichsbahngesellschaft) as a separate company and made it a direct agency of the Government. This trend was carried farther by the comprehensive railroad act of July 4, 1939, which had the following principal provisions:

1. The Reichsbahn belongs to the Reich central government. However, its finances will be administered separately from other Reich finances. It operates under its own name and has its own directorate.

2. The leadership of the Reichsbahn rests in the hands of the Reich, i. e., under the Minister of Transport. All railroad employees are Government officials * * * The board of directors of the Reichsbahn is abolished; in its place a board to advise the Minister of Transportation on railroad questions is established.

---

[2] Statistical Yearbook of the League of Nations, 1938–39, Geneva, pp. 200, 201.
[3] Herbert Block, German Transportation Policy During the War, New York, 1944, pp. vii–viii.
[4] Adolf Sarter and Theodor Kittel, Was jeder von der deutschen Reichsbahn wissen muss, 8th edition, Leipzig, 1943, pp. 13, 15.
[5] Block, p. viii.

144 . FASCISM IN ACTION

3. As Government officials, the employees of the Reichsbahn no longer have
their own separate personnel regulation but are subject to the same employees'
law as other Government employees.[6]

As state employees, all railroad officials had to swear personal allegiance to Hitler.

Political and other noneconomic considerations were major factors
in rate making. In 1938 only 27.3 percent of railroad passengers paid
full fare; thus nearly three-fourths received some sort of reduction.
The special Strength through Joy trains provided travel at greatly
reduced rates for many groups of German workers and youth. These
excursions accounted for a considerable share of the reduced fares.
In freight traffic, 70.6 percent of the freight was carried at reduced
rates. The average revenue per passenger-mile dropped from 4.06
pfennig in 1932, to 3.94 pfennig in 1937.[7]

On the whole, while German railroads prior to Hitler had been
developed with an eye to both their economic and strategic advantages, and for these reasons should have been especially favored by
the Nazis, nevertheless, after 1933, highways and airways were
given more and more attention, frequently at the expense of the railroads. By 1937 there was an acute shortage of freight cars. Later
the military problems of the railroads were enormously increased as
the German armies penetrated eastern and western Europe. While
the victories in the West resulted in the requisition of large numbers
of captured locomotives, freight and passenger cars, the war in
Russia produced many problems. Particularly vexing were the
different railroad gauges. Many restrictions were imposed on the
use of railroads in order to compensate for the increasingly severe
shortages encountered.

Finally it should be noted that, when the building of the superhighways was inaugurated in 1933, it was done largely with funds
and technical experts from the Reichsbahn. After the outbreak of
the Second World War, the Reichsbahn, however, gradually withdrew from the project because it needed its own technicians and
engineers for railroad activity.

Italy [8]

In Italy the railroads gave the Fascists a chance to develop their
prestige. Mussolini boasted that trains ran on time in Fascist Italy.
He speeded up and improved schedules. From 1922 to 1940, the
rail distance from Milan to Rome was shortened 20.5 miles, or 5
percent, and the running time was reduced from 12 hours 40 minutes
to 5 hours 38 minutes, which represented an increase in speed of 114
percent. The stretch from Rome to Naples was shortened and completely rebuilt at a cost of 1,700,000,000 lire ($85,000,000) in the
early years of the Fascist regime, with no grade steeper than 1 percent, and with no grade crossing. Direct connection between Bologna
and Florence was established in 1934 through construction of an 11.5
mile long tunnel. This tunnel had strategic significance in that it
facilitated operations on the main axis route from Rome to Milan,
avoiding coastal stretches that would be exposed to bombardment
from the sea.[9]

[6] Sarter and Kittel, p. 11.
[7] Sarter and Kittel, p. 42.
[8] Information on Italian railroads, except as noted in footnotes, taken from: Wernecke, Die ersten Hundert
Jahre der Italienischen Eisenbahnen, 1839-1939, Archiv fur Eisenbahnwesen, 1941, note 2, pp. 305-330.
[9] Ernst-Gunther Schrader, Verkehrsprobleme und Verkehrswandlungen in Italien, Gelnhausen, 1936,
p. 50.

Only about a quarter of the railroad mileage in Italy was double track before the outbreak of the Second World War. At the beginning of the war, there were 6,290 train-miles run daily at 56–62 miles an hour; 4,035 train-miles at 62–68 miles an hour; and 1,326 train-miles at 68–73 miles an hour.

A principal objective of Fascist railroad policy was the electrification of much of the mileage. Italy was among the first countries to undertake an extensive railroad electrification program, and in April 1947 had electric routes amounting to 4,400 miles, the longest of any country in the world. Sweden ranked second with 3,421 miles, the United States third with 3,091 miles, and Switzerland fourth with 2,793 miles.[10] This program aimed at diminishing coal imports and making Italian railroads independent of foreign supply. It also sought to make use of the water power in the Alps and the Appenines, and thus secure the advantage of electric power on the steep grades and in the numerous tunnels which characterized Italian railroad construction. Plans were made in 1932 to have about 5,600 miles electrified by 1944. As of 1939, 3,181 miles of these had been electrified.

Fascist Italy inaugurated special excursion trains, at the behest of Mussolini, in 1931. In the summer months of 1938, there were 1,538 Sunday trains which carried 1,201,000 excursionists to Rome, Naples, and Venice at extremely low fares. Special trains patterned after the German Strength through Joy were run to Budapest and Vienna in 1939. As a result of these innovations Italian railroads remained in a financially precarious position during the Fascist regime. Competition of trucks and busses led to the abandonment of many branch railroad lines, especially because the railroads were expected to limit themselves more and more to long-distance travel for the masses. An increase in the railroad deficit was practically inevitable, due to (1) increased highway competition, (2) the writing off of capital with the abandonment of branch lines, and (3) the high cost of the electrification program. While there was considerable potential demand for railroad transportation, especially if one considered the density of population, only a marked increase in the purchasing power of the people could bring about the economic progress necessary to make the railroads profitable.

During the Second World War Italian railroads became an integral part of the German war transportation machine. German officials replaced Italians at headquarters, and the direction of Italian railroads actually came from Berlin rather than from Rome.

Spain

The destruction of rolling stock, rails, and bridges in the civil war confronted the Franco government with a serious railroad rehabilitation problem. The principal railroad development in Spain after the civil war was the nationalization of all normal gage railroads on February 1, 1941. This was carried out by expropriation in accordance with conditions set forth in the statute of 1924, with certain important modifications which worked to the advantage of the private interests whose properties were being absorbed. In addition to the state-owned normal gage railroad, Spain's railway system included 17 small, state-owned railways of varying narrow gage; about 75 small, private-company, narrow-gage railways of between 2,100 and 2,400 miles of

10 Universal Directory of Railway Officials and Railway Yearbook, 1946–47, London, pp. 411, 415.

track; and about 50 street-railway companies which operated or participated in the ownership of urban or short interurban traction systems. In spite of the nationalization, railroad equipment had not been brought back to 1936 levels by 1942.

Motorization of much traffic, especially passenger traffic, was the goal of both Nazi Germany and Fascist Italy. In 1930 Germany produced 60,000 passenger cars and 14,000 trucks. In 1938 this had been increased to 277,000 passenger cars and 65,000 trucks. The automobile industry in Italy was much smaller. It produced 48,000 motor vehicles in 1930, and 69,000 in 1938.[11] Highway construction was emphasized in both countries.

Germany

In Germany the smaller passenger cars with relatively low fuel requirements were advocated—this in line with the aim of making Germany as self-sufficient as possible. On the other hand, larger trucks were required for military purposes. Taxes on new cars were abolished in 1933, but were offset later by increased gasoline taxes. The Nazi government appointed a special commissioner general to bring the automobile industry in line with war requirements. In order to increase production at the outbreak of the war, passenger models were cut from 52 to 30, and in the case of trucks from 113 to 19.[12] A great fanfare was made about the people's car (Volkswagen) which was first displayed at the domestic automobile exhibition in Berlin in 1939. The scheduled price was about 950 marks ($380 at an exchange rate of 40 cents to the mark).[13] To encourage workers to purchase these cars, a scheme of advance payment was devised which required the purchaser to make all payments before receiving the car. This device was adopted in order to help finance the large plant at Fallersleben which was to produce the people's cars. However, the advent of the war caused the plant to be entirely converted to war production, so that very few people's cars were delivered, and most persons lost the payments which they had made.

Civilian use of cars was sharply curtailed during the war. While 306,000 passenger cars, trucks, and motorcycles were in use in 1939, by April 1, 1942, this figure had dropped to 42,000.[14] The shortage of gasoline was so critical that all except the most essential motor transport was strictly forbidden. The superhighways (Autobahnen), the pride of Hitler, were almost deserted after 1939.

The Autobahnen were probably the most noteworthy transportation accomplishments of Nazi Germany. They constituted a network of 4,350 miles which was doubled after the annexation of Austria and Sudetenland. These highways consisted of two strips having a width of 24 feet each, with a separating grass strip of about 15 feet. No grades exceeded 8 percent. The right-of-way was carefully landscaped in harmony with the surrounding countryside. In some places the center strip was also paved so it could be used as an emergency or auxiliary landing field. The construction cost, over RM

[11] Statistical Yearbook of the League of Nations, 1932–33; 1938–39.
[12] Wolfgang B. Lengercke, Kraftfahrzeug und Staat, Heidelberg, 1941, p. 96.
[13] The Motorisation of Germany, The Economist (London), vol. 135, June 10, 1939, p. 599.
[14] Block, p. 44.

500,000 per kilometer ($320,000 per mile), compared with the 1937 average of about $39,000 per mile for ordinary Reich highways.[15]

The initial capital was RM 50 million (approximately $20,000,000) furnished by the Reichsbahn, which also carried materials for construction at reduced rates. Contributions were made by various cities and states to further the project in their particular areas. The Reich contributed the remainder. It was pointed out that in considering the cost to the Government, the reduced expenditure for unemployment compensation had to be taken into account. Revenue was gained from increased gasoline taxes and taxes on goods carried by truck.

The following figures indicate the size of the Autobahn project as of December 31, 1940.[16]

Mileage of Autobahn open to traffic_____ 2, 323
Mileage of Autobahn under construction_____ 1, 465
Man-days of work since Sept. 23, 1933, beginning date of Autobahn
   construction_____ 164, 908, 000
Construction steel used since Sept. 23, 1933, tons_____ 367, 249
Amount of cement used since Sept. 23, 1933, tons_____ 7, 220, 000

The three principal motives for this expansive highway program were prestige, employment-creating potential, and military preparation. Hitler wanted to live in history as a great builder of roads. The Inspector General for the German Highways, Dr. Fritz Todt, said:

The purpose of the Reichsautobahnen is to become the roads of Adolf Hitler. They are the first technological achievement which bears his name. To do him honor, not only for today but for generations to come, is the greater obligation of the Autobahnen, within which all lesser purposes are contained.[17]

Rapid reemployment was possible. A large proportion of the labor was unskilled or semiskilled. Construction was undertaken at many different points.

As an employment-creating device the Autobahnen were successful. During the main periods of construction 130,000 men were employed; 30,000 were housed in specially constructed workers' camps; the remaining 100,000 lived in more permanent dwellings and came to work on foot, bicycle, or bus.[18]

The military effectiveness of the Autobahnen has been debated. They served to unite the border areas of Germany with the main production and communication centers of the country, but could not be effective in filling the transportation needs of extended warfare beyond the borders of the Reich. Finally, it may be noted that it was hoped that the Autobahnen would attract considerable tourist trade from abroad, but the increase was small.

In addition to the Autobahnen, the network of other primary and secondary roads was expanded under the Nazi regime.

Italy

In Italy the Fascist government took an active interest in the development of highway transport, though not to the extent the government did in Germany. Mussolini said, "Highways are the nervous system of a people." [19] In 1924, he founded a state corporation to

---

[15] Block, p. 87.
[16] Statistisches Jahrbuch fur das deutsche Reich, 1941–42. Berlin, p. 266.
[17] Eduard Schonleben, Fritz Todt, der Mensch, der Ingenieur, der Nationalsozialist, Oldenburg, 1943, pp. 38–39.
[18] Hans Pflug, Germany's Reich Motor Roads, Berlin, 1941, pp. 62–63.
[19] Schrader, p. 65.

modernize old state highways (Azienda Autonoma Statale delle Strade), to take charge of their upkeep, and to build new ones. Revenue was to come from automobile and gasoline taxes, tolls on special roads, sale of advertising space, concessions along the highways, and state subsidies. The corporation employed an average of 40,000 men at a time on construction. By the middle of 1934, 6,567 miles of roads had been put into good condition, as compared with 287 miles in 1928. This modernization involved building nearly 2,000 new bridges, and was carried on mostly in the north (especially on those routes which led to the Swiss-Italian lakes and which served international traffic), along the entire west coast, and on the roads leading out of Rome and other major cities. Secondary roads were seriously neglected, due to lack of funds.

The first major through-highway (comparable to the Autobahnen and our own modern parkways) was begun in 1923, and opened in September 1925. It ran from Milan to the Swiss-Italian lakes, and had a width of from 36 to 46 feet. The average cost of construction exceeded 1 million lire per kilometer (about $80,000 per mile). By June 1934, only 338 miles were open to traffic. Except for the stretch from Naples to Pompei, the new highways operated at a loss because the tolls charged were so high that they kept away many who would have been willing to pay a smaller fee. Mussolini himself confessed that these superhighways were only a "glorious anticipation." [20] Financing was by a combination of private and public funds. Private investment was found to be unprofitable in almost every instance, due primarily to overestimating the amount of traffic the toll highways would carry, and underestimating the competition of other state highways.

As in Germany, motorization was fostered as a military measure. Automobile manufacturers were subsidized by the state, both directly and indirectly. The manufacture of trucks was considered to be especially important. The Ministry of War was allowed to sell at a low price trucks it had used and to purchase new trucks so as always to have a fleet of modern trucks on hand. Truck purchasers were granted certain tax exemption.[21]

Spain

In contrast to the conditions in Italy and Germany, the automobile and highway development in Spain was quite backward. The national highway system in April 1947 consisted of about 45,750 miles of roads, not including 6,100 miles maintained by the provincial governments. The serious damage to road transportation caused by the civil war resulted in a decrease of about 65 percent in automobile registrations between 1935 and 1940.

<h3 style="text-align:center">INLAND WATERWAYS</h3>

Germany

The Nazi government desired the expansion of inland waterways to be second in importance only to the development of superhighways. Aid to inland waterways seems to have been publicized more than any other development in the transportation field. The extensive river and canal system of Germany even before 1933, meant that an

[20] Guerin, p. 224.
[21] Information on Italian highways taken from Schrader, pp. 63-84.

unusually high proportion of freight was carried by water. This freight averaged about one-fourth of that carried by rail, was twice that of ocean shipping, and was much greater in volume than that carried by highway transport. The total length of inland waterways open to traffic in Germany (including Austria and the Sudetenland) in 1940 was 7,800 miles, as compared with railroad mileage of 40,700.

In August 1939, State Secretary Gustav Koenigs, of the Transportation Ministry, stated the objectives of German inland waterway policy to be: (1) To develop waterways so as to further the interest of German harbors (e. g., divert traffic from Antwerp and Rotterdam to Hamburg); (2) to strengthen the border provinces by uniting them with the waterways network; and (3) to connect the various German rivers to make more complete the network of inland waterways.[22]

Germany assumed complete control over her waterways after November 14, 1936, when Hitler repudiated article 331 (1) of the Treaty of Versailles, which put the international waterways within Germany under the control of an international commission. The German Government then fixed all rates on its own waterways and planned future expansion of the canals in the interest of the greater German Reich.

The most important canal construction during the Nazi regime was the Mittelland Canal connecting the Rhine and Elbe Rivers. Many sections of this canal had long been in operation, but not until October 30, 1938, when the lock at Magdeburg was put into operation, was the entire stretch opened to traffic. The Mittelland Canal was particularly important because it carried coal and ore eastward from the Ruhr. The location of the huge Hermann Goering Works (Reichswerke A. G. fuer Bergbau und Eisenuetten "Hermann Goering") and of the People's Car Works were materially influenced by the Mittelland Canal. The smelting plants of the Goering Works were connected to the Mittelland Canal by a branch canal over 9 miles long; the People's Car Works had a direct connection with the canal. It was anticipated that about 14 million tons of cargo would pass along the canal from the Hermann Goering Works alone.[23]

Next to the Mittelland Canal, the Adolf Hitler Canal in eastern Germany was the most important waterway opened up under the Nazis. It brought inland shipping facilities to the industrial area of Upper Silesia, by connecting it with the Oder River, and thus joined Upper Silesia with the center of the Reich. Traffic was opened in December 1939. There were plans, at the outbreak of the Second World War, for a Rhine-Main-Danube Canal and a Rhine-Neckar-Danube Canal.

The shortage of all types of carriers in September 1939 was acute and led to a sharp increase in the procurement programs of railroad and waterway equipment. By the beginning of 1941, there were 2.3 times the number of tugs in use that there were in 1939. Additional new tugs were under construction,[24] and in 1939 a 50-percent increase over 1937 had occurred in the amount of tonnage handled by tugs.

The Nazi purposes in the waterways system were: (1) to effect a more rational distribution of industry, (2) to relieve the districts of

[22] Fritz Markmann and Johann Thies, Die deutschen Flusse und Kanale, Leipzig, 1942, p. 14.
[23] "Mittelland Canal as an Economic Factor," Bulletin of the Hamburg World's Economics Archives vol. 5, November 1938, p. 215.
[24] W. Kleinmann, Die deutschen Verkehrsmittel in der Friedens-und Kriegswirtschaft, Der Vierjahresplan (Berlin), January 1941, p. 27.

greatest industrial concentration, and (3) to introduce new industries in areas that were economically less advanced. The reorganization of the German economy under the 4-year plan facilitated the use of the canals to such ends.

Although the waterways suffered some disadvantage from competition by rail and truck, their importance was sufficiently recognized to assure continued operation as carriers of bulk goods on a large scale. For a time the freight tariffs set by the railroads on the feeder stretches and along routes paralleling rivers and canals were highly disadvantageous to the waterway traffic. A coordination of the various methods of transport aimed at alleviating this competitive, disadvantage.

With the absorption of Austria in 1938, inland waterways assumed an even greater importance. Commerce along the Danube River became an important part of the German expansion plans. Control of the Danube facilitated the penetration of the Balkans.

MARITIME SHIPPING

Germany

Ocean shipping under the Nazis was considered less important than inland shipping because inland shipping could be used to fuse the various parts of Germany together and thereby increase economic self-sufficiency, while ocean shipping tended to make Germany dependent on foreign raw materials and finished products. Nevertheless, ocean shipping was of great importance to the German economy as a whole, and had to be maintained at a high level for purposes of military preparedness, prestige, and appearance both in German and in foreign eyes. It was also a source of badly needed foreign currency.

The increased economic activity after 1933 was reflected in the increased shipping receipts. Gross shipping receipts jumped from $243,000,000 in 1929 to $266,000,000 in 1937.[25] German merchant tonnage also increased from 4,093,000 tons in 1929 to 4,493,000 tons in 1939. Of course, the situation changed radically during the war. Thus, the Foreign Commerce Weekly estimates that merchant tonnage of German vessels of 1,000 tons and over dropped from 3,973,893 gross tons on June 30, 1939, to 1,068,000 tons on June 30, 1945.[26]

The German merchant marine had been severely curtailed as a result of the First World War, and although it made a notable recovery during the 1920's, it was hard hit by the depression and experienced serious financial difficulties. In 1933 the two largest shipping companies, the North German Lloyd and the Hamburg-America Lines, were united as a result of the heavy indebtedness of both. The Government sponsored the new German Levant Line, for Mediterranean commerce (this had formerly been operated as part of the Hamburg-America Line), and stimulated the operation of fishing and whaling vessels.

Much financial aid was given the lines by the German Government. A credit of 77,000,000 marks (70,000,000 marks to the Hamburg-America and North German Lloyd companies, and 7,000,000 for tramp operations), guaranteed originally in 1932, was extended in 1933 to the beginning of 1935. This enabled the ship companies to cover a floating debt amounting to between 170,000,000 and 180,000,000

[25] Foreign Commerce Weekly (Washington, D. C.), April 29, 1944, p. 3.
[26] Foreign Commerce Weekly (Washington, D. C.), February 23, 1946, p. 4.

marks. On May 26, 1933, the Government decided to distribute an outright subsidy of 20,000,000 marks to the vessels in service. This decision was taken instead of compensating the shipping companies, which were suffering from the unfavorable foreign exchange position of the Reichsmark, for their losses due to the exchange rates. About 75 percent of the merchant marine benefited. Finally, in 1933, a shipbuilding fund of 8,700,000 marks was set aside from the general fund for the national work-creating program.[27] Under the Nazi policy of autarchy the port of Bremen was particularly vulnerable. It had traditionally imported far more than it exported, and the diminishing imports, especially of cotton from the United States, was a blow to that port. Hamburg was a little more advantageously situated during the 1930's since exports were increased and a major share of the exports of Germany went by way of Hamburg. With the occupation of the Netherlands and Belgium, the Nazis intensified their efforts to divert traffic from the western ports of those countries to German ports. As mentioned above, the Germans already were using their inland waterways to bring this about. During the war publicity was issued to show the preparations made to handle the purchase of cotton for the whole continent and also to make Hamburg the center for the wool and tobacco trade. It was anticipated that Bremen and Hamburg would play an outstanding part in future colonial trade.

The outbreak of the Second World War drove virtually all overseas shipping off the high seas, except for a few trips for highly essential raw materials, or for short trips to neutrals such as Sweden. In order to coordinate shipping still more completely, and to maintain shipping lines at a maximum of economic strength, a Maritime Shipping Office, (Seeschiffahrtsamt) was established in April 1940.

Italy

In contrast with its negligible inland waterways traffic, Italy's overseas and coastal trade were extensive and important. Before Fascism, emphasis had been placed on passenger traffic, in part due to the high Italian emigration rate before the First World War. With the virtual exclusion of most immigrants by the United States after 1920, Italy tried to maintain her passenger traffic by seeking American tourist business. This involved the construction of luxury liners heavily subsidized by the Fascist government. It was in this manner that the *Rex* and the *Conte di Savoia* were constructed. Both were 50,000-ton vessels. The former made a record transatlantic crossing in 1932, which resulted in so much business that the Italian Line carried more passengers between North America and Europe in 1933, than did any other line, although the advantage did not last long.

The subsidies required to achieve this position of predominance in passenger traffic were heavy. During the fiscal year 1933–34 almost 287,000,000 lire ($14,350,000) were paid in operating subsidies to steamship lines. Contrast this with 26,900,000 lire ($1,350,000) paid in 1914. In addition, there were numerous concessions, Government loans and bonuses for speed and safety.

An extensive program of consolidation of steamship lines was carried out under Fascist direction. The first major consolidation was that of Lloyd Sabaudo, Navigazione Generale, and Cosulich, into

[27] U. S. Bureau of Foreign and Domestic Commerce, Merchant Marine Policy and Shipping and Shipbuilding Subsidies (U. S. Congress, 74th Cong., 1st sess., S. Doc. No. 60), March 13, 1935, pp. 12-15.

the one company Italia, which was to handle transatlantic and all other Atlantic traffic. This took place on November 12, 1931. On February 15, 1932, the Tirrenia was formed to serve in the Mediterranean and Red Seas, and 2 weeks later the Adriatica was formed from those lines serving the Adriatic and Aegean Seas. These consolidations facilitated more direct control by the state.

Before the Fascist regime, Italian harbors suffered from neglect. What state aid there was had been spread over 98 harbors. On December 31, 1922, the Fascist government dissolved all independent harbor authorities and established a central administrative agency which was instructed to concentrate on 14 major harbors. Genoa, which customarily handled 30 percent of Italy's overseas import trade, was given particular attention. From 1922 to 1933, more than 600,000,000 lire ($30,000,000) were spent on harbor improvements and expansion. This expansion was particularly difficult on account of steep rock formations and other natural barriers. Livorno's harbor capacity was almost doubled between 1925 and 1933, and its dock equipment was improved. Naples' service as a passenger port of embarkation grew rapidly after the fall of Abyssinia. Venice, the second leading freight harbor in Italy, had both strategic and commercial significance. It would have to be ready to handle greatly increased traffic in case of an attack on Italy from the west. Thus, it too was improved and expanded.

Like Germany, Italy sought an economic self-sufficiency which was detrimental to her own shipping. Italian foreign trade had long been characterized by a heavy excess of imports over exports. This operated as a handicap to the merchant marine. The electrification of railroads, the elimination of sizable imports of coal, and the attempts to become self-sufficient in wheat, reflected adversely on Italian shipping.

Spain

In June 1945, the Spanish merchant marine of about 850,000 gross tons had increased by 74,000 tons over that of 1939. Spain was reported to be embarking, under Government direction, on a program to attain 2,000,000 gross tons by 1953, a level declared to be absolutely necessary for Spanish national requirements.

The insufficiency of the merchant marine for national needs after the civil war was ameliorated by a series of government measures which encouraged and supported shipping expansion. The Naval Credit Law of 1939 was supplemented by the law of May 6, 1941, whereby loans were furnished to naval construction firms amounting to 1,175,000,000 pesetas, an amount which was considered sufficient for 10 years of construction work. A law of October 4, 1942, gave priority rights to the shipbuilding industry as regards concession of construction materials and declared shipbuilding to be of "national interest." Plans were made to expand the shipbuilding facilities at Barcelona, Seville, and Valencia. In April 1947, the estimated rate of construction in Spain was approaching 50,000 gross tons per year.

The president of Garcia & Diaz, agents for the Compaña Transatlantica (Spanish line) revealed plans for the construction of two 20-knot passenger vessels and a series of 16-knot combination passenger and cargo ships, with a passenger-carrying capacity of 500. He also disclosed the company's desire to operate American vessels. That organization, presupposing favorable sale or charter conditions, appeared ready to purchase or charter a number of United States surplus ships.

The importance of aviation to military power and world prestige was quickly recognized by the fascist government, both in Italy and in Germany. Therefore, they encouraged new commercial air lines. The Lufthansa in Germany and the Ala Littoria in Italy more than doubled their operation between 1932 and 1938. Flights of the German line increased from 5,800,000 miles a year to 13,000,000 miles a year in this time, and the Italian from 2,900,000 to 8,500,000 miles. After 1938, commercial flights in Germany dropped as the need for military use of planes and flight facilities became paramount.

Germany

From the beginning, all aviation activity in Germany was coordinated by the Nazis with military considerations in mind. In May 1933, the Ministry of Aviation (Reichsluftfahrtministerium) was created to control both civil and military aviation. Hermann Goering was made the head of all aviation. His subordinate, General Milch, was placed in charge of civil aviation. One of the most quoted phrases of Goering, "The German people must become a people of fliers," indicated the importance which the Nazis placed on all types of aviation. This was also made clear in the final paragraph of a study, Die deutsche Luftgeltung (Germany's Recognition in the Air), by Heinz Orlovius, an official of the German Ministry of Aviation in 1939. That paragraph reads:

Air force, aircraft industry, aviation research, air sport and air transport with airplanes and airships—they all constitute a unified whole. They are all conscious of their great obligation. With justifiable pride they look back on the accomplishments of the last 6 years and with a passionate will to accomplish new deeds, they stride forward to achieve the recognition of Germany in the air.[28]

German commercial aviation was centered entirely in one company, the Deutsche Lufthansa. The Lufthansa took over the assets of the Austrian company, Osterreichische Luftverkehrs A. G., when Germany absorbed Austria in 1938. The Lufthansa was useful to the Nazis in extending German influence over most of the European Continent. It constantly attempted to expand and extend its field of operation within Germany, on the European Continent, and overseas to the United States, South America, and the Far East. It was heavily subsidized by the state. In 1937, 40 percent of the gross income was subsidy. With few exceptions, passenger flights on the European Continent were daytime flights, there being little demand for night flights, due to the relatively short distances covered on the European Continent. The longest distance regularly flown by the Lufthansa on the European Continent was from Berlin to Lisbon, a distance of 1,607 miles; the average flight within Germany was under 350 miles.

Italy

Italian civil aviation was well behind that of Germany, due to lower industrial development, the concentration of industry in a small area, and the difficulty of constructing adequate landing fields on

[28] Heinz Orlovius, Die deutsche Luftgeltung, Berlin, 1939, p. 35.

account of the mountainous terrain. The first regular commercial air line was established on April 1, 1926, between Trieste and Turin, via Venice and Padua. With political expansion into Africa, air lines to Tripoli, Rhodes, and Tunisia assumed considerable importance. Rome was the most important air center; Venice and Milan ranked next. The Fascist regime required the consolidation of all air lines into a single company, Ala Littoria, formed in 1934. A large portion of Italian air travel was devoted to the American tourist trade.

Fascist interest in aviation was intense, but it tended to be more military than commercial. Mussolini himself did considerable flying and used aviation as a means to foster his own and his government's prestige. A considerable number of aviation experiments were successfully undertaken, and several speed and distance records were established. Such flights as Balbo's massed flight of 24 planes to Chicago in 1932, had considerable publicity value, and were undertaken with that in view.

COORDINATION OF TRANSPORTATION

The subjection of all modes of transportation to a high degree of government direction and control characterized fascist government policy. This government control can also be seen in the policy covering competition between various types of carriers.

Germany

In Germany, coordination of the transportation system had the avowed purpose of avoiding economically wasteful competition, but at the same time it attempted to retain the advantages of healthy rivalry. The law of February 27, 1934, established the "unity of transportation policy" to be enforced by the Reich Minister of Transportation. He was made responsible for the unity of the transportation policy and for settlement of all conflicts between various kinds of transportation services. He had the deciding voice in the establishment of rates and fares. The law of December 4, 1934, providing for land transportation of persons, stated the national objective as follows:

In the National Socialist State, the direction of transportation is one of the duties of the State. The means of transportation may be privately or publicly owned. All transportation agencies, however, must hold themselves to standards set uniformly for the whole Reich. To each branch of transportation must be directed those obligations which it is best able to fulfill within the framework of the total transport and economic situation of the country.[29]

Similar statements of objectives appear in the law on long-distance freight traffic of June 26, 1935, and the decree on the organic growth of transport of September 25, 1935.

The most critical sphere of competition in transportation, namely that between rail and highway freight, was strictly controlled by the Freight Traffic Law of June 26, 1935, which became effective April 1, 1936. This law provided that all common carrier trucking over 50 kilometers (31 miles) had to have government approval and the number of common carriers was strictly limited.

This policy had unfortunate repercussions. The responsibility centralized in the government meant that any mistakes in policy

---

[29] Hermann Haemmerle, Zur wirtschaftlichen and rechtlichen Organisation der deutschen Seehafen, Verkehrswissenschaftliche Abhandlungen: Schriftenreihe des Verkehrswissenschaftlichen Forschungsrats beim Reichsverkehrsministerium, Berlin, 1938, Heft 1, p. 5.

were more serious than would be the case if some discretion were left to the individual transportation agencies. Thus it is generally believed that the Nazis made a decisive mistake in concentrating on the construction of superhighways, canals, and, to a lesser extent, railroad track expansion, while neglecting the procurement of vehicles.[30] The forced coordination was often resented by officials of individual agencies. The inauguration of the Autobahnen as a subsidiary of the Reichsbahn was more a source of friction than a promise of cooperation. Also, the appointment of Dr. Dorpmueller, head of the Reichsbahn, as the Minister of Transportation was greeted with little enthusiasm by the proponents of water and highway transport.

Italy

In Italy the competition between automobile and railroad traffic was severe and the subject of some governmental decrees. In 1932, the Minister of Transportation ordered numerous railroad lines, which were suffering a continual deficit, to be abandoned and bus and truck lines to be opened instead. It was planned to put the entire bus traffic under state control so as to prevent unhealthy throat-cutting competition between trains and buses. At the outbreak of the Abyssinian war, special taxes were placed on truck transportation largely to conserve gasoline, needed for the African campaign.

CONCLUSION

In general, fascist governments have assumed direct and, for the most part, exclusive control of all means of transportation, in order to carry out military preparation, to attain a high degree of economic self-sufficiency, and to exercise a direct control over the citizenry. Germany and Italy used their transportation projects for (1) combatting unemployment, and (2) increasing the prestige of the government both at home and abroad. The construction of the Autobahnen in Germany was incorporated in all of these objectives. But they were most successful as construction projects. Aviation was emphasized for its obvious military objectives.

The centralization of all transportation, however, created fatal weaknesses which were revealed during the Second World War. The overwhelming attention given to highway and air transportation led to the neglect of railroads and canals. The procurement of railroad rolling stock in Germany was notably inadequate. And the lack of sufficient motor vehicles and petroleum fuel meant that the Autobahnen were almost deserted during much of the war. In the final analysis, the transportation system in all warring fascist countries proved inadequate despite the intensive efforts to develop facilities which would not fail in times of crisis.

---

[30] See Block, p ix.

PART III—INDIVIDUAL
CHAPTER XI—LIVING STANDARDS

Fascist efforts at improving living standards, especially for party members, were moderately successful. This was partly due to fascist governments having acquired control during periods of depression and chaos. Consequently they benefitted from normal gains arising from improved world conditions. Also they exploited successfully their controlled and planned economies which administered industrial, trade, and labor monopolies and set wages and prices. But conversely they suffered from depressions fully as much as democratic states did.

In the case of Germany, in particular, official statistics showed an improvement in living conditions between 1932 and 1938. But such statistics are only a part of the story. They do not measure individual requirements in goods and services, availability of supplies, fluctuation of consumer demands, extra and unmeasured costs of buying due to inadequate substitute products, stocks reserved by the state, and the abnormal activities due to expanded armaments programs, all of which enter into and constitute basic parts of living standards.

Since education, recreation, and transportation, which are important to the standard of living, are discussed elsewhere, this chapter concerns itself with what M. K. Bennett calls "the per capita quantum of goods and services used annually by the inhabitants of a country." [1] Attention is given particularly to food, clothing, and shelter as they concerned Germany, Italy, and Spain. Social-security measures, as they represent services, are briefly reviewed. A preliminary discussion of cost of living in the three countries sets a background in terms of the buying power of the available currency.

COST OF LIVING

Germany

The Nazi program of rigid economic controls was designed in part to increase production of war equipment while controlling prices to keep rearmament expense within bounds. Although it is difficult to measure the bolstering influence of Germany's enormous armament expenditures, which could hardly be classified as normal to its economy, clearly, by 1938, Germany had come out of the depression and had reached approximately the 1929 level of income and consumption. According to Prof. Otto Nathan:

> The explanation is not far to seek. The German economy was put to work at full capacity. In 1932 only about two-thirds of the labor force were gainfully occupied; even in 1929 considerable unemployment obtained. In 1938, on the other hand, practically every employable man and many women had jobs. Since the population as a whole increased and since numerous people worked who had not worked before, the total number of wage and salary earners in 1938 was about 60 percent greater than in 1932 and about 14 percent larger than in 1929
> * * *[2]

---

[1] M. K. Bennett, On Measurement of Relative National Standards of Living, in The Quarterly Journal of Economics, vol. LI, February 1937, p. 321.

[2] Nathan, p. 364. Professor Nathan served as Statistical and Economic Adviser to the Reich Department of Economics from 1920 to 1933, and is at present a professor of economics at New York University.

Meanwhile, according to official figures, the cost of living from 1933 to 1937 had risen only 6 percent: a figure which, Nathan suggests, may actually have varied anywhere between 5 and 15 percent.[3] His computation of the total of real income of employed persons, for the significant years of 1929, 1932, and 1938, adjusted for changes in taxation, social insurance, contributions and savings, show: RM 25.6 billions in 1929, RM. 19.2 billions in 1932, and RM. 32.7 billions in 1938.[4]

Since any increase in living costs falls most heavily on the lower-income groups, their expenditures at the family level furnish a guide to living conditions. An investigation by the Labor Front, in 1938, of household account books kept for a year by 2,600 workers' families in rural and urban districts all over Germany, was a good measuring rod. In the lowest group, consisting of about 40 percent of the cases, the average income was RM. 1,549 (about $620). One-third of these families derived small supplemental incomes from subleasing or the sale of garden truck, but 94 percent received state relief. Only 50 percent bought newspapers or went to the movies, but they all made donations to party organizations and to the Winter Relief, averaging RM. 4.50 ($1.80) per year. In one-third of the cases both husband and wife worked as did the children in 10 percent.[5]

An increasing degree of price control, with stability as its goal, was characteristic of Nazi policy and practice especially after 1934. With the invasion of Poland, in August 1939, this policy was reinforced. The War Economy Act of September 3, 1939, froze wages and salaries, prohibited excessive profits, and provided that the prices of goods be reexamined and, if necessary, adjusted to wartime conditions. Since this policy was carried out with comparative efficiency in a disciplined and highly integrated economic structure, wholesale prices apparently rose only about 10 percent in Germany from 1932 to 1939, in contrast with increases of from 50 to 100 percent in other western European countries.[6]

These official figures, however, do not allow for hidden reductions in real buying power especially when they took such forms as virtually compulsory contributions to the Labor Front and other party organizations, or in deterioration in the quality of many products due to the development of substitute materials.

Italy

In Italy, as in Germany, self-sufficiency was the primary aim of the controlled and planned economy. In both countries, the purpose was to be achieved within an area already intensely cultivated, whose product must meet the needs of a population increasing yearly as a result of an expanding birth rate and reduced emigration. In Italy in contrast to Germany, the standard of living had always been relatively low, and the agricultural group had remained the largest single element in the population (47 percent in 1936). Self-sufficiency in

[3] Nathan, p. 344. In August 1938, Die Wirtschaftskurve, XVII (1938), p. 301 ff., estimated the raise at between 5 and 15 percent. For the annual index figures, Nathan has converted the indices given in the International Labour Review, vol. XLI (1940), p. 99, to use 1929 rather than 1913–14 as 100, with the following results: 1930, 96; 1931, 88; 1932, 78; 1933, 77; 1934, 79; 1935, 80; 1936, 81; 1937, 81; 1938, 82.
[4] Nathan, p. 345. These figures are taken from a table showing wages and salaries, total deductions (including taxes, social insurance, contributions, and savings); net wages and net real wages for the three years. Salary deductions were tabulated as follows: 1939, 5.4 billions; 1932, 2.1 billions; 1938, 6.8 billions. Sources used were Statistisches Jahrbuch fuer das Deutsche Reich, Wirtschaft und Statistik, and Halbjahresberichte zur Wirtschaftslage.
[5] Heinrich Hauser, Battle Against Time, New York, 1939, p. 187.
[6] Helen C. Farnsworth, Wartime Food Developments in Germany ,Food Research Institute, Stanford University, War-Peace Pamphlets ,No. 1 ,1942.

Italy, represented by a bare margin of subsistence, was seriously threatened by even a moderate decline in available supplies. In general, therefore, the Italian cost of living was more difficult to measure than the German and showed greater variation as to area, being higher in the industrial North than in the agricultural South.

From the establishment of the Fascist state in 1922 until 1926, both prices and the cost of living rose in Italy. They declined after the revaluation of the lira in 1927; fell rapidly during the depression to reach their low point in 1934. Then there was a gradual recovery following an increase in world prices, the Ethiopian campaign, the new devaluation of the lira (October 5, 1936), and, of course, as a result of the Second World War.[7]   It should be noted that Fascist syndical and party organizations participated in the enforcement of control regulations. When, for instance, the decree of November 18, 1930, reduced the wages and salaries of public and semipublic bodies, private syndicates soon followed suit to bring about general reductions.

With the outbreak of the Second World War, both prices and salaries were frozen. But in Italy at any time, and particularly in a short wartime market, stability was more easily ordered than administered. Labeling government efforts at control "a serious test of regulated and corporative economy," La Stampa (Turin) commented wryly on August 27, 1943:

> Salaries and wages have remained frozen; but prices, from semester to semester finally with an always more rapid rhythm, continue to soar   *   *   *   Since the quantities released by (ration) tickets are insufficient, all citizens, it is useless to hide, are compelled to resort to illegal markets. On the so-called black market the prices of goods of prime necessity are often tenfold.[8]

Spain

The local conditions which made Italian Fascism less efficient and living conditions more variable in Italy than in Germany, were extended and magnified in the Spanish state. Spain has normally had a provincial, agricultural economy. To the difficulties of establishing a planned and disciplined economy in such an economic pattern, the years of civil war added their own disruptions of production and transportation. The food supply had always been unbalanced and lacking in variety, and the productivity of the land was low.

In theory, at least, the Franco government attempted extensive and complicated controls over all prices, using the party organization as an administrative unit; the military as the policing power. The mayor of each town, as head of the local syndicate, was given complete power to distribute seeds, calculate crop quotas, and to collect a set quota of produce. But even such extensive authority, administered at a local level, did not seem to have been effective in the control of prices or commodities. Such fragmentary data as were available placed the cost of living in April 1947, at from three to four times prewar levels.[9] Ordered distribution had failed to materialize largely as a result of an extensive black market in nearly all products, in which party officials often seemed to have taken a prominent part.

---

[7] For the period 1928 through 1938, the cost of living index figures are quoted by William G. Welk, Fascist Economic Policy, Cambridge, Mass., 1938, p. 234. They are as follows: 1928, 100; 1929, 101.15; 1930, 97.73; 1931, 88.26; 1932, 84.10; 1933, 80.50; 1934, 76.39; 1935, 77.48; 1936, 83.52; 1937, 91.74; 1938, 99.25.

[8] DCF, La Stampa, Turin, Italy, Friday, August 27, 1943. Part of the source material for this chapter was taken from the files of the Office of International Trade in the United States Department of Commerce. Footnote citations of such material are preceded by the letters DCF (Department of Commerce files) as above.

[9] DCF. From Barcelona, for instance, David McK. Key, American consul general, estimated on April 17, 1945, that current costs were four to five times above the prewar levels. An official index for Barcelona in September 1944 was 255.6 (1936 as 100) for working class families, including rationed goods on which prices were controlled.

FOOD

Germany

Deeply imbedded in German consciousness was the memory of the starvation years of 1917–19, when war shortages and blockade took their heavy toll. The Nazi regime, from its inception, viewed self-sufficiency in food production as a primary object. How far this policy was prompted by the widely publicized concern of the Hitler regime for the "security" of the German people, and how far it was preparation for another war, it is difficult to determine. But on May 24, 1940, Volkswirt claimed that the basis of the war food economy had been laid before the Nazis came to power: as early as June 1, 1930, when Hitler, "preconceiving the preponderant significance of agriculture in the construction of a strong Germany, gave R. Walther Darré the task of organizing the farmers on National Socialistic lines." Stressing the importance of an organized domestic food production as a vital factor in over-all war strategy, Volkswirt concluded, "When one states that modern war must be waged, not only militarily, but with an equal intensity economically, it follows that the role of economics must also be defined by the principles of military science." [10]

Production of food.—As early as 1933, the Reich Food Estate assumed complete responsibility for the administration of food, including both production and distribution. As a result, Germany's food economy in 1939, was well prepared for war. According to most estimates, over 85 percent of the Nation's food supply for that year was produced within the country, the only substantial deficit was in fats and oils. Even the war did not radically alter this balance. According to J. H. Richter, the losses occasioned by shortage of labor, fertilizer, and machinery during the wartime were "more than offset by a diversion of production from feed to food and of consumption from foodstuffs of animal origin to foodstuffs of vegetable origin." Allowing for the substantial imports and requisitions of food from the occupied countries, Richter concluded that "* * * the country's own production remained the backbone of its wartime food supply." [11]

Since the living standards of the German people were inevitably linked with domestic production of foodstuffs, the activities of the Reich Food Estate in the field of food self-sufficiency were important. In 1934, when the "battle of production" began, there was a protein deficit of over 1,000,000 tons (15 percent) of the total requirement. To add to the problem, all available land was already under cultivation, and the Nazi defense program called for conversion of part of this land (2,225,000 acres by 1938) into roads, airdromes, and cantonments.[12] Meanwhile, the movement of farm workers into the city (1,800,000 by 1938) was not compensated to any degree by increased mechanization. In January 1939, less than 2 percent of German farms were equipped with tractors.[13]

The emergency farm measures of 1934, therefore, put particular stress on higher yields, more-intensive farm methods, mechanization where possible, and especially on increases in fertilizer production. As a result, average yields increased in 1937–39 over 1934–36 in the

---

[10] DCF. A free translation from Volkswirt, May 20, 1940. See also Ch. IX, Agriculture and the Farmer.
[11] J. H. Richter, Food in Germany, Foreign Agriculture, Washington, February 1944, pp. 43–44. Richter's estimates have been used throughout the paragraph.
[12] Konrad Meyer, Gefuege und Ordnung der deutschen Landwirtschaft, Berlin, 1939, p. 241.
[13] DCF, Guenther Pacyna, farm labor expert of the Reich Food Estate, in Nationalsozialistische Landpost, March 3, 1939.

following percentages: Wheat, 16; rye, 13; barley, 12; oats, 15; potatoes, 15; sugar beets, 9.[14]   Subsidies were used to stimulate production of much-needed foods such as milk, butter, cheese, vegetables, hogs, and oil seeds.[15]

Distribution of food.—Nazi blueprints called for wider distribution and consumption of foods by means of regulated produce collections on a quota basis, improved transportation facilities, and especially a controlled price policy.   The principles of a free market were soon discarded, and price control became one of the basic instruments of total economic control.   The law of October 29, 1936, extended the authority of the Price Commissioner to include agricultural prices. This price power, it should be noted, was coordinated with and subordinated to the program of the Commissioner for the 4-year plan,[16] thus tying it into the German economic strategy and warfare.   The effect of such a program on the annual price index has already been indicated.   In terms of the average German family, prices were held within the range of wages, but with some striking changes in the dietary habits of the German people.   The consumption of potatoes rye bread, and fish, for instance, grew while that of milk, meat, white bread, tropical fruits, and, especially, fats and eggs, decreased.   The average family of low-wage workers consumed weekly 9.1 liters of milk in 1927, as against 3 liters in 1936; 7.21 kilos of bread as against 2.4 kilos; 2.8 kilos of meat and meat products as against 1 kilo; 9 eggs as against 3.   The use of vegetables dropped only from 2.43 to 2.0 kilos; while fish, which was not listed in the 1927 figures, appeared in 1936, in the amount of 1.25 kilos.[17]

But comparing consumption during 1936 and 1938 shows a very different result.   Using the diet of the adult consumer as a base, and calculated in percentages, the heavy manual workers had on the average 28.7 percent more bread; 73.1 percent more meat; 120.6 percent more fats; 89.1 percent more vegetables; and 11.9 percent more potatoes than the average adult consumer.   Soldiers averaged 105.4 percent more bread; 62.8 percent more meat; 47.7 percent more fat; 120.7 percent more potatoes; and 85.9 percent more vegetables for a a total over-all average increase of 61.7 percent.[18]

Controls.—Although official rationing was not instituted until August 27, 1939, with the invasion of Poland, informal rationing procedures, especially in the form of "guided consumption," and purchase licenses were features of the prewar economy.   Faced with a fat shortage, the Berlin Butchers' Guild, as early as mid-December, 1935, issued fat ration cards.   Many Berlin storekeepers maintained lists of their regular customers who had almost exclusive purchasing rights to the decreased stocks of foodstuffs.   In spite of official disapproval, tie-in sales (Koppelgeschaefte) were used for such scarce articles as butter.   Indeed, Henry P. Leverich, American vice consul, reported in 1936, that the Government considered official rationing "a highly desirable step" but they feared the psychological effect

[14] Frederick Strauss, The Food Problem in the German War Economy, Quarterly Journal of Economics, Cambridge, Mass., vol. LV, May 1941, p. 377.
[15] Farnsworth, Wartime Food Developments in Germany. *See* also ch. IX, Agriculture and the Farmer.
[16] Nathan, Ch. 8, Control of Prices, pp. 214–275.
[17] Hugh Corby Fox, DCF, United States vice consul, Decrease in the Standard of Living of German Workers, Berlin, September 18, 1936. A liter equals .9 qt.; a kilo 2.2 pounds.
[18] Table by U. S. Department of Agriculture, Office of Foreign Agricultural Relations, German Food Consumption and Requirements, Washington, January 1940, p. 19. Sources were Wirtschaft und Statistik, Die Ernaehrung des Arbeiters, and W. Ziegelmayer, The Nutrition of German Soldiers.

on the public of issuing "ration cards reminiscent of those used during war years."

By December 1936, a campaign for the so-called "political stomachs" called for increased use of potatoes, sugar, jam, skimmed milk, and honey to replace imported meats, fats, and vegetables.[19] The Institute for Business Research believed that bread, grains, potatoes, sugar, drinking milk, and coarse vegetables could be supplied by domestic production but the use of meat was discouraged during May of 1936, while beef consumption was recommended only for October and November.[20] The shortages which had resulted from three successive drives for rearmament and industrial self-sufficiency were serious, especially as a result of the poor grain crop in 1936. Concurrently, food substitutes began to appear more frequently on the market, and white flour was almost entirely replaced by darker and coarser grades. Typical of these new products was "migetti," made of potatoes and whey, which was used as a substitute for rice.[21]

The official food rationing system, instituted on August 27, 1939, shortly before the invasion of Poland, covered all principal foodstuffs with the exception of bread, flour, and potatoes. By September 27, bread was included. Workers engaged in heavy and "heaviest" work were entitled to extra rations of 490 grams of meat per week and 350 grams of fat. The number of workers thus covered was given by the German press as 1,100,000 of whom 600,000 were miners. Children under 6 received an additional 0.5 liter of milk per day, and expectant and nursing mothers an extra 0.3 liter per day, but milk sales to the average adult were limited.[22] During the first year of the war, the consumption of unrationed fruits and vegetables is estimated to have increased by about 350 percent. Approximately 13 percent of the fruits and vegetables came from small gardens, which covered only 0.1 percent of the total agricultural and forestry areas.

As the war progressed, newspaper reports gave evidence of black markets in operation. The Reich, by decree and by storm troop investigation, moved to suppress them. Penalties, including even the death sentence, were set up as warning, but the illicit trading continued. The organized black market dealt more often in commodities totally lacking in the open market: tea, chocolate, fresh fruit, and coffee. The "back door" trade originated with the farmers who found it difficult to resist such profitable but illegal practices as processing milk into butter by night, to be sold directly to the consumers.[23]

On the whole, however, the black market seems to have been less widespread in Germany than in any other European country, partly because food supplies were more adequate. On July 12, 1941, a report of the Military Intelligence Division of the United States War Department gave a quick summary of the situation after two years of war. According to this document:

There are few reports of the rations not being available and it would seem that such shortages are local and temporary, due to a delay in transport or some similar reason. There was no shortage of potatoes this winter. Information suggests

[19] DCF, Henry P. Leverich, Growth of "Informal" Rationing of Certain Foodstuffs in Germany, Berlin, December 27, 1935.
[20] DCF, Henry P. Leverich, Campaign to Readjust Consumption to Conform with Domestically Produced Supplies * * *, Berlin, December 18, 1936.
[21] DCF, Sam E. Wood, Economic and Trade Report No. 704, March 19, 1940.
[22] DCF. Food rations in force on September 15, 1939, were as follows (in grams per week): Meat, 500; butter, 90; cheese, 80; fats and oils, 250; sugar, 335; coffee substitutes, 100; coffee, 20. Milk was allowed in the amount of 0.20 liter per day. See Sam E. Woods, Economic and Trade Report No. 85, Berlin, September 15, 1939.
[23] DCF, Halleck L. Rose, vice consul and third secretary, letter from Berlin. February 18, 1941.

that wages are high enough to permit of the full rations being bought and to allow something over for unrationed foods * * *. In Germany the control exerted by the administration over food supplies is probably as |complete as can be achieved. The system of rationing is more comprehensive than in any other country in Europe, and distribution between classes is probably more equitable than in most European countries.[24]

How far this result had been achieved as a result of the forced labor of Germans, foreigners, and prisoners, or through the exploitation of conquered territory, it is difficult at this writing to determine. But most evidence seems to indicate that the battle for production still furnished the backbone of the German food supply.

Italy

In 1938, · Italy was about 94 percent self-sufficient in foodstuffs, but the 6 percent deficiency included the two staples, wheat and olive oil.[25] It is not surprising that the Fascists early instituted land reclamation schemes and launched the extensive Battle of Grain "to free the Italian people from the slavery of foreign bread." [26]

From 1928 to 1938, the total production of wheat did increase as a result of reclaimed lands and increased yields per unit. But these increases were sometimes made at the expense of pasture land and the yield of other ,crops.[27] After 1938, wheat production declined as a result of the war, and the resultant loss of agricultural labor to the army and to industry; smaller supplies of fertilizer; lack of implements and machinery, and adverse weather. A decline in all crops, for the same reasons, and a drop in supplies of meat and dairy products due to plowed-up pastures, further decreased food supplies.

Consumption and distribution of food.—Such shortages of food as are indicated above were, of course, most serious in the cities and large towns. The peasants, who considered stores of food more desirable than lira with little purchasing power, hoarded what they could of crops. For the industrial population (29.3 percent in 1936), consumption in terms of buying power is, perhaps, most quickly revealed in the following table which shows real monthly and hourly wages, and production and unemployment figures for the years 1922 through 1934.[28] These figures are significant because they show a steady decline in purchasing power, as represented by real wages, in the years least affected by the war economy:

[1929=100]

Year	Production	Unemployment	Real wages	Year	Production	Unemployment	Real wages
1922	72.3	112.3	106.4	1929	100.0	100.0	100.0
1923	88.8	53.4	108.4	1930	93.8	115.5	97.6
1924	87.4	39.8	106.5	1931	89.2	185.3	97.4
1925	93.9	23.1	100.4	1932	117.5	225.7	96.3
1926	91.1	27.3	96.5	1933	106.9	243.5	97.7
1927	80.9	84.5	102.8	1934	101.2	221.3	97.9
1928	86.2	80.5	103.7				

[24] DCF, U. S. War Department, Military Intelligence Division, Food Consumption in the German Hegemony, July 12, 1941, pp. 6, 8.
[25] Italian Wartime Economy: Part II—Food Production and Trade, Foreign Commerce Weekly, Washington, December 6, 1941, p. 6.
[26] Mussolini's Words, Welk, pp. 191-194. See also Italian Wartime Economy * * * Average wheat production, 1931–35 was 267,140,000 bushels. The record 1938 crop of 297,317,000 bushels was nearly equalled in 1937 and 1939 but unfavorable weather was partly responsible for declines in 1940 and 1941 to 260,880,000 and 262,717,000.
[27] DCF, Col. G. H. Paine, military attaché, C-2 report, April 12, 1939. Deficiency items included meat and poultry, eggs, fish, wheat, edible olive oil, rye, corn, oats, coffee, tea, and cocoa. See Welk, pp. 196-197.
[28] Welk, p. 238, reproduced this table prepared by Pier Bertani for Economia, May 1936, p. 383. Prepared from wage statistics of the Confederation of Italian Industry.

When it is considered that the indices of unemployment increased between 1929 and 1934, from 100 to 357.6 in industry, and from 100 to 221.3 in agriculture, it will be obvious that the increases in real wages did not represent over-all gains for Italian laborers.

Controls.—Control of prices had existed in Italy as early as 1927 when costs of bread and macaroni were closely regulated by local authorities.[29] Informal rationing in the form of forced pooling of wheat in district collection centers (ammassi) was begun in 1936. By 1939, compulsory pooling had been extended to corn, rice, hemp, cotton, wool, silk cocoons, olives and olive oil, saffron, manna, and bergamot essence. Oats were added in July 1940; barley, rye, and beans in May 1941.[30]

Meanwhile, the food shortage grew more acute, due primarily to army requirements. Owing to the meager diet of the men as civilians, Italian army rations represented a large increase over normal consumption. Supplies lost in Greece and Africa, or sunk in the Mediterranean, added to existing shortages. When formal rationing of basic foods began, late in 1940, the quota amount of the important alimentary pastes, including macaroni and spaghetti, was only 4.4 pounds per person monthly, about one-third of normal consumption.[31] The diet, especially of the lower income groups, was further limited by exorbitantly high prices in other foods, notably the fresh vegetables which had been cheap and abundant.[32] Adulteration cut down nutritive value, and even early ration quotas were not always met.[33] During 1941 rationing was extended to include nearly all available items of the food supply. By February 1943, it was estimated that the diet of the Italian light worker had suffered a total calorie drop of 45 percent (67 in fats and oils, 42 in carbohydrates, 37 in proteins).[34]

During the same period, penalties for violations of regulations were tripled, and the Government increased its powers to requisition foodstuffs, to commandeer stocks in warehouses, and to supervise all phases of production, sale, and conservation. The shortage of food supplies, inadequate transportation, and a relative inefficiency of the price control system inevitably produced flourishing black markets which expanded as supplies decreased. Early estimates put their operation at from 5 to 10 percent of food sales.[35] The chief patrons were, of course, people with cash reserves, the chief sufferers, the low wage or salary earners in the large cities.

Did the Italian laboring classes benefit under Fascism? On the basis of his exhaustive studies, William G. Welk concludes that they did not. He comments

Disregarding such benefits as are implied in extended social insurance and the social welfare activities of the regime our general conclusion about the condition of Italian labor under fascism as measured by prevailing wage and employment conditions must be that on the whole it has not only failed of improvement but has been made worse—certainly in agriculture, and most probably in industry.[36]

[29] DCF, A. A. Osborne, American commercial attaché, Rome, May 4, 1927.
[30] DCF, Bureau of Foreign and Domestic Commerce, European Unit, Italy's Food Position • • • April 1943, p. 12.
[31] DCF, John L. Goshie, Assistant Trade Commissioner, Rome, January 10, 1940.
[32] DCF. On April 27, 1940, Lester L. Schnare, American consul in Milan, noting the scarcity and cost of vegetables, added that German importers in the wholesale markets were "purchasing vegetables by the carload practically without question as to price."
[33] DCF, Alexander Kirk to Secretary of State, December 29, 1940, by cable.
[34] Italy's Food Position, pp. 16–19.
[35] Philip M. Copp, Italy's Food—in War and Peace, Foreign Commerce Weekly, Washington, vol. 12, August 28, 1943, p. 5.
[36] Welk, pp. 241–242.

Spain

Although figures are fragmentary, of only local significance, or are open to suspicion, one fact is clear: after 1935, Spain had an inadequate supply of food. The official figures show that daily çalorie consumption for the typical Spaniard had been reduced from 2,752 in 1935, to 1,605 in 1942.[37] According to the Government viewpoint, the food scarcity was due to lack of imports and to lowered Spanish production by destruction of crops, farm implements, and fertilizers during the civil war, to lack of internal transportation, and to widespread hoarding of foodstuffs for sale on the black markets. Spanish critics of Franco blamed heavy exports to Germany, disorganization of the rationing system, and corruption on the part of Government officials.[38]

Franco attempted to control living conditions through licenses for imports, distribution of imported raw materials among producers, governmental determination of goods to be manufactured from imports, transportation priorities, and price controls at all stages of production and distribution. Through an elaborate enforcement and administrative system, using the syndicalist pattern, he attempted to regulate the food supply of every Spanish citizen, with little success. Worn railroad rolling stock was constantly breaking down, available foodstuffs for the rationing system were completely inadequate, and producers, merchants, and distributors became experts in evading government regulations.[39]

As a result, reports from Spain told of three prices for most products: the official price, at which practically no goods were available; the the prices in the "official black market" (*estraperlo*), operated largely by the Party itself; and the regular black-market prices (*mercado negro*) prices, which were the highest of all.[40] The law of June 24, 1941, added the death penalty for black-market transactions. But, according to Temple Wanamaker, in 1942:

Penalties * * * will have no effect on curbing bootleg activities in Spain unless there is an administrative force that is incorruptible. Most charges can be fixed with a little influence and money * * *. The idea is now so thoroughly rooted in the Spanish mentality that the only possible way of stamping it out is to make it unprofitable.[41]

HOUSING

Germany

In all three countries, the fascist governments, upon advent to power, found some provisions for public housing already in effect, as well as a housing shortage which threatened to undermine the state's program for larger families and an increasing birth rate. In general, the Hitler government concentrated its plans for building in the direction of low-cost housing for workmen and employees. The old "rent tax mortgages" [42] supplied between 40 and 70 million

---

[37] Typical of the unreliability of any statistics is the fact that, although the population of Spain in 1942 was around 26 million, some 30 million names were inscribed on ration cards, which failed to allow for approximately 500,000 people in transit.
[38] DCF, Temple Wanamaker, Jr., American vice consul, Food Conditions in Spain, Barcelona, April 4, 1942.
[39] DCF, John A. Caragol, High Cost of Living in the Barcelona District. Office of the United States consulate general, Barcelona, Spain. March 4, 1942, p. 2.
[40] DCF, European Unit, Bureau of Foreign and Domestic Commerce, Spain: State Control or Regulation of Private Enterprise, October 1945, p. 6.
[41] Wanamaker.
[42] The rent tax, a measure of the Weimar Republic, financed the construction of some 1,853,000 new dwellings between 1924 and 1931. But by October 1, 1931, it was reduced to 20 percent and rent-tax revenues were diverted to other uses. As a result, the German building industry was, in April 1932, operating at only 15.4 percent of its capacity. See Diversion of Rent-Tax Revenues Seriously Affects Construction in Germany, Commerce Reports, Washington, August 1, 1932, pp. 196–197.

Reichsmarks each year for new loans, closing the financial gap for about 75 to 90 percent of total construction costs. Indirect financing by the Reich, in the form of guarantees for mortgages (other than first), tax and fee alleviations on new buildings, and loans to provinces and municipalities assisted in the construction of modest homes and tenement flats.

The small settlement (Kleinsiedlungen) program planned to create annually about 100,000 small plots of at least 800 square meters of usable land for "racially highly qualified carriers of best blood heritage."[43] Its purpose was to promote the stability of the working population by giving them a home which provided room for a truck garden and small domestic animals at a monthly cost of RM. 30 to 35. This program at its height produced only about one-fourth of the annual quota: 24,513 settlements in 1936, and 25,868 in 1937.[44] The people's flats (Volkswohnungen) were designed to meet the housing needs in industrial areas at rents ranging from RM. 20 to 30. Most of these flats were built by the municipalities or social building enterprises (Gemeinnuetzige Bauunternehmungen).[45] In Berlin, for instance, where it was estimated in 1934, that some 85,000 families were inadequately housed,[46] Reich funds were used by the city to clear slum areas in the Frankfurter Strasse and Horst Wessel Platz and to build low-priced workers' apartments which rented at RM. 25 to 30 monthly for 1½ rooms, and RM. 41 for 2 rooms including kitchen and bath.[47]

The Weimar Republic had, between 1924 and 1932, furnished loans for 67,000 homesteads (Landarbeiter-Eigenheime) and flats (Landarbeiterwohnungen) for farm workers and laborers in their concern to check the "flight from the land." The Nazis, in 1934, authorized the Reich Labor Exchange to take over the program. At the expiration of its authority in 1937, the Exchange had granted subsidies for 25,000 such dwellings.[48] In 1938, both funds and materials were being diverted to new public and industrial buildings and armament construction; the biggest construction job in that year was the west wall. And, although Hitler continued to talk of postwar housing plans, by March 17, 1942, an official decree ordered that —

all building construction in Germany * * * must be reduced to a minimum in order to provide the arms industry with necessary labor forces, to assure the food supply, and to decrease the difficulties in the transportation situation.[49]

Italy

The housing program under Mussolini followed the same general pattern using and extending pre-fascist measures, and functioning in the form of loans which bolstered and syndicalized the private building industry. Special governmental credit facilities were furnished to the Istituto Case Popolari and the Institute for Houses for Civil Servants (both established in 1908) for construction of apartments to be sold

[43] D C F, Sam E. Woods, commercial attaché, Housing Programs in Germany, September 27, 1939, pp. 4–5; Frieda Wunderlich, the National Socialist Agrarian Program, in Social Research, vol. 12, No. 12, March 1946, p. 40.

[44] D C F, Sam E. Woods, commercial attaché, Housing Programs in Germany, Berlin, September 27, 1939, pp. 3–5. For details on the program see Bestimmungen ueber die Foerderung der Kleinsiedlung of September 14, 1937 and Schmidt-Bellinger, Die Kleinsiedlung, Berlin, 1937.

[45] D C F, Robert M. Stephenson, Workers' Houses in Berlin, Municipal and Other Projects, Berlin, April 30, 1936. Stephenson estimated that some 10,000 flats and houses had been built by the city.

[46] 43,000 in individual huts and shanties; 22,000 in basement apartments; and 20,000 in garrets.

[47] Stephenson.

[48] Woods.

[49] D C F. Quoted from the Frankfurter Zeitung, No. 174–5, April 5, 1942, by Harrison Lewis in a report from Berne, Switzerland, April 24, 1942.

on the hire-purchase system.   The 25-year exemption from house-tax
for new buildings, and generous credit facilities through state-controlled banks were retained and .extended to small apartments until
Italy's housing program, too, was gradually liquidated by armament
and war.

CLOTHING

The drive for German self-sufficiency failed most obviously in the
area of clothing for, as late as 1938, only 26.3 percent of the requirements of textile fiber was supplied from domestic sources.   When it is
considered that about half of all available textiles was used to equip
the army, the problem of clothing for the people becomes clear.   Such
substitutes as were developed were generally inferior both in quality
and quantity.   The following table, based on official figures, illustrates
the sustained shortages in clothing supplies which even the best Nazi
planning and heavy governmental subsidization could only partly
alleviate.[50]

Textiles—Supplies for clothing industries, 1932–38 [1]

	1932	1933	1934	1935	1936	1937	1938
Total supplies (1,000 tons)	504	583	578	601	547	673	757
Domestic production (1,000 tons)	38	42	59	84	128	200	258
Percentage of domestic production to total supplies	7. 5	7. 2	10. 2	14. 0	23. 4	29. 7	34. 1

[1] Source: Wochenbericht des Instituts fuer Konjunkturforschung, XII (1939), p. 65. The figures are based
on domestic production plus imports minus exports.   Included are cotton, wool, flax, rayon, silk, and textile
fibers.

The rationing system, instituted at the outbreak of the war in 1939,
revealed the shortage of supplies at that time, since the quota of
150 points represented a reduction to 30–40 percent for a middle-
class family, and 40–50 percent for a worker's family.[51]   By September 1, 1941, the third clothing card had cut the point allowance to
90 points a year, and there were not always enough supplies to meet
the rations.   Clothing obtained in various ways by the occupation
armies undoubtedly did much to supplement domestic supplies, for
actual shortages were far less than statistics indicate.

Clothing shortages, in much the same proportion, existed in Italy
and Spain, but were somewhat less serious owing partly to the milder
climates.

SOCIAL SECURITY

All three of the fascist countries found systems of social insurance
in operation when they took over, which were incorporated, extended,
and adapted by the new governments.   The changes lay not so
much in the programs as in the fact that they came to be administered,
almost exclusively, by and for the party in power.   Developments
in Germany showed this pattern with special clarity.   Compulsory
social insurance had existed for half a century before Hitler.   By
1927 such insurance covered unemployment, sickness and accidents,
and old-age pensions, on a contributory basis except for accident
insurance which was financed entirely by the employers.   When

[50] DCF, Sam E. Woods, commercial attaché, Rationing of Clothing in Germany, Berlin, December 15,
1939.   According to Nathan, p. 359, importation of cotton increased only slightly between 1932 and 1938.
from 96,000 to 101,000 tons.
[51] DCF, Sam E. Woods, Berlin, December 15, 1939, Economic and Trade Note.

Hitler came to power he retained the general structure, but transferred the authority to special public organizations functioning as a part of the Nazi party. Surplus funds collected for social insurance were channeled directly into the Reich Treasury, thus becoming a source of public revenue available for [government credit, and relieving it of expenditure which it otherwise would have been forced to carry.[52]

In the same way public welfare, which before 1933 was largely under local and district authorities, was partially transferred to such Nazi party organizations as the NS Public Welfare and the Winter Relief.[53] In theory, collections for such charities were voluntary. Campaigns were conducted as popular crusades under slogans such as "Everyone in our nation helps the next fellow." Storm troopers, the Hitler Youth, and members of party organizations often acted as collectors. Distribution of relief on an individual basis was the concern of these agencies. (In the case of the Winter Relief fund, for instance, the work income of low-wage families was supplemented usually by about 10 percent.) At the same time, Winter Relief became "the biggest consumer of foodstuffs and the biggest wholesale house in the Reich. When the government wants to introduce any new ersatz product * * * it always turns to WHW."[54]

If statistics alone told the story, the social-security program under the Nazis was quite complete. Under a full-employment economy, need for social services decreased, while collections and deductions increased, finding their way into the Reich treasury. A typical example of how social-security measures served as a form of government control was the substitution (September 5, 1939) of unemployment relief for unemployment insurance, thereby enabling the authorities to subject the recipient not only to a means test, but to a course of retraining as well. In the same way, unemployment exchanges usually gave preference to party members. In Italy the decree establishing such exchanges specified that preference be given "to members of the Fascist party and of the Fascist syndicates according to the priority of registration."[55]

The Italian social-security system, codified in 1927, reorganized the existing municipal boards of charity (Congregazioni di Carita) to consist of members representing the registered occupational union or syndicate, and appointed by the Podesta, or Government-appointed heads of cities.[56]

Similarly, in Spain the Instituto Nacional del Previsión, established in 1908, was restaffed by Franco to carry out the Government's program for old-age pensions, workmen's and unemployment compensation, sickness and maternity benefits, and family allowances. Family subsidies, maternity benefits, and other measures designed to increase the birth rate in all three countries, included in Spain a provision that marriage loans were automatically reduced with the birth of each child. No complete study of the Spanish system is available, but there is evidence that contributions were very high

---

[52] Nathan, p. 322.
[53] Hauser, p. 188–189. The Adolph Hitler Collection was another important organization of this type which obtained contributions by firms in the amount of 0.2 percent of total pay roll above RM 5,000.
[54] Hauser, p. 189.
[55] Welk, p. 291.
[56] At the end of 1938, the old-age and invalidity pensions in Italy totalled 466,262,218 lire annually; unemployment insurance payments, 166,100,000 lire; tuberculosis insurance payments, 239,800,000 lire; and maternity benefits, 30,200,000 lire. Encyclopaedia Britannica, 1945 ed., vol. 12, p. 825.

(10 to 30 percent of base pay), and that the funds were used by the Falange.

CONCLUSION

Did standards of living improve under fascism? Germany, where records were most complete and controls seem to have been most efficient, was the most successful of all fascist countries. If the average German claimed more buying power in 1938 than during the depression period of 1932, so did workers in most countries, as a result of improved world conditions. More to the point was the fact that the Nazis had, by 1939, often only succeeded in reaching the levels achieved by the democratic Weimar Republic in 1928–29. Of overwhelming significance was the fact that the Nazi Party was the chief, or often the only, administrative unit for the distribution of the basic necessities of life. Sometimes, as in the case of clothing ration books, denied by law to German Jews, discrimination was boasted policy. In less dramatic cases, party loyalty offered the key to special privilege. If the Germans under fascism had, therefore, a reasonable security in return for the surrender of their freedoms, it was a security which Americans understand only in its military sense: where food, clothing, shelter, medical care, and the prospect of a pension are given by the state in exchange for unquestioning obedience, rigid discipline, and expendability of the individual.

The efficiency of a fascist economy of control, as has been seen, depends upon manipulation of monopolies of producers, of management, and of consumers; on rigid control by the state; and on a one-party system which uses the party's powers to create cohesive and disciplinary measures. Regulation was, therefore, more easily accomplished within industrial units than in the more self-sufficient agricultural regions. Indeed, improvement in fascist living standards seems to have occurred in direct ratio to the percentage of people engaged in industry. It was highest in Germany, somewhat lower in Italy, and almost negligible in Spain. This conclusion was best illustrated by the operation of the black markets. Such markets were less prevalent in Germany than in any other European country. In Italy they constituted a more serious threat to the control of inflation (estimated 5 to 10 percent of sales in 1939), while in Spain, with a predominantly agricultural population, illicit sales overwhelmed the controlled market and sent living costs soaring for all classes.

CHAPTER XII—USE OF LEISURE TIME

Nowhere do fascist states show more clearly their inexorable regimentation than in the control of leisure time. Here may be seen the completeness with which the individual must submerge himself into the so-called larger purposes of the state. Work, play, joy, and sorrow must be molded into community interests.

A detailed examination of the German system and a less thorough survey of the Italian will serve to give the pattern. Space does not permit examination of leisure-time organizations of other fascisms.

German and Italian leisure-time regimentation began with the seizure of existing private recreational organizations and their resources by the Fascist and Nazi Parties. In Germany, the Nazi-sponsored Strength through Joy organization took over the previously voluntary Wandervoegel, while in Italy the Fascist Dopolavoro or after-work institution, absorbed the private employees' welfare and recreational groups attached to factories. The new organizations regimented the popular and welfare aspects of recreation while the German Chamber of Culture and the Fascist Institute of Culture regulated the arts and the cultural use of leisure time. State control of the popular and cultural uses of leisure time in both Fascist Italy and Nazi Germany showed a striking resemblance to state control in Soviet Russia.[1]

In Germany and Italy there were systems of age groups for young people which might, at first glance, appear to be like the boy and girl scouts of democratic countries. Actually, however, in Germany and Italy youth groups were compulsory, not voluntary; state controlled, not private. Their purpose was regimentation for industrial, agricultural, and, ultimately, military use. Youth were compelled to belong regardless of their parents' wishes. Thus youth groups in fascist and democratic countries were poles apart in purpose and control.

The German and Italian regimes made wide and frequent use of dazzling spectacles. Anniversaries of political significance and other celebrations, held on the average of once a month, were designed to occupy the time of the energetic and to impress the onlookers with the power of the party. The frequency of events left little opportunity for individual use of leisure time. Allied with the cultural controls and with the excursions sponsored by Strength through Joy and by Dopolavoro, they constituted a complete device for the regimentation of all leisure time.[2]

Running throughout the pattern for leisure-time use was a fanatical emphasis on nationalism and "national culture." In a world growing progressively smaller with the lightning-like advances in air transport and radio communication, the fascist nations deliberately seemed to

---

[1] See The Use of Leisure Time, Communism in Action, H. Doc. No. 754, 79th Cong., 2d sess., 1946, pp. 117-125.
[2] See also in this connection, ch. II, Education and Thought Control.

turn the clock back to medieval and reactionary exclusion of every cultural influence they interpreted as "foreign."

GERMANY

The first impression captured from a perusal of the literature on leisure-time use in Nazi Germany is one of extraordinary improvization. Every possible need in leisure-time use was taken care of and, within the space of a few years, thoroughly and intensively organized under the Nazi government. Upon closer and more detailed examination, however, the improvization seems less important in the light of the thorough-going and intensive organization of all leisure-time activities which was already in existence before the Nazi advent to power. It remained for the latter to coordinate and merge a bit here and there, adopting a few ideas from Italy and Russia, and finally to place the entire leisure-time organization under certain party and state officials. As far as the adaptation of leisure time to state and military purposes was concerned, the improvization was sometimes carried out in brilliant strokes, sometimes in obtuse moves with negative effect.

To be completely logical, the state, which regulated the working time of the individual, should also have governed his play time. It would hardly have been practicable or safe to allow individualism in recreational and leisure-time activity when all the rest of life was regimented under the totalitarian state. Yet Nazi statements of the ends and means involved in the use of leisure-time organization, curiously enough, sometimes paid lip service to the free, individual use of leisure time.[3]

Even recreation during working hours was organized, so that all moments of work, play, and rest were carefully linked into a well articulated system.[4]

Leisure-time organization also sought to provide the change and relaxation needed where workers were tied down to machines and immersed in the ceaseless grind of the stepped up program of rearmament and heavy industrial production initiated by Hitler. The Germans, like other human beings, craved relaxation and relief from the pressures of this immense effort in spite of the fanatical zest with which the party zealots drove their work program. The demand increased for rest, travel, sport, and other methods of getting away from the driving pace of occupational activity. Individual parts of the recreational program were fitted in nicely with rearmament. The

[3] "(1) Our leisure-time organization is self-help; that is, the individual is left free and uninfluenced in the disposal of his leisure time. (2) But with a view to a utilization of leisure time that shall be of value for the whole community, instead of a mere spending of leisure time, a central organization for all work in the interests of recreation, so far as this is concerned with the German people as a whole (in contrast, for instance, to confessional leisure-time organizations) has been set up. The National-Socialist Organization Kraft durch Freude has, within the scope of the German Labour Front, the task of leisure-time organization for the whole people, from the humblest upwards. By superintending all the work of leisure-time organization, Kraft durch Freude at the same time prevents the atomizing effects of individualistic use of leisure time, which is not leisure-time organization, since it has no relation to the natural form of human life; that is, to the community of the people." From World Congress for Leisure Time and Recreation, Report Berlin, 1936, p. 77. Hereafter cited as World Congress.
[4] "Our leisure-time organization therefore wins the approval of the whole people, because it comprehends the whole of life, from its most essential conditions down to the last details of practice. We must distinguish between true and false leisure-time organization, and finally reject the mere spending of leisure time to which I have referred. Leisure-time organization is not confined to that part of the week or the day that is left after work is done and after the satisfaction of the requirements of eating and sleeping; but in addition to the week end, feast days, and holidays, leisure-time organization is bound up with work itself, so that the rhythm of life, which is mainly determined by the work achieved, may not be disturbed or the unity of work and leisure destroyed.
"This is also an explanation of the fact that the National-Socialist Organization Kraft durch Freude finds its most important sphere of activity in the working establishment itself." World Congress, pp. 77-78.

popular radio receiving set was designed to bring in only German programs. The people's car was proposed with a view to making the German people mechanical-minded and for possible military use. Such sports as skiing and gliding were designed for combative situations of war.

The Strength Through Joy Organization

The Strength Through Joy (Kraft durch Freude), the most gigantic attempt in history to organize the leisure-time activities of an entire nation, was created in November 1933, on the model of Mussolini's National After-work Institution (Opera Nazionale Dopolavoro). The German organization quickly outstripped its Italian predecessor in range and complexity. Strength Through Joy reached its height in 1936, at the time of the Olympic Games in Berlin. In that year representatives of leisure-time associations of most countries of the world met in Berlin and founded an international leisure-time organization, which was to have its permanent headquarters in that city.[5]

The subsequent history of Strength Through Joy was uneventful. In 1938, it was taken under the wing of the German Labor Front and after the start of the Second World War its activities were sharply curtailed by military needs. In its latter days it was chiefly concerned with the maintenance of morale among the armed forces at the front and in hospitals. In October 1944, it was completely disbanded.

After 1938, the membership in the Strength through Joy organization was made up of the following groups: (1) Labor Front members, 20 millions; (2) collective members, 5 millions, and (3) household associates, 12 millions. In 1939 there were estimated to be from 40 to 45 million members throughout Germany. Only Nazi Party members were eligible to become officials.

The financial turn-over is estimated to have exceeded 2 billion marks yearly. The organization itself contributed from 15 to 20 millions toward its own expenses. The salaries of officials totalled about 20 millions. Dues of Labor Front members reached 400 to 500 millions. Other sources of income were contributions from corporations and voluntary labors performed by the workers themselves. Thus, sports teachers were provided by the Nazi Sports Organization and military bands contributed musical entertainment.

This immense bureaucracy destroyed all individual initiative in the use of leisure time.[6] As a national organization it was divided into 32 Gaue (regional or provincial units), 771 districts, 15,000 town units, and 18,000 local groups. There were some 57,000 leaders in the separate divisions including the very small primary units or cells in factories or offices. In the cities the organization possessed a block warden for every 25 persons and this official looked after the special interests of his group. He worked in conjunction with the block steward of the German Labor Front in keeping tab on every individual within his block. Information was collected constantly concerning marital and home conditions of every individual, his housing, his occupation, his avocations, his state of health, and above all, his attitudes toward the government. This information was passed along to the central office in Berlin.[7]

[5] Ernest Hamburger, Significance of the Nazi Leisure Time Program, Social Research, vol. 12, No. 2, May 1945, pp. 227-249.
[6] The previous paragraphs are all based on Hamburger.
[7] World Congress, pp. 129, 680-696.

In addition to its geographic divisions and subdivisions Strength Through Joy was sectioned off into separate compartments by type of activity. The more important were: (1) travel; (2) popular education; (3) sports; and (4) beauty of labor.

Travel

The "Travel, Excursions, Hiking, and Holidays Section" stimulated popular interest in, and provided facilities for, travel. City workers were taken to the country, beaches, and forests; fishermen were sent to the mountains and places away from the sea; mountain dwellers were given a chance to see the lowlands and the cities. Changes of scenery were provided. Sea voyages were arranged for the romantic, and vessels were chartered for Norway, Portugal, the Azores, Madeira, Spain, Italy, and the Italian Colonies. During 1934–35, there were 384 sea voyages. Seven oceanic steamships were continuously occupied with Strength Through Joy tours. Naturally the trips were confined to countries with a fascistic form of society. This use of leisure-time allowed no opportunity for dangerous contacts with non-fascist influences. After the start of the war in 1939, all sea trips were canceled.[8]

Within Germany some 5 million persons went on tour each year on trips of 3 days or less in length. Low-cost skiing trips to the Alps were made available to organization members and similar facilities were developed for use of bathing beaches.[9] More will be said on holidays later in this chapter.

In the interests of road travel within Germany Hitler made his sensational announcement in 1937 that the new people's car would be ready soon at a low price; but the car never materialized. The system of strategic automobile highways (Autobahnen) throughout the Reich also had a recreational purpose, which was never realized.[10]

Popular education

Popular education over and above the regular school system through 300 adult education centers in various parts of Germany offered courses in Nazi race science, heredity, public health, national and local history, political science, economics, art, technical subjects, and natural sciences.[11] Formal course work was amplified by work in small study groups or circles ostensibly designed to improve the critical faculties of the individual citizens on all questions of interest to the nation, but actually to sharpen his appreciation of National Socialist ideas. The study circles allowed "personal creative work" in music, painting, modeling, and handicrafts. Much attention was also devoted to practical subjects such as arithmetic, shorthand, and foreign languages.[12]

In addition to the lectures and circles, the popular education section arranged for visits of workers to museums, industrial centers and similar escorted excursions to places of great Nazi historical and cultural interest. Popular libraries were also assembled and made available in connection with the adult lectures and study circles. Evening programs of study and related diversion of several kinds were stressed. After the start of the war in 1939, popular education was

---

[8] Hamburger, pp. 227–249.
[9] Wallace R. Deuel, People Under Hitler, New York, 1942, pp. 318–333.
[10] See ch. X, Transportation.
[11] See ch. II, Education and Thought Control.
[12] World Congress, pp. 690–691, 614–16; Hamburger; Cesare Santoro, Hitler Germany (3d Eng. ed.), Berlin, 1939, pp. 184–5.

largely confined to work with the inhabitants of newly acquired territories.[13]

Sports

In 1934 there were 48 regional sport departments scattered throughout the Reich. Special facilities were provided in all local sports offices for medical advice and counsel. Each factory provided facilities for physical sports while in rural areas camps were available. Almost all branches of sport were recognized and fostered.[14]

The sports section of Strength through Joy cooperated with individual sport groups and organizations in stimulating and directing athletic activities. "Exercise evenings" were promoted, and sport equipment could be purchased at low prices on easy terms. Contestants were granted national sports badges in recognition of their interest, and special attention was given to participation by older persons and young children.

The German Reich Sports League, sponsored by Strength through Joy, was divided into 17 Gaue or regions. Each region was subdivided into districts. The district sports authority acted as mediator between the regional authorities and the governing bodies of the individual sports and physical-culture societies. The House of German Sport in the Reich Sports Field at Berlin was the headquarters for the League. Here also the headquarters of the Reich Academy of Physical Culture was maintained. Among the many activities sponsored by the League, attention might be drawn to the German Gymnastic and Sports Festivals, the first of which was held at Breslau in June 1938.[15]

Beauty of Work

The Beauty of Work section devoted its efforts to the improvement of working conditions in the factory and on the farm. These consisted chiefly of providing facilities for recreation and exercise. Amateur theatricals, dances, and music were emphasized. Model villages were established in each province. The factory was made more pleasant and healthful by a program of improvements and cleaning up, which constituted a part of the leisure-time activities.[16]

In every large city at least one House of German Labor, modeled along the lines of the Russian Workers Clubs, was organized. The club quarters were connected with factories, and they fostered art and an interest in factory products. Exhibits of the manufactured goods characteristic of the locality were frequent. Business Community Evenings provided a chance for labor and management to get together and to cooperate in play as well as in work. Out of these institutions grew a specially selected or elite corps of workmen who as "factory shock troops" gave popular demonstrations of the Nazi way of life in industry and repaired break-downs in factory production where they occurred.[17]

In addition to the foregoing divisions of Strength through Joy, there was the Evening Leisure Section with the task of "awakening and shaping a National Socialist way of life." Its program related to the stimulation of folk culture through a revival of antiquated and traditional forms of German life. Singing of old folksongs was encour-

[13] Santoro, p. 184; World Congress, p. 616.
[14] Santoro, pp. 405–12; World Congress, pp. 692–3.
[15] World Congress, pp. 692–3; Hamburger; Santoro, pp. 185, 405–12.
[16] World Congress, pp. 693–6.
[17] Santoro, p. 186.

aged through music clubs. Employers arranged meetings in which costumes of the guilds were worn and explained to the employees. Folk dances were given at specified times. Arrangements were made for the workers to attend concerts, plays, operas, operettas, vaudeville, and motion picture performances. These activities, however, outside observers asserted, were mainly propaganda for Naziism under a gloss of entertainment.[18]

Leisure of village and housewife

"Village Community Evenings" were organized by the Strength through Joy workers in the rural areas as monthly events. The local educational officer of the party generally presided. Hitler Youth and the League of German Girls took prominent parts in these events which were used for indoctrination and propaganda under the guise of dancing and theatricals.[19]

Strength through Joy did not neglect the housewives. It furnished them with special radio programs and films on domestic matters. "Trips to relatives," who had been separated for a long time, were made possible by special financial aid.[20]

The Institute of the Land Year was also brought to the aid of housewives, especially those in rural area. This organization consisted of young girls from the cities, who had just left school and were sent in groups to help country women in their tasks and incidentally to learn the virtues of rural life.[21]

In 1934, an assistance organization called Mother and Child was founded for the purpose of fostering family life and leisure time for mothers. Especially favored were mothers with more than two children, delicate mothers, young married women, and expectant mothers up to the fifth month. Arrangements were made to take care of the families during the mothers' vacations. A substitute was generally found among relatives, acquaintances, neighbors; or, failing this, the service provided an unpaid girl from the Girl's Labor Service or, as a last resort, a paid housekeeper.[22]

During their vacations, which lasted from 3 to 4 weeks, mothers were lodged in groups of 40 or 50 persons in holiday houses specially arranged for the purpose. The matrons of these houses were trained nurses or experienced women who had responsibility for the maintenance of order and the arrangement of activities. The latter consisted of group discussions, games, singing, needlework, systematic sport, and nature studies. Rest homes of a similar nature were open to mothers with babies and very young children and in these places instruction in child care was a part of the daily program. For mothers who could not leave their families, local recreation houses for a day's stay were provided in which emphasis was placed on rest, walks, and good food.[23]

Leisure of youth

The Hitler Youth (Hitler Jugend), the Association of German Young Girls (Bund Deutscher Jungmaedel), the German Young People (Deutsches Jungvolk), the Young Girls (Jungmaedel) and the

[18] World Congress, pp. 690–71; Deuel, p. 322; Santoro, p. 184; Hamburger.
[19] World Congress, pp. 563–66.
[20] World Congress, pp. 397, 472–4.
[21] World Congress, p. 483.
[22] World Congress, pp. 477–478.
[23] World Congress, pp. 478–479.

Little Fellows (Pimpfe) were organized into local groups ranging down to 15 members.[24] Each unit was headed by a leader who was responsible for the activities and utilization of leisure time of the members. Meetings were held every Wednesday evening at headquarters when a special radio program was broadcast from the Berlin Central Office for Youth. On Saturdays, there were special youth festivals and celebrations while during week'days before and after school hours there were always parades and demonstrations. Early in the morning and late at night the whistle of the leaders of marching groups of youth could be heard in city and country. Youth organizations were under the direct control of the Nazi Party and in turn controlled all of the athletic programs in school and out. Much of the sports program of the youth groups emphasized military preparedness, as the early separation of boy and girl activities abundantly testified. Success in sport and in mental tests led to the coveted proficiency badge for some of the contestants.[25]

The Heim was the core of the smaller units and the center of activities. Wednesday evenings were exclusively retained for the Heimabend which was inevitably accompanied by the radio program known as Young Germany's Hour. About 6 weeks of the year were given over to tenting or camping out. The German Youth Hostel Association under Nazi auspices maintained 2,000 hostels with 25,000 beds. These hostels were located in castles, city towers, and even in stationary ships in port. At a small price both food' and lodging could be secured by youthful travelers.[26]

National Youth Service Duty for a limited period was required of all German young men. If the families resisted, their sons were subject to Youth Service Arrest and could be taken from their homes, treated as orphans, or placed with more tractable families.[27]

The youthful factory workers were given special opportunities to attend technical schools and to make use of recreational facilities for noon and evening activities. Arrangements were also made on week ends for conducted hikes to the woods and hills, to museums and national monuments, and for annual vacation trips to places of interest to youth.[28]

The Press and Propaganda Department of the Hitler Youth organization supervised every magazine or book which the Hitler Youth would have a chance to read. This was especially important because the main channels of direct propaganda were the 10 Hitler Youth periodicals, each of which was designed to reach a particular age group and sex.[29]

Every summer several thousand German students worked on the farms. In the same way the student's factory service gave relief to the factory workers over a period of several months. Thus the factory and farm workers were able to take paid holidays.[30]

The League of German Girls met weekly at the home evenings which brought the members together for discussion, reading, and singing. There were also occasional excursions or camping periods,

[24] See ch. II, Education and Through Control; World Congress, p. 505; Santoro, pp. 319-20.
[25] William Ebenstein, The Nazi State, New York, 1943, p. 187; World Congress, pp. 504-507; Santoro, pp. 319-23.
[26] Santoro, p. 321.
[27] Ebenstein, pp. 191-194.
[28] See Ch. II, Education and Thought Control.
[29] Ebenstein, pp. 188-9.
[30] World Congress, pp. 225-7.

which were featured by fairy tales, shadow and puppet pantomimes, and other forms of entertainment. Arrangements were also made for excursions to factories and workshops.[31]

The Community of Culture, organized by Rosenberg, had a special division known as the Cultural Community of Youth designed to unify all efforts at cultural education and propagandizing of youth. In order to "create receptivity for the great master works of German art," it promoted youth theaters and films, puppet shows, lay and folk plays, folk music, and writing competitions.[32]

Vacations, holidays, and anniversaries

The law for the regulation of national labor (January 1934) required the employer to care for his workers and provide for vacations. The length of the vacation period was adjusted to the needs of the work. Special regulations were made for young workmen and laborers physically handicapped by war disabilities. A minimum vacation of six working days was mandatory for employees of from four to 12 months' service. Two weeks or more could be given to those who had worked over 12 months.[33]

Dates and lengths of vacations were fixed by agreements between self-administering bodies, the labor committees, labor boards, and committees of experts. The Labor Gazette regularly gave information on the subject.[34] The majority of German employees actually had a vacation of seven working days annually. The maximum period was determined by length of employment or in some cases by the particular occupation according to age. Vacations could not be spent at paid employment and a violation of this regulation was punished by dismissal and forfeiture of the money earned.

The workweek extended from Monday through Saturday between one and four o'clock, except in factories employing shift labor. The closing time on weekdays, fixed by law, was seven o'clock.[35]

Local and national holidays were common. Local patriotic assemblies met weekly, sometimes daily, in every town and village of the Reich. About once a month some colossal demonstration of national scope was staged.[36]

Spectacular display was most extensive at the Party Day celebrations in Nuremberg extending from September 1 to 3. The number of participants about equaled the number of the audience. In 1934, for example, there were 180,000 party officials, 110,000 storm troopers, 50,000 labor service men and women, together with 120,000 ordinary party members who took part: a total of 460,000 people, equal to a military force of 30 divisions. In addition, the spectators from all parts of Germany numbered 550,000 or the equivalent of another 35 divisions.[37]

The scenes enacted at these memorable occasions were sufficient to stir even the most impassive of Germans and often to transform him into a zealot for the National Socialist cause. At night there were massed torchlight processions which reflected weirdly against the waving banners and marching men. In daytime it was a sea of gaudy colored banners and parades. The constant roar of massed bands and

[31] World Congress, pp. 544–6, 505–7.
[32] See ch. II, Education and Thought Control.
[33] World Congress, pp. 214–220.
[34] World Congress, p. 216.
[35] World Congress, p. 446.
[36] See ch. II, Education and Thought Control.
[37] Derrick Sington and Arthur Weidenfeld. The Goebbels Experiment, New Haven, 1943, pp. 40–44.

the sounds of countless marching feet and "heiling" voices were most impressive. The sight of thousands of uniformed men and women marching beneath majestic arches and columns arranged in long rows gave an effect of a colossal and irresistible force. Unbelievably large masses of people assembled in large stadiums for ceremonial events also impressed the onlooker. The program of events went on interminably as Hitler Youth choruses with thousands of voices sang party songs or recited in unison, party leaders made rousing speeches, the bands gave their stirring open-air concerts and long Labor Service roll calls were completed. Such an event was a superspectacle, a religious saturnalia, and a mass emotional spree.[38]

The preparation was in the hands of the Office of Cultural Activities, which designed, ordered, and assembled all the necessary banners, streamers, loudspeakers, torches, and the show columns crowned with brass eagles clutching swastikas. Every badge or emblem adopted by the party was also supervised and prepared with care. These items included mottoes, quotations for inscription on banners, and badges for uniforms. The Office also prepared the architectural effects in which they followed the Caesarean or conqueror's formula of tall columns in long rows together with archways and huge arenas. Interiors, where used, were decorated with chandeliers and movable trappings along the lines of a supercinema.[39]

Besides the Party Day celebrations there were a number of other national holidays which were the occasion of party propaganda and efforts to arouse mass emotions. On October 1 the Harvest Thanksgiving Day was celebrated with speeches, concerts, parades, and picnics throughout Germany. On one such occasion a half million peasants gathered at Buckeberg near Hameln where they were entertained by music, parades, and military maneuvers. On November 9 there was an annual solemn celebration at Munich in honor of Hitler's unsuccessful beer hall putsch of 1923. Christmas was the occasion of nationalistic rallies and cultural harangues, and New Year's Day furnished an opportunity for more speechmaking, proclamations, parties, and parades. February 24 was the anniversary of the first promulgation of the party program and was honored by a great festival at Munich in which loyalty was sworn to Hitler. The day following, February 25, was National War Heroes Day, on which occasion the dead war heroes were honored by a gigantic nation-wide demonstration. May 1 was the Day of National Labor and was celebrated with parades and festivities.[40]

The National Chamber of Culture

The cultural employment of leisure time was regulated by the National Chamber of Culture (Reichskulturkammer), established on September 22, 1933. Its function was primarily to decide on the fitness of cultural productions in Germany for presentation to the people, and it included everyone who earned a living by practicing any of the arts. By law it comprehended all who were engaged in audible, written, or visual instruction or entertainment in Germany. The National Chamber of Culture was presided over by Dr. Goebbels in his capacity of Minister of Propaganda and Peoples Enlightenment. This Ministry had an organization of its own which was concerned, in the main, with the same activities as the chamber of Culture.[41]

---

[38] Sington and Weidenfeld, pp. 40–44.
[39] Sington and Weidenfeld, pp. 40–44.
[40] Sington and Weidenfeld, pp. 36–44. See also ch. II on Education and Thought Control.
[41] See ch. II, Education and Thought Control.

Since membership was compulsory for any persons engaged in production, reproduction, dissemination, or distribution of cultural matter, undesirable persons such as Jews, Communists, Masons, and other non-Nazis might be excluded from the fields of artistic, literary, or professional activities by simply denying them membership.[42]

Seven corporations were included in the German National Chamber of Culture as constituent bodies: (1) National Music Chamber; (2) National Plastic Arts Chamber; (3) National Theater Chamber; (4) National Literature Chamber; (5) National Press Chamber; (6) National Radio Chamber; and (7) National Film Chamber.

Each chamber included all activities within the entire Reich which could be classified under its subject matter heading. The first four and the last were geographically divided into 31 regional and local representative bodies. In the case of the Radio and Film Chambers, the local officers were under the direct control of representatives of the Nazi Party.[43]

The entire system was graded under a hierarchy of leaders. Dr. Goebbels appointed the officers presiding over each member chamber and also the president, vice president, and secretary of the over-all Chamber of Culture. Each leader below Goebbels in turn conferred authority on each subordinate leader. Theoretically, the cultural chambers were self-governing bodies made up of the industries concerned in cultural production. They were directly paralleled by the Divisions of the Propaganda Ministry.[44]

The National Chamber of Music had total control over that art. Cultural orchestras were created to cultivate approved music. Only music by Aryans was acceptable. Under the Chamber's auspices about 1,300 towns appointed municipal musical counselors to develop musical life in their respective communities. Scholarships were provided for promising students of music. Folk music, community singing, and the revival of older folk tunes were stimulated. A "State Society for the Utilization of Musical Copyrights" (STAGMA) was given a monopoly over the granting and withdrawal of musical copyrights. The latter were extended to from 30 to 50 years after the composer's death. Unemployed musicians of approved race were given financial aid from a provident fund.[45]

The National Theater Chamber concerned itself with the monopoly of all affairs pertaining to theatrical exhibitions. It authorized the opening of new theaters and supervised the activities of 250 big theaters, 81 smaller ones, 90 opera companies, 45 itinerant theaters, and 46 private ones. Theaters were encouraged to engage in local festivals, cultural weeks, concert try-outs, special broadcasting programs, and variety performances. An Artists' Benevolent Fund for Actors and Actresses in distress or old age was established. The Reich Supervisor of Drama by the law of May 15, 1934, was made the head of the Theater Division of the Propaganda Ministry and was empowered to grant or withhold subsidies to the individual theaters. A censor was provided by the Chamber of Culture to examine the manuscripts of new plays for their social fitness. Prize competitions were offered for works written by youth and children.[46]

[42] Ebenstein, p. 126 ff.
[43] Ebenstein, p. 126.
[44] Santoro, pp. 349–368. The divisions are given in ch. II, Education and Thought Control.
[45] Sington and Weidenfeld, p. 246 ff; World Congress, pp. 630–31; Santoro, pp. 312–25.
[46] Santoro, pp. 312–25; Sington and Weidenfeld, pp. 224–5.

Allied to the National Theater Chamber was the National Socialist Community of Culture, organized by Alfred Rosenberg, which has already been noticed in connection with youth groups. This institution was organized primarily with the intent of comprising all theatergoers. At one time it had over a million and a half members. Its major activity lay in the organization of clubs and circles through which the stimulation of approved plays was fostered. Nor was the theater the only phase of culture in which it was interested. There were also art circles, book circles, and lecture circles. Any German citizen might belong to a circle by paying the dues of 1 mark per year for each circle.[47]

The Community of Culture bought theater tickets in blocks and was thus enabled to secure reduced rates for its members. The rates were generally one-half the market price or less. It also undertook active management of theatrical productions, exhibits, and prize competition in writing of plays. Some 2,000 local groups were organized by the Community of Culture, each with its culture guardian or supervisor. The Community of Culture worked in two ways, namely: (1) Through direct dealings with theaters; and (2) through agreements for cooperation worked out with other Nazi corporate formations, such as the army, police, National Association of Jurists, National Socialist Students' League, the Labor Service, Strength through Joy, and the Hitler Youth.[48]

The coordination of the theater with the National Socialist way of life was regarded as of the greatest importance. This function was discharged through sponsorship of the correct and approved plays, through the advice given to party officials who had charge of conducting large groups to the theater, and through the support of plays written by Nazi playwrights only. In Berlin certain theaters served as cultural laboratories for model plays by model playwrights, portrayed by model players before model audiences. Thus a new German style in drama was developed with emphasis on historical drama, folk plays, and spectacles which emphasized the German role in leadership of other nations.[49]

The Chamber of Art sponsored the House of German Art in Munich. Another example of its activities was the exhibit of the so-called Soviet Paradise which toured the Reich in 1941 and 1942. This exhibit displayed in visual form the national wealth and riches of the Soviet Union. Also displayed was an OGPU torture chamber. A similar exhibit called German Greatness and Glory was sent out in the fall of 1941.[50]

The Reich Chamber of Literature included in its compulsory membership all those in any way concerned with book writing or book publication, such as authors, publishers, book sellers, and proprietors of circulating libraries. The function of this institution was to screen the works of all authors before publication. An Examining Committee for the Protection of National Socialist Literature censored all political writing. Special attention was devoted to calendars, which in Germany contained all sorts of almanacal and other material which might have some political slant. Marks of approval given books were as follows: A triangle for a book of recog-

[47] Ibid.
[48] Ibid.
[49] Ibid.
[50] Sington and Weidenfeld, p. 79 ff.

nized Nazi standards; a triangle plus a circle indicated a hundred percent Nazi book, and finally a triangle plus an asterisk was indicative of a book specially recommended by Rosenberg for ideological education.[51]

An Advisory Committee for Popular Literature was created by the Chamber of Literature for the guiding of publishers in the selection and utilization of manuscripts submitted to them. Book sellers were controlled through the Union of German Booksellers. Another group connected with the Chamber of Literature was the Reich Union of German Authors which comprehended all of the recognized writers and was supported by the Chamber.[52]

The Chamber of Literature was delegated powers to rid libraries of undesirable publications, such as writings of Jews, Communists, liberals, and Masons, and to encourage the publication of recognized Nazi literature. It was given police authority to prohibit the circulation of books which it considered trash or filth. Books censored might be divided into two categories: (1) undesirable for any circulation; and (2) undesirable for circulation beyond a limited group.[53]

Library personnel in Nazi Germany were all members of the party or of one of its subdivisions. Foreign books, periodicals, and newspapers were kept out of book stores and libraries by the requirement of a government permit for each importation of foreign goods. Many leading foreign newspapers and authors were thus definitely shut out of the Reich. Foreign exchange for the purchase of foreign reading matter was also difficult to obtain.[54]

The National Press Chamber included in its membership the personnel of newspapers and other periodicals. Every editor, journalist, or contributor was required to be a member of this organization. There were 14 national groups of member trade associations and each of these was subdivided territorially into regional and local groups. Control of the press was primarily evident in the outlets rather than through the guilds of authors and journalists. Editors and publishers were left to decide what was unfit or fit on the basis of general instructions issued by the Ministry of Propaganda. The latter was more interested in control of the content of publication than of the business itself. In some instances daily hand-outs were issued by the Propaganda Ministry, instructing on what to print, what to stress, and what not to print.[55]

The National Radio Chamber supervised the manufacture of radio sets and the distribution of the "People's Radio Set," a special make which could be bought on the installment plan and was good for domestic reception only. Germans were forbidden to listen to any except certain specified foreign stations by a very strict law with extremely heavy penalties (including capital punishment) attached to it. Communal listening to important broadcasts was common. Considerable time and effort was expended in the investigation of the reactions of radio listeners and the collection and digesting of criticisms and suggestions regarding programs. Amateur nights to cultivate new talent and inspire listener interest were instituted. Interval broadcasts scheduled to coincide with recreational periods in factories afforded

[51] Sington and Weidenfeld, pp. 231–35.
[52] Santoro, pp. 365–68.
[53] Santoro, pp. 365–68.
[54] Ebenstein, p. 131. See ch. IV, Finance and Fiscal Policy; also ch. V, Foreign Trade
[55] Ebenstein, p. 115 ff.; Brady, pp. 84–101; Santoro, pp. 365–68; Sington and Weidenfeld, pp. 60, 112.

music for the relaxation of workers and helped stimulate interest in
the People's Radio Set. Propaganda cars were sent to rural districts
to familiarize country folks with radio.[56]

The Nazi Party, by means of its radio wardens and block wardens
in every village and town, helped to install communal radio sets and
organized communal listening. The content of the programs was
mainly light and classical music, news bulletins and Party propaganda.
As in other European countries advertising in the sense that it is
developed on the American radio, was absent.[57]

The National Film Chamber comprised all persons engaged in the
production of films with the exceptions of authors and composers who
were members of the Literature and Music Chambers respectively.
The purpose of the Film Chamber was to supervise the production of
films, their propaganda use, their exhibition and advertising. Film
techniques as well as the film industry as a whole were supervised. A
Film Credit Bank was organized to finance the production of films
regarded as necessary. In 1934, a gigantic (Government-owned)
holding company called UFA-Film was formed which absorbed all the
preceding private companies and was designed to monopolize all film
production in Europe. A film city was constructed at Babelsburg near
Potsdam for production. An Institute for the Production of Docu-
mentary and Educational Films was initiated for propaganda purposes and official newsreels were prepared for compulsory showing at
all motion picture houses. Foreign films were carefully screened
before admission into the country.[58]

ITALY

The after-work institution

The Fascist Government hereby recognizes two distinct necessities as indispensable to the workers: The necessity of work, as a means of earning a living,
and the necessity of leisure-time organization as a means of imparting the fullest
and finest content to life.[59]

These words indicated the reasoning which lay behind the leisure-
time organization in Italy. An 8-hour day and the 40-hour workweek in 1923 were accomplished by agreements between representatives of industrialists and workers. These allowed more leisure time
for the workers than had formerly been possible. The extended week
end periods were sometimes denominated "Fascist Saturdays" or
"Fascist week ends" in tribute to the Fascist Party as the initiator
of the new way of life.[60]

As early as 1920 the Fascist Party organized in various parts of
Italy a few groups of workers for the utilization of their leisure time.
The idea spread rapidly to other parts of the country. National recognition was granted the movement in 1923, with the founding of the
central office of Dopolavoro and with its subordination to the Confederation of Fascist Trade Unions. Agreements were made with employers' associations for the founding of Dopolavoro centers in factories and business concerns. On May 1, 1925, Mussolini founded the
Opera Nazionale Dopolavoro by Decree No. 582. The formal purposes of the organization were stated as follows:

[56] Ebenstein, p. 121; Sington and Weidenfeld, pp. 47 and 143; Santoro, pp. 356–57.
[57] Sington and Weidenfeld, pp. 138, 152–4.
[58] Santoro, pp. 355–56; Ebenstein, p. 143.
[59] World Congress, p. 93.
[60] World Congress, pp. 90–95.

64304°—47——13

(1) To stimulate the healthy and beneficial employment of the workers' leisure time by means of local centers for developing physical, intellectual, and moral capacities of the workers.

(2) To provide for the increase and coordination of these centers by furnishing them and their members with whatever assistance may be necessary.[61]

Dopolavoro was guided by a general directorate under the secretary of the Fascist Party. The organization was divided into six departments, namely: (1) Administration; (2) sport; (3) art; (4) culture; (5) touring; and (6) welfare. There were 15 district inspectorships, 94 provincial offices, and a personnel of 726 officials or employees. The rural and communal Dopolavoros have boards of directors each composed of from 5 to 6 persons and a president. Altogether there were 98,000 directors and 3,680 technical managers. In 1936, there were about three million members all told in the various branches of the Dopolavoro throughout Italy. Every worker was entitled to a free card of membership which gave him the right to all the privileges and conveniences furnished by the organization.[62]

The state, during the years from 1925 through 1927, established Dopolavoro centers throughout the large government enterprises such as the railways and the postal and telegraph services. These centers were administered by central offices with independent managers (subject to general regulation). There was also a large Dopolavoro organization in the merchant marine.[63]

Collective labor contracts entered into between the Fascist labor organizations and the syndicates of employers were endowed with legal force by the Fascist Government. These agreements included the granting of paid holidays and the observance of Fascist Saturdays as leisure time.[64]

The sports activities were administered by a central commission subordinate to the general directorate of the National Recreational Association. National championship contests were organized, and district and provincial sports activities were promoted. Technical offices in the local areas were subordinate to the district inspectorate or the Dopolavoro organizations in the provinces. Sports badges were given to those participating in competitive sport. In general, sports and recreations associated with Italian history or held to be of Italian origin were promoted above all others. Among the most notable were tug-of-war, rowing with fixed seats, push ball, boccia, and tambourine playing.[65]

Traveling and hiking to historic places in Italy was encouraged. In this way a sense of national pride and a familiarity with national history were inculcated. Excursions to the Alps and highland areas were connected with skiing competitions. Mountain marches and target shooting, exploration of caves, voluntary forestry work, popular trips to factories and places of interest, such as museums and national monuments, were carried on by Dopolavoro groups. Special rates for travel and hotel expenses were secured as well as reductions in the price of sports clothing and equipment. Free insurance was provided to members.[66]

Dramatic activities were encouraged by means of Thespis Vans or troupes of traveling players carrying stage equipment with them,

[61] World Congress, p. 91.
[62] World Congress, pp. 161–169.
[63] World Congress, p. 701 ff.
[64] World Congress, pp. 161–169.
[65] World Congress, pp. 430–431.
[66] World Congress, pp. 435–438.

who gave dramatic performances to Saturday afternoon audiences in particular. The lowering of theater prices for workers was also used as an inducement to theater attendance. Allied to the theater were the numerous bands and choruses. The National Motion Picture Institute (Luce) produced sports, educational, and historical films for Dopolavoro members.[67]

There was a special 10 minutes Dopolavoro radio broadcast daily for cultural and propaganda purposes.

Evening vocational schools, schools for the illiterate, and lending libraries were also developed. Traditional religious and civic festivals in even the smallest villages were revived.[68]

At the better furnished centers there were radios, phonographs, billiard tables, pianos, gymnasiums, fencing and lecture halls, libraries and reading rooms, and movie apparatus. Throughout the year recreation fitted to the season was cultivated. In the spring there were supervised excursionist rallies, mountain trips, archery, and shooting; in summer, camping, cruising, and exploratory trips; in the fall bicycle races, motorcycling, fairs, and more excursionist rallies; and, in the winter, special rallies for winter sports such as skiing and snowshoeing.[69]

The revival of Italian folk culture was a primary aim of Dopolavoro. Special associations were organized for the cultivation of local popular traditions and these groups served as centers of propaganda for folk competitions, meetings and rallies. Costumes characteristic of the peasants and of other classes in earlier times were worn and displayed. In September 1928, for example, there was an Italian costume rally at Venice in which thousands participated. In local villages displays of costumes, decorated carts, implements, and processions were conjoined on gala occasions. Special photographic records were taken of these events and made the occasion of patriotic displays. Folklore films showing local customs and beliefs were produced for circulation throughout the country. Shows of rustic arts included special sections for decorative art on working implements executed by peasants during their leisure hours. Folk musical performances included obsolete instruments and concerts of almost forgotten melodies. Even the guild festivals of the patron saints were revived and their elaborate pageantry was given modern day interpretation. Every effort was made to link medieval customs of work and play with modern life and, in so doing, to stress strictly Italian contributions to civilization.[70]

Youth groups and leisure time

The Opera Nazionale Balilla was organized in 1926, to bring all young people from 8 to 18 into activities considered fitting for the Fascist state. Young women were divided into Piccole Italiane, from 8 to 14, and the Giovani Italiane, from 14 to 18 years. Similarly young men were divided into the Balilla proper, from 8 to 14, and the Avanguardisti, from 14 to 18 years. The local organization of these youth groups in each community had a governing council with a presiding officer or committee. Sections were set up for sailing, cycling, skiing and other sports. Great stress was laid on physical

---

[67] See Chapter II, Education and Thought Control.
[68] World Congress, pp. 607–608.
[69] World Congress, pp. 430–438, 701 ff.
[70] Opera nazionale dopolavoro ,The National Dopolavoro Foundation (2d ed.), Rome 1937, pp. 79–89.

education and vocational training.   Group insurance against accidents
was furnished by the state.[71]

Holidays and celebrations

In Fascist Italy as in Germany, there were numerous occasions for
patriotic celebrations.   October 28 was celebrated as the anniversary
of the Fascist March on Rome.   Parades were followed by a gathering
in the Colosseum at Rome where Mussolini made the only speech.   It
was primarily a military celebration followed by several military
holidays.

Another notable day was the Fascist Levy (Leva Fascista), which
was held on the nearest Sunday to March 23rd.   On this day graduates
of the Avanguardisti were initiated into the Fascist Party.   The
chief ceremonies revolved around the symbols of the initiation as
Party membership cards and rifles were presented to the new members.
The day was devoted to the interests of the youth organizations.[72]

April 21 was commemorated as the anniversary of the founding
of Rome and constituted the Fascist Labor Day.   It took the place of
the former May 1 celebration which, on account of its connection with
socialism and communism, was forbidden.   Speeches and general
festivities were used to celebrate this event.[73]

The Constitution (Statuto) was commemorated by a celebration on
the first Sunday of June.   It consisted of the glorification of Italian
unity by elaborate military parades.   November the 4th was celebrated
as the anniversary of the victory over the Central Powers in the
First World War, and November 11 or Armistice Day with military
events.   Other anniversaries which were the occasion of public
celebration were the King's birthday, the Queen's birthday, the
anniversary of the taking of Rome (September 20), and the declaration
of the First World War (May 24).[74]

The specifically Fascist and military celebrations greatly eclipsed in
importance all of the older traditional and religious holidays.   From
time to time special commemorative ceremonies were held in connection with various economic battles being waged by the Government.
Such, for example, were the celebrations at harvest time when prizes
were given for the best results in the Battle of Grain.[75]

The National Fascist Institute of Culture and Censorship

Of some significance in connection with the use of leisure time in
Fascist Italy were the devices used to mold the reading matter which
was presented to the Italian people.   The National Fascist Institute
of Culture maintained a special library of Fascist books dealing with
the Fascist world outlook, published a review of Fascist education, and
edited a series of historical and political works interpreted from the
Fascist viewpoint.[76]

The press was strictly subject to the authority of the local prefects
and a firm censorship was maintained on all printed matter.   When
Party decisions were made, no details were given out regarding the
debates or details of the controversies preceding them.   Editorial
responsibility of individuals for newspaper contents was firmly fixed

[71] Herbert W. Schneider and Shepard B. Clough, Making Fascists, Chicago, 1929, pp. 178–182.
[72] Schneider and Clough, pp. 193–195.
[73] Schneider and Clough, pp. 193–195.
[74] Schneider and Clough, pp. 193–195.
[75] Schneider and Clough, pp. 193–195.
[76] Tomaso Sillani, ed., What Is Fascism and Why, New York, 1931, pp. 167–8.

also. New printing establishments required police authorization. No opposition press was permitted since the establishment and recognized list of journalists were the only ones who might write for publication.[77]

Periodicals were, in the main, political reviews designed to propagate Fascism. Some of them contained semiscientific matters, literary and popular reviews. The Fascist Publishing House (Libreria del Littorio) had a monopoly over printed matter.[78]

CONCLUSION

Democratic citizens are prone to look upon leisure time as their own and to regard such time as no concern of the state except in cases of gambling and vice, where leisure-time use contravenes the law. This results from the individualistic philosophy of democracy. On the other hand, equally logically, fascist societies conclude, because of their beliefs in the predominance of the state, that the state has the power to regulate and dispose of the individual both at work and at play as it wishes. This includes leisure time. Because recreation rebuilds tired minds and bodies so that they are again able to work; because impressions gained during leisure activity are among the most lasting of mankind; because the fascist citizen must never swerve from the role assigned to him, and especially because opposition and revolt may be bred during leisure moments, the fascist states have regarded the organization, use, and control of leisure time as a most important state function.

Leisure time was seized upon by the fascist states for the inculcation of doctrines of Deutschtum, Hispanidad, and a return to Roman greatness. The blending of work programs and leisure-time programs made possible an uninterrupted series of propaganda pressures throughout the day. Vacations too and holidays were no escapes for the individual.

In both Germany and Italy the use of leisure time was carefully articulated with the other controls of the state. As noted in the preface all waking moments were regimented and regulated. In the case of Germany, at least, this control was facilitated by the preexistence of many extensive and highly organized voluntary groups for sport and recreation. The earlier voluntary organizations were taken over by the state and woven into a network of leisure-time planning, programming and regulation.

With control over the masses as the broad objective of both Italian and German leaders, the Strength Through Joy and the Dopolavoro were concerned most with organizations of a popular nature such as the sports groups and evening recreational associations. Leisure-time control was combined with a tight censorship giving the state complete domination over all cultural organizations. The fascist leaders arrogated control over both the physical and the mental aspects of leisure-time use.

Especially clever was the manipulation of the individual through mass psychology. His feelings were played upon by appealing to ultra-nationalistic sentiments, revival of traditions, and folklore. His loyalty was exploited through games, sports, and recreation.

[77] Schneider and Clough, pp. 159–177.
[78] Ibid.

There was also the constant repetition at frequent intervals of rallies, demonstrations, celebrations, anniversaries and spectacles, a species of event which kept the spirits keyed up and moving in a constant, guided direction.

Youth especially experienced emotional stimulation from the many activities of the all-embracing youth organizations controlled by the state. This state paternalism stressed achievement by group rather than by individual resourcefulness. This was linked with the militaristic emphasis which lay heavily upon all youthful employment of leisure time.

In closing this section, it should be noted that the chief distinction between totalitarian leisure-time organizations and the democratic lay in that in democracies leisure time belonged to the individual primarily and almost entirely, while in the totalitarian state leisure time belonged to the state primarily and to the individual only secondarily and incidentally.

What has been said for Germany and Italy applies to all fascist states, not as a peculiar malady or perversion, but rather as an inexorably logical outcome of the fundamental tenets of fascism, namely (1) predominance of the state, and (2) subordination of the individual.

CHAPTER XIII—RELIGION

FASCISM VERSUS CHRISTIANITY

As already noted in the preface, fascism, which mobilizes the total human personality in the interests of the power of the state, cannot accept the principle of independent religious direction of the individual. It cannot accept the basic tenets of the Christian Church which consider God as the highest authority and individuals as his children with equal rights. Fascism and Christianity are therefore basically incompatible. Nevertheless, the two beliefs can and have lived side by side for a time in an uncertain peace. It is only when fascists attempt a militant subordination of the church to their purposes that a clash becomes inevitable.

The antagonism between fascism and Christianity expressed itself in varying degrees in the different fascist countries. Outright struggle took place in Germany. Mussolini and the Pope frankly proclaimed their differences but managed to maintain a tenuous peace. The issue in Spain was and remained in 1947 somewhat obscured by the unique historical position of Catholicism in that country and by the comparative weakness of the Spanish fascist movement. But beneath the façade of cooperation in Spain there existed the necessary elements for conflict.

An examination of church-state relations in Germany, Italy, and Spain reveals the basic similarity of objective in the religious policies of all the fascist countries. Techniques, of course, have varied. Whether fascism attacked the church, showered favors upon it, or posed as its defender against Communism depended upon the opportunities of the moment. The purpose of the policy, however, remained constant—to enhance the power of the state and its leaders, either by distorting Christianity or by destroying it.

GERMANY

War against the Church

From the very first Adolf Hitler desired to establish complete state control over religion. He moved slowly, however, for fear of alienating support during the period of his rise to power. His real intent with regard to Christianity, therefore, was carefully concealed in the language of Point 24 of the National Socialist Party program.

We demand religious freedom for all denominations so long as they do not endanger the stability of the State or offend against the German people's instincts of morality and decency. The party as such takes its stand on a positive Christianity, without committing itself to any particular creed * * *.[1]

Recognizing the inherent threat in this statement, Catholicism began to resist National Socialism as early as 1930. But during the next 3 years the fever of National Socialism spread rapidly throughout the Reich. Opposition was stilled by nationalist appeals or was

---

[1] Quoted in Michael Power, Religion in the Reich, London ,1939, p. 7.

bludgeoned into silence by terrorist squads. Furthermore, the impassioned Nazi denunciations of "Godless" Bolshevism and vague promises to uphold the churches allayed Christian suspicion, and many "Protestant and Catholic leaders alike welcomed Hitler's success in January 1933." [2]

Shortly after becoming Chancellor, Hitler made a conciliatory gesture to religion in an address before the Reichstag on March 23, 1933. He declared that:

> The National Government sees in the two Christian confessions most vital factors in the survival of our nationality. Their rights will not be touched. The National Government will accord and secure to the Christian Confessions the influence that is due to them in schools and education.[3]

Despite this pledge nothing was done to curb the rabid elements in the Nazi Party who were advocating a neo-paganism built around the gods of German mythology. Instead, measures were undertaken immediately to end the independent influence of both Protestantism and Catholicism.

The Protestant Church

The strategy against the Protestants was designed to unify the numerous sects into a single national church responsive to the will of the state.[4] For this task Hitler chose Ludwig Mueller, an obscure pastor of the so-called German Christians, (Deutsche Christen) organized in 1932, in full support of National Socialism.[5] A series of astute maneuvers in the church synods and elections were engineered by Mueller and Dr. Jaegar, another appointee, who was Minister of Church Affairs. Their machinations, coupled with direct pressure on the clergy, secured the election of Mueller as Reich bishop and insured dominance of the German Christians in the state-sponsored organization of all Protestantism.[6]

The speed with which the Nazis had brought about the unification stunned the regular Protestant groups. There were no public protests until Dr. Reinhold Krause, speaking at a German Christian mass meeting in Berlin on November 13, 1933, said:

> We must get rid of the Old Testament. The Old Testament has rightly been called the most questionable book in the whole history of the world, it does not, cannot, fit with a racially correct Christianity. A radical revision, too, must be made of the whole theology of the Rabbi Paul * * *[7]

The immediate result of this statement was the formation of the League of Defense of the Pastors which rapidly expanded into the Confessional Front. Despite threats and attacks, these independent churchmen repeatedly denounced Mueller and proceeded boldly to form a "true" Confessional Church government in defiance of his state-dominated organization.[8] Alarmed by the popular enthusiasm for the Confessionals, the state retreated. Dr. Jaegar resigned as Reich Minister for Church Affairs and Reichbishop Mueller was forced into the background.

The Confessional Church was encouraged by its success. On February 21, 1935, it ventured to publish a cautious statement warn-

[2] Power, p. 8.
[3] Quoted in Arthur S. Duncan-Jones, The Crooked Cross, London, 1940, pp. 8–9.
[4] Two-thirds of Germany's 65 million inhabitants were Evangelicals. The principal divisions were United Prussian, Lutheran, and Reformed. Power, p. 104.
[5] Power, p. 105.
[6] Duncan-Jones, pp. 15–16.
[7] Power, p. 115.
[8] Duncan-Jones, p. 19.

ing against the "new heathenism" as a denial of Christianity. The Nazis reacted swiftly and ruthlessly. Seven hundred pastors were placed under arrest. The secret police warned thousands of others not to read the statement. A mass meeting in Berlin emphasized the state's support for heathenism by acclaiming the "German Faith of Blood and Soil." Finally, in May 1935, the Confessional Church was placed under police jurisdiction.

A new phase of the struggle began in July. Hitler appointed Dr. Hans Kerrl, an uncompromising foe of the Confessionals, as Reich Minister for Church Affairs. Kerrl permitted the clergy to establish an independent committee to work out a satisfactory nation-wide organization. At the same time, however, he arbitrarily instituted "legal" attacks on the Confessional Churches. Ordinances were promulgated seeking to strip the churches of their remaining freedom and of all significant administrative and executive authority. To combat this new wave of persecution, the leading Confessionals formed the Provisional Church Administration in the spring of 1936.[9] They appealed secretly to Hitler for clarification of his attitude with regard to Dr. Kerrl's attacks against the Church. The only response was intensification of the pressure on the Confessionals. On February 12, 1937, the independent Church Committee was forced to resign. Its efforts to form an all-German Protestant organization had been continually frustrated by Kerrl in the interests of the German Christian group. After the resignation, Kerrl boldly declared:

There has now arisen a new authority concerning what Christ and Christianity really is. This new authority is Adolf Hitler.[10]

After Kerrl's statement, the emphasis of state policy shifted to attacks on pastors in their person and property. Pastor Martin Niemoeller was arrested in July 1937. In his last sermon on June 27, 1937, he had said:

We have no more thought of using our own powers to escape the arm of the authorities than had the Apostles of old. No more are we ready to keep silent at man's behest, when God commands us to speak. For it is and must remain the case, that we must obey God rather than man * * * [11]

Niemoeller's arrest climaxed the state's war on Protestantism. During 1938 and 1939, pressure on the remaining independent evangelical thought increased in line with war preparations. Nevertheless, despite enormous difficulties, many of the Confessional pastors went on with their spiritual work wherever possible, undeflected, though the organization of the Confessional Church had practically become nonexistent.[12]

The Catholic Church

While the Nazis were engaged in harnessing Protestantism to the state system, they waged a simultaneous campaign against Catholicism. In some respects, the latter presented more formidable problems. "The postwar years were the most brilliant in the history of German Catholics." [13] Although numbering only 20 millions, they were well-organized and united. The clergy was numerous, and the monastic orders extensive. The Catholic Centre Party in the Reichstag exercised real power. Lay and youth organizations flourished. The Catholic press wielded great influence. Nevertheless, within a

[9] The organization included Pastor Niemoeller, Dr. Boehm and Pastor Albertz.
[10] Quoted in Duncan-Jones, p. 28.
[11] Quoted in Power, p. 143.
[12] Duncan-Jones, p. 30.
[13] Robert d'Harcourt, The German Catholics, translated by Robert J. Dingle, London, 1939, p. 101.

few months after the National Socialist ascent to power, the "vast facade of organized Catholicism—so carefully built, so apparently unshakable—was to crumble." [14]

The Nazi request for a concordat with the Vatican was the first step in the destruction of organized Catholicism. An agreement was signed by Cardinal Pacelli (later Pope Pius XII) and Franz von Papen on July 20, 1933.[15] The National Socialist government guaranteed absolute protection for Catholic education, complete freedom of religious practice, and abstention from interference in religious affairs. In return the Vatican agreed that the German Catholics should refrain from organized political action and that the church would swear allegiance to the state.[16] In effect this agreement meant the dissolution of the' Centre Party in the Reichstag.

The treaty brought only a brief respite to the church. The Nazis soon began to violate indiscriminately the 33 articles of the Concordat.

By the end of 1933 * * * not a week passed without several brutal and arbitrary arrests of faithful Catholics and ecclesiastics.[17]

The appointment of Alfred Rosenberg, in February 1934, as "cultural" head of the Reich introduced a new phase of the conflict. The battle for control of youth and the destruction of Catholic lay organizations began. The familiar Nazi techniques of propaganda, restriction, and violence were used to discourage membership in the Catholic youth organizations. On June 7, 1934, the German bishops protested in the Pastoral Letter of Fulda. On June 26, Hitler gave them his personal reassurances. Four days later Dr. Erich Klausener, leader of Catholic Action, was assassinated on Hitler's orders, and the secret police confiscated the Fulda Pastorate.[18]

After the Saar plebiscite of 1935, the Nazis dropped all pretenses in their attacks on Catholicism. The leading spokesmen of National Socialism in a series of speeches announced their determination to end what they termed "political Catholicism." The campaign of calumny, economic pressure, and physical terror waged throughout 1935 and 1936 was effective. By the beginning of 1937, Catholic education and the Catholic Youth Movement were doomed and the Catholic press had been suppressed.

The war of attrition against Catholicism continued unabated through the opening months of 1937. In the spring the German bishops made a final attempt to come to an understanding with Hitler. When it failed they appealed to Rome.[19] Pope Pius XI responded with the Encyclical, "With Burning Anxiety" (Mit brennender Sorge). In defiance of the Gestapo, the Encyclical was read in the Catholic Churches of Germany on March 14, 1937. It was a complete condemnation of Reich religious policies.

It illuminated * * * the whole nature and extent of the attack upon the church, the width and the depth of the gulf that separates National-Socialism from the Christianity of Christ.[20]

[14] In 1927-28 there were 20,410 priests for the 20,000,000 Catholics. Protestantism had only 16,244 pastors for 40,000,000 followers. Catholic lay organizations had 800,000 members. Almost all units had newspapers. 12,000 parishes had been established. Power, pp. 18-19.
[15] Baerwald asserts that von Papen and Professor Karl Schmitt were the only two Catholic leaders of any national standing in the territory held by Germany before 1933 who voluntarily participated actively in the Nazi movement. Friedrich Baerwald, Catholic Resistance in Nazi Germany, Thought, vol. 20, June 1945, p. 227.
[16] Power, p. 26. Prior to 1933 the Vatican had concordats with several German States, Baerwald, p. 219
[17] D'Harcourt, p. 149.
[18] D'Harcourt, p. 151.
[19] Power, pp. 75-77.
[20] Power, p. 82.

The state retaliated with a new wave of arrests and sensational smuggling and morality trials against nuns and priests. Increased financial and police pressure was also applied. The burst of persecution, however, soon died away. "The main body of Catholicism, rallied by the Encyclical, stood firm." [21]

The new German church

Hitler repeatedly denied that there had been any persecution of religion in the Reich. In January 1939, he pointed out that financial aid to the churches had been increased from RM 130 million in 1933 to RM 500 million in 1939. These contributions, derived from the church tax, were in line with the Nazi policy of giving a semblance of morality to their acts, while at the same time destroying by any means available the foundations of all opposition to their totalitarian objectives. [22] The real intent of the party toward Christianity was made clear in Alfred Rosenberg's 30-point program for a new German church announced in January 1942 [23]— the time of flourishing Axis military success. The plan was a natural elaboration of the National Socialist religious policies of the previous decade. It was also the final crystallization of Nazi "religious" thought as represented principally by Alfred Rosenberg, Ernst Bergmann, and Wilhelm Hauer. Rosenberg had even anticipated the program in his early book, Der Mythus des 20. Jahrhunderts, when he wrote:

  * * * the German religious movement which some day may develop into a national church, must declare that the ideal of love among men is to be absolutely subordinated to the national honor * * * [24]

The 30-point program proposed that the German National Church with its single doctrine of "Race and People" take over all parishes, churches, and cathedrals disseminating "the imported Christian belief," and especially those "based on international bodies or directed from abroad." Under the new plan Hitler's Mein Kampf was expected to supersede the Bible for religious purposes. It would be propounded and interpreted by National Church "orators" rather than priests or ministers. It was also planned to substitute National Socialist symbols for those of Christianity. This involved replacing the cross with the swastika. Finally the ceremonies and holidays of the Christian Church were to be stripped of their religious context by creating corresponding Germanic substitutes. [25]

The plan was to go into effect immediately upon Hitler's acceptance. On March 22, 1942, at the "first office" of the New National Church, it was revealed that the compulsory features of the program, which would have doomed the Christian Churches, had not yet been adopted. Nevertheless, the situation was so serious that in May, Cardinal Faulhaber closed his report to the Vatican with a prayer that:

  * * * the church stand together for the fight of its existence. Today it is a question of life or death for Christianity, for in its blind rage against religion the Nazi "faith" does not or cannot distinguish between Protestantism and Catholicism. [26]

Under the stress of continuing war, Nazi religious policies were increasingly determined on the basis of expediency. This is especially

[21] Power, p. 83.
[22] Power, pp. 88–96.
[23] New York Times, January 3, 1942, p. 1.
[24] Quoted in Andrew J. Krzesinski, Religion of Nazi Germany, Boston, 1945, pp. 10–11.
[25] New York Times, January 3, 1942, p. 10.
[26] New York Times, May 9, 1942, p. 5

evidenced by the measures that were taken in the occupied and conquered countries. In Belgium and Holland attempts were made to
undermine the loyalty of Christians, and in the latter country,
Catholic priests were compelled to resign from teaching positions.[27]
In Poland the physical oppression was even more severe than it had
been in Austria in 1938. Cardinal Hlond, primate of Poland, states
that in addition to the secularization of all church property:

Ninety-five percent of our priests have been imprisoned, expelled or humiliated
before the eyes of the faithful.[28]

Policy in Eastern Europe, however, varied. In some instances
there was severe persecution. In others, the Nazis "sedulously
fostered certain Orthodox groups." [29] Always the basic criterion was
what helped or hindered the plans of the Nazi state.

ITALY
Compromise with the Church

In contrast with German Nazism, Italian Fascism, except on
occasion, did not openly fight Christianity but rather sought to avoid
conflict and to convert the Papacy into an ally of Fascism. Mussolini
made repeated concessions to Catholicism and offered it a leading
place in the Fascist way of life.[30] This reflected a realistic adaptation
to the existing religious situation. Catholicism is the religion of an
overwhelming majority of the Italian people.[31] But in spite of the
long Catholic tradition of Italy, and the intimate historical association
between the Papacy and the country, the pre-Fascist government had
pursued a policy of rigid secularism. The Popes since 1870, had confined themselves within the Vatican, assuming before the world a role
of "prisoners" of the Italian state.[32]

Mussolini recognized the desirability of eliminating this impasse and
hoped thereby to create of Catholicism an instrument for the promo-
tion of Fascism in Italy. He submerged his own anticlerical feelings,
held in check those of his extremist followers,[33] and "linked the solution
of the ecclesiastical problem with the revival of Italy's political fortunes." [34] He laid the groundwork for a rapprochement by acts of
official courtesy.

Public functions * * * always included a mass, attended by royalty and
members of the government. The crucifix returned to the walls of the schoolroom,
the university, the tribunal, and all other institutions * * *.[35]

Early Fascist legislation constituted even more tangible evidence of
the party's efforts to win Catholic support. Religious teaching was
reintroduced into the primary schools. The military forces and the
Fascist militia were assigned chaplains. Some religious festivals were
made national holidays. The clergy received salary increases. The

[27] Liam O'Connor, Hitler's War on the Church, New York, 1941, p. 18.
[28] O'Connor, p. 8.
[29] Christian Science Monitor, December 12, 1942, p. 5.
[30] Daniel A. Binchy, Church and State in Fascist Italy, London, 1941, p. 695.
[31] In the Italian census of 1931, of a reported total population of 41,709,851 all except 154,247 returned themselves as Catholics. Binchy, p. 470.
[32] Relations improved steadily, however, and with the growth of the Catholic-influenced Popularist
Party after the First World War I, the Church's position was better than at any time since 1870. Binchy,
pp. 69-70.
[33] Mussolini had been violently and vulgarly anticlerical during his Socialist days. Even the program
which he drew up for the first Fasci in 1919 contained a provision for the confiscation of all ecclesiastical
property. Binchy, p. 106.
[34] Samuel W. Halperin, The Separation of Church and State in Italian Thought * * *, Chicago, 1937,
p. 99.
[35] Binchy, p. 140.

church recovered some of the property seized from it by the pre-Fascist government. Freemasonry was suppressed. Most significant of all, the state appointed a commission to revise the entire body of ecclesiastical law on a basis satisfactory to the church. The favorable reaction which greeted these concessions was indicated by the Pope on December 14, 1925, when he publicly thanked the government for "everything that is being done in favor of religion."[36] Furthermore, Mussolini sought to introduce a modern corporative economic system which appeared to be in accord with older corporate ideas long advocated by the church fathers.

The Concordat with the Vatican

In spite of these overtures, in 1926, the politically absolute Fascist regime still lacked the moral endorsement of the church. Mussolini, therefore, turned his attention to a final settlement of the long-standing dispute between the Italian Government and the Vatican.[37] Three years of preparation and negotiations produced the Lateran Accords or Agreements signed on February 11, 1929.[38]

The settlement included a political treaty, a financial convention, and a concordat.[39] Thus it was believed that all outstanding issues between the Vatican and the Italian Government had been eliminated, and the course of amicable future relations had been laid. In part, the Lateran Accords provided for: The establishment of an "independent Vatican state;"[40] a two billion lire compensation to the church for state-inflicted losses since 1870, and numerous other material benefits for the clergy; the recognition of Catholicism as the religion of Italy; and the right of organizations of Catholic action "to diffuse and encourage Catholic principles * * *"[41]

Church-state relations after the concordat

The publication of the Lateran Accords was generally acclaimed throughout Italy.[42] Almost immediately, however, discord appeared over the precise role of the Church in the organization and education of youth, and the status of Catholic lay organizations. Agreements could not wipe out the incompatibility "between the Fascist view of religion as something that fell under the control of the state and the Catholic doctrine of the primacy of spiritual power."[43]

Sporadic incidents against the Church broke out almost immediately after ratification of the accords, but the full force of the state attack came in May 1931. The Fascist press raised the charge of anti-Fascist influence in the Catholic lay organizations, and the party unleashed the anticlerical group who had been held in check until now. Brutal attacks against persons and properties associated with Catholic lay organizations followed. On May 30, Catholic Youth and the Catholic University Federation were ordered dissolved.

[36] Binchy, pp. 140–3.
[37] Herman Finer, Mussolini's Italy, London, 1935, p. 457.
[38] Rino Longhitano, La politica religiosa di Mussolini, Rome, 1938, p. 115. The Italian King authorized the Government to enter into formal negotiations on December 10, 1926. By May 20, 1928, substantial agreement had been reached. Mussolini and Marchise Pacelli (later Pius XII) personally conducted the final stages of the negotiation. Binchy, pp. 176–178.
[39] Ratification of the three treaties took place June 7, 1929. Statesman's Year Book 1945, New York, 1945, p. 1209.
[40] The Vatican has an area of 10,817 acres and a population which in 1932 was reported to total 1,025. Stateman's Year Book, pp. 1209–1210.
[41] Finer, pp. 457–459.
[42] There was some concern expressed by non-Catholics who feared that the Accord would end the religious parity they had previously enjoyed. A law issued on June 24, 1929, however, granted religious freedom to all religions not contrary to public order or morality. Binchy, pp. 584–586.
[43] Binchy, p. 219.

In answer to these attacks, Pius XI ordered the publication on June 29, 1931, of his Encyclical, "We Have No Need"(Non abbiamo bisogno). The document refuted Fascist charges of disloyalty leveled at the Catholic organizations and went on to condemn "some of Fascism's most cherished doctrines." It countercharged the party with seeking to raise the young in a "pagan worship of the state" and in "a species of religion which rebels against the direction of the highest religious authorities."[44] Neither Mussolini nor the Pope, however, were seeking a general conflict. The dispute, therefore, was suddenly settled by an agreement reached on September 2, 1931. The state withdrew the ban on the youth and university organizations, and Catholic action was allowed to continue, confined in activity to strictly religious functions.[45]

After the publication of the famous Encyclical, there were additional flareups between the church and state. On the whole, however, "formal collaboration * * * (was) the rule and open disagreement the exception * * *"[46]. Outwardly, the Italian church gained from the patronage of the state, but the advantages of association were partially offset "by the anti-Christian glorification of violence in the youth organizations and the neopagan elements in the scholastic programmes" and by the eclipse of the Catholic press.[47]

Clerical support for Fascism began to wane shortly after the African campaign, and "the steady drift towards Hitler's Germany, culminating in the Rome-Berlin Axis—silenced even the warmest admirers of the regime."[48] It should be pointed out that there were always individual officials of the Italian church and numerous humble parish priests who opposed Fascism. Many were jailed or terrorized for their beliefs. Furthermore, the entire hierarchy invariably repudiated those acts of the regime that conflicted with basic Catholic doctrine, as in 1938, when the Italian church echoed the Pope in denouncing the anti-Jewish racialist doctrine imported by Mussolini from Germany. Thus, despite the support Mussolini received from a substantial part of the Catholic priesthood:

> The Church as a whole, in its structure, activities, and corporate life (was) * * * the only institution * * * not fitted into the totalitarian machine.[49]

SPAIN

Collaboration with the Church

Most of the higher Spanish Catholic clergy gave wholehearted support to the Nationalist rebels during the Civil War.[50] The cardinal primate of Spain and other leading clerics regarded the struggle as a crusade and the Nationalists as saviors of Christianity.[51] The Vatican, however, although it vehemently condemned the persecution of the church in Loyalist Spain, maintained formal connections with the Madrid government until 1939, and avoided all association with the authoritarian principles of General Franco.[52]

---

[44] Binchy, pp. 522–5.
[45] Finer, p. 467.
[46] Binchy, p. 685.
[47] Binchy, pp. 685–7.
[48] Binchy, p. 679.
[49] Binchy, p. 684.
[50] A. de Castro Albarran, Guerra Santa, Burgos, 1938, pp. 104–108. Exceptions were the bishop of Victoria and the priests of the Basque provinces and Catalonia. Hamilton, 1943, pp. 95–96.
[51] Albarran, pp. 25–30.
[52] Camille M. Cianfarra, The Vatican and the War, New York, 1944, p. 79; see also Binchy, p. 653.

The unique traditions of Spanish Catholicism and the situation in which the church found itself under the Republic, determined its stand during the Civil War. For centuries Spain had been an intensely Catholic country.[53] The clergy dominated education. The Catholic Church was the greatest single property owner. It was closely linked with the Spanish state. Until recent years it had been the decisive factor in politics. The leaders of the church had frequently been famous warriors and statesmen as well as priests.[54] New recruits for the priesthood, drawn from the lower and middle classes, were instilled with this aristocratic, political, and fervently nationalistic heritage.[55]

The coming of the Republic in 1931, upset the traditional position of the church. Catholicism was disestablished and subjected to rigorous anticlerical measures. Some physical attacks on the clergy and church property took place. The Jesuits were banished. The Catholic hierarchy, nevertheless, accepted the republic, stating in the collective declaration of the episcopate of December 20, 1931, that:

> The Church has never failed to inculcate the respect and obedience due to constituted power, even in those cases where its holders and representatives have abused it. * * * [56]

The sporadic attacks of the early Republican period flared into a wave of violence after the election victory of the left coalition government in February 1936. During the first 4 months of the new regime, church property was confiscated and the clergy were subjected to indignities and violence.[57] The very existence of the Spanish Catholic Church seemed to be threatened. When the Nationalist revolution broke out in July, the church no longer supported the declaration of December 20, 1931, and upheld the rebellion.[58] Moreover, it looked upon Franco as a good Christian and upon the other side as composed of atheists, communists, and anarchists who were seeking the destruction of the Catholic Church.

Religion in Spain after the civil war

Spanish Catholicism emerged from the Civil War restored to its traditional position of political influence and subsidized to the extent of some $5,400,000 annually.[59] It resumed a dominant role in education.[60] The Jesuit orders, expelled by the Republic, were permitted to return and were granted increased rights and privileges. Free Masonry was suppressed.[61] New Spanish laws were drawn in conformity with Catholic precepts of morality.[62] Pope Pius XII indicated the extent of the Catholic resurgence in April 1943. At the presentation of the new Spanish Ambassador to the Holy See, he said:

> We have seen the Church rise out of smoking ruins to infuse the Christian spirit into your laws, your institutions and all the manifestations of official life.[63]

---

[53] In 1933, the total evangelical community in Spain numbered only 21,900 out of a total population of 23,500,000. E. Allison Peers, Spain, the Church and the Orders, London, 1945, Burns, Bates and Weshbourne, p. 4.
[54] Spanish Catholicism, New Statesmen and Nation, London, January 25, 1941, p. 79.
[55] Arturo Barea, Struggle for the Spanish Soul, London, 1941, p. 55-57.
[56] Alfredo Mendezebal, Church and Democracy in Spain, New Europe, New York, April-May 1945, p. 23.
[57] According to the report of the Spanish Government agency in charge of reconstruction (Dirección General de Regiones Devastades), damage to the Catholic Church during the entire Civil War amounted to 150 churches totally destroyed and 4,850 damaged, including 1,850 which were more than 50 percent destroyed. Hamilton, p. 24.
[58] Peers, pp. 158-162.
[59] Mendezebal, p. 23.
[60] Julio Alvárez del Vayo, Freedom's Battle, New York, 1940, p. 329.
[61] The New Order in Spain, Christian Century, Chicago, Oct. 30, 1940, pp. 1332-1333.
[62] Divorce and civil marriage have been abolished. Christian Century, Oct. 30, 1940. p. 33.
[63] Michael Kenny, Pius XII and Franco on Spain, Ave Maria, Notre Dame, Ind., vol. N. 8. 59, Mar. 1, 1944, p. 297

The few Spanish Protestants and the English Evangelical missions in the Iberian Peninsula did not share in this religious revival. According to an open letter of the World Evangelical Alliance issued in 1944, Protestantism was being systematically rooted out of the national life of Spain, and there had been instances of the direct persecution of non-Catholics.[64]

In spite of the revived strength of the Spanish Catholic Church, it would appear that there still was in April 1947 an ideological incompatibility between the Church and the fascist wing of the Falange similar to that which once existed in Nazi Germany and Fascist Italy.

The Falangists had experienced a tremendous growth of influence during the period of Axis military success during the Second World War. It enabled them to launch press attacks against individual clergymen, to bar Vatican criticism of Germany from free circulation in Spain, and to curb Catholic action.[65] The situation became serious enough to move some Spanish bishops to issue warnings against idolatry of the state.[66] However, for the most part Falangists proclaimed their Catholicity, and the Spanish church steadfastly supported the state.

CONCLUSION

Generalizations about fascism in religious matters are dangerous because each country had its own peculiar experiences. Emperor worship and Shintoism were integral parts of Japanese fascism. Outright conflict characterized relations between the German Christian Church and the National Socialist Party. Between these two poles one found the Italo-Papal modus vivendi and the Spanish cooperation between the church and state.

If religious tenets make the state supreme on earth, then a basic conflict between religion and fascism may not be necessary. If, on the other hand, a religion such as Christianity "renders unto Caesar that which is Caesar's," but correlatively insists that one "render unto God that which is God's," then ultimately such a religion will conflict with fascism, for which the state is God. Politically it may be inexpedient for fascism to challenge an established religion. In such case it makes adjustments as in Italy until the time is propitious for an attack upon the church. Sometimes too, the fundamental conflict may not be apparent, as was the case in Spain. But it must be repeated that under fascism the state comes first, and if religion conflicts with the state, so much the worse for religion.

[64] Christian Science Monitor, Dec. 9, 1944, p. 8. See also Christian Century Chicago, June 22, 1947, p. 103; New York Times, Dec. 4, 1946, p. 23; Gabriel Javsicas, Spain Divided, Harpers, November 1945, p. 428; Washington Post, Dec. 22, 1946, p. 1b.
[65] Wilhelm Solzbacher, The Church and the Spanish State, The Commonwealth, New York, vol. XXV, Feb. 27, 1942, pp. 454–458. See also, Arturo Barea, Spanish Catholicism New Statesmen and Nation, London, Mar. 15, 1941, p. 267.
[66] Solzbacher, p. 456.

CHAPTER XIV—FREEDOM

FASCIST THEORY

Anti-individualistic, the Fascist conception of life stresses the importance of the State and accepts the individual only insofar as his interests coincide with those of the State. * * * [1]

In these words Mussolini flatly rejects the liberal democratic idea that the purpose of the state is to serve the individual. The subordination of the individual to the state in National Socialist theory is equally complete, although in the latter case the state itself is made an instrument of a still higher entity, the community (Volk).[2]

In modern democracies it has been accepted that some spheres of human endeavor should be removed from the realm of the state. Fascist theory recognizes no limits on the subordination of the individual to the state.

The Fascist conception of the State is all-embracing; outside of it no human or spiritual values can exist, much less have value. Thus understood, Fascism is totalitarian, and the Fascist State—a synthesis and a unit inclusive of all values—interprets, develops, and potentiates the whole life of a people.[3]

Nazi theorists likewise have stressed the idea that political authority carried with it absolute spiritual and moral authority. Not even in his own soul is the individual supposed to have any obligation except to the state.[4]

The subordination of the individual in fascist theory is rounded out by the doctrine of leadership. Both Italian Fascism and German National Socialism make the will of the state synonymous with the will of the ruler, and vice versa. The individual is supposed to give unquestioning obedience to his rulers. Particularly in National Socialist theory the idea is expressed that the citizen should not merely obey his rulers; he should have it as his mission to make himself in the image of his rulers, so that he will have no will to do other than their bidding. The Nazi concept of leadership, however, was more complex than sheer domination.

What Fuehrertum really means * * * is * * * that German people are to be ruled by masters so eminently incarnating their peculiar "kind" or "essence" as to be able to divine—and to decree—in their stead, what they want; indeed, to conceive and prescribe the essence and character of the "guided" on behalf of their racial "genius" who is truer to their soul than their own conscious thinking could possibly be.[5]

It follows that the fascist theory of the state has no patience with the "rights" of individuals. Their rights are duties, the primary one of which is absolute obedience to their rulers. Fascist and National Socialist theory insists, however, that democratic freedom is a sham. Man is really free only as he is true to his inmost nature. In National

---

[1] Benito Mussolini, Fascism, Doctrine and Institutions, Rome, 1935, p. 10.
[2] For a summary of National Socialist theories of community, see Aurel Kolnai, The War Against the West, London, 1938, ch. II.
[3] Mussolini, p. 11.
[4] See Kolnai, pp. 159 ff.
[5] Kolnai, p. 160.

197

Socialist theory, his inmost nature is membership in a race. "Real" freedom, therefore, is conceived of as "the full expression of the racial soul in a cohesive social order which brings forth human types finding their highest satisfaction in serving the organic life of the folk." [6] According to Mussolini:

> Far from crushing the individual, the Fascist State multiplies his energies, just as in a regiment a soldier is not diminished but multiplied by the number of his fellow soldiers.[7]

The idea is that in return for the surrender of "useless or harmful" liberties, namely those of the democratic state, the individual under fascism actually gains liberty, in that he becomes a participant in a positive, dynamic and undivided, hence more powerful and prosperous state. It is contended that the individual cannot have both of these kinds of freedom. The traditional democratic type—freedom of press, speech, religion, and association—is viewed as actually harmful to the individual in that it leads to disunion and friction, thus weakening the nation and consequently subjecting the individual to the restraints of poverty and national weakness and insecurity. This is, of course, in sharp contrast to democratic theory, which holds that the strength and prosperity of the state are best promoted by tolerating individual dissent and by placing limits on the scope of state activity.

METHODS OF CONTROL

It is one thing to develop a theory in which the individual is at all points subordinated to the will of the state, as expressed by its rulers. It is quite another to develop a system of control which will in practice achieve the desired result. Fascism was successful in this respect to a far greater degree than the peoples of democratic countries at first thought possible. Its success was due in considerable measure to certain undemocratic devices, notably the securing of a dominant position in all kinds of groups and associations, the monopolization and skillful utilization of all methods of influencing opinion, and the development of extraordinary agencies and procedures for dealing with opponents or potential opponents of fascist rule. The use of these devices is illustrated by the following brief account of the regulation of the conduct of the individual in his political, economic, and cultural activities.[8]

Political freedom

Except for the fascist elite, the individual's participation in the process of government was confined chiefly to obeying the commands of his superiors.[9] The privilege of voting at elections was widely extended, but had little significance because of the absence of choice in elections, and because of the relative unimportance of elective bodies. In Italy national elections were altogether abandoned in 1938. In both Germany and Italy only one party was recognized. All others were outlawed, their funds confiscated, and their leaders imprisoned or otherwise removed. Membership in both the Fascist and the National Socialist Parties was reserved for the relatively

[6] Albert R. Chandler, Rosenberg's Nazi Myth, Ithaca, 1945, p. 75.
[7] Mussolini, pp. 29–30.
[8] A more detailed account of the restrictions imposed on specific aspects of individual behavior will be found in other chapters of this study.
[9] See chapter on Government for detailed discussion.

small number who could meet the rigorous qualifications. Office-holding, even as applied to the judiciary, was confined to those of demonstrated party loyalty. The party was identified with the state and criticism of party leaders or policies was prohibited. The influence of public opinion was negligible, since opposition to established policies was prohibited. In short, the individual had available to him almost none of the methods of political participation taken for granted in a democratic society.

The virtual elimination of all except underground political opposition required numerous departures from generally accepted democratic legal safeguards.[10] The category of political crimes was greatly extended both in Italy and Germany, and the definition of the crime was often extremely vague. For example, a National Socialist law of 1934, providing punishment for insidious attacks on the state and the party, extended even to utterances "likely to undermine the confidence of the people in the political leadership".[11] Moreover, the Nationalist Socialists repealed the principle *nullum crimen sine lege* (there is no crime unless defined by statute) by the law of June 28, 1935. This statute provided for the punishment of anyone committing an act declared punishable by statute or deserving a penalty according to the basic principles of a criminal statute and to the people's sound sentiment. It was provided that if no particular criminal statute directly applied to the act, the act should be punishable under the statute, the basic principles of which best fitted the act.[12] Another feature of the National Socialist administration of justice was that the discretionary powers of the police and of administrative officials were broadened, and the extent of judicial review of police and administrative action narrowly confined. An example was the authority conferred upon the Italian police to deal with persons politically suspect. Under the Public Security Act of November 6, 1926, persons could be classed as "infamous" if "public rumor" indicated that they were "dangerous to the national order of the state." They were then subject to police "admonishment," which was in effect a rigid surveillance. The police could deport an "admonished" person or any other person who "has committed, or manifested the intention of committing, acts which may disturb the national, social, or economic order of the state or obstruct public authority in such a manner as to jeopardize the national or international interests of the state." There was no judicial appeal.[13]

Repressive criminal laws, almost unlimited police and administrative discretion, and party domination of the regular police and courts were not, however, the chief weapons of fascism in dealing with political opposition. Both in Italy and Germany great reliance was placed on special political police and on extraordinary tribunals established to deal with political offenses. In Italy the early Blackshirts or Fascist "squads of action" were eventually organized as the Voluntary Militia for National Safety (generally referred to as the militia). It was in essence the army of the Fascist Party, and was an official part of the party. In the late 1930's it had a membership of about 400,000,

---

[10] A compact description of Fascist and National Socialist methods of dealing with political opposition will be found in James T. Shotwell et al., Governments of Continental Europe, New York, 1940, which is used as the basis of this discussion.
[11] Shotwell, p. 474.
[12] War Department Pamphlet No. 31-122, Military Government Information Guide, The Statutory Criminal Law of Germany, War Department, August 1946.
[13] Shotwell, p. 720.

most of whom, however, were called out only occasionally for emergency police duty. The real espionage agency was the secret political police (OVRA), made up of a selected number of the militia. Its primary function was to search for and spy on political suspects.

Even more famous were the German secret police, notably the Gestapo and the S. S. A powerful influence since its organization in 1933, the Gestapo was given a legal basis in 1936, being empowered "to uncover and combat all tendencies and developments inimical to the State, and to take for this end all measures deemed necessary and expedient." [14] Its actions were legally uncontrolled, except by Himmler and by Hitler himself. An accused person was given a complaint, but could take no appeal from the decision of the chief of the political police. Many of the tasks of the Gestapo were executed by the S. S., or Elite Guard. It was this agency which ran the concentration camps. Commitment to a concentration camp, legally designated as preventive custody, was the Nazi counterpart of the Fascist administrative remedy of deportation. Both remedies were entirely extra-judicial. It seems certain that the Nazi measure of commitment to concentration camps for political reasons was much more frequently used than deportation in Italy, but official figures are not available.

The Fascist Special Tribunal for the Defense of the State and the National Socialist People's Court exercised broad jurisdiction in cases involving political crimes. The members of the Fascist Tribunal were military or militia officers, and the procedure was that of a court martial. There was no appeal. The National Socialist People's Court had a majority of lay judges from the Elite Guard and party leaders, chosen for their special knowledge of subversive activities. Proceedings were secret.[15]

<h3 style="text-align:center">ECONOMIC FREEDOM [16]</h3>

The fundamental economic freedom virtually eliminated by fascist states was that of free, private, competitive enterprise, the type one sees operating on Main Street in thousands of American cities, where some 3,000,000 individually owned and operated businesses compete vigorously for the patronage of the public. Under fascist regimes there was but little freedom of occupation, or freedom of contract. Of free markets, free trade or free movement of capital, labor or goods there remained only so much as served the interests and purposes of the ruling clique which comprised the state.

The precise methods whereby the fundamental economic freedoms of free, private enterprise, free markets, free collective bargaining, free trade, and freedom of contract were emasculated or abolished, varied from country to country.

[14] Shotwell, p. 490.

[15] With respect to the treatment of political opposition, as in many other matters, the Franco regime in Spain appears to have followed the Fascist and National Socialist examples. After the defeat of the Loyalists, the Franco decree of February 9, 1939, known as "The Law of Political Responsibilities," provided for the punishment of those who, through their acts or serious failure to act, were deemed to have contributed to Spain's plight. It outlawed 26 specified organizations, including many moderate political groups. The decree established special agencies and courts, headed by a National Tribunal of Political Responsibilities, to enforce the decree. Through the actions of these special courts and of the military courts a large number of persons were executed, put in concentration camps, or otherwise punished for political reasons. See London Times, March 7, 1939, p. 7. Also, A. Randle Elliott, Spain after Civil War, Foreign Policy Reports, vol. XVI, No. 5, May 15, 1940.

[16] See chs. VI and VII on Organization of the Economy; also chs. VIII and IX on Labor and Agriculture for details.

In Germany, for example, the National Socialists found ready to hand an elaborately organized economy which merely required modification to their own ends. The voluntary labor service of the Republic was transformed into compulsory service in labor camps, under military discipline. Independent trade unions were abolished, and membership of workers in the Labor Front was in practice compulsory. As the land of cartels and state-sanctioned monopolies, it required mere logical extension to organize all entrepreneurs into an elaborate framework of estates, associations, and cartels, under the Ministry of Economics.

Developments in Italy and other fascist regimes differed considerably in detail from those in Germany. But the ultimate status of economic freedom in all these fascist regimes was the same. The small independent shopkeeper, tradesman or manufacturer found himself a cog in a monopolistic cartellized "new order" which took from his hands nearly every important managerial decision. The laborers and farmers likewise lost their freedom of contract and of movement and were forbidden autonomous, self-governing organization. The powerful combines, the high party leaders, the army generals and the bureaucrats were giving the orders. Economic freedoms for the individual were lost.

CULTURAL AND SOCIAL FREEDOM

Virtually all forms of cultural and social expression were thoroughly controlled under fascism. The one important exception was in matters of religion. Even here there were drastic restrictions, particularly under National Socialism, but fascism was not successful either in capturing religious organizations or in limiting religious activities to an extent comparable to that in other areas.[17] Apart from this partial defeat, however, the fascist goal of the "totalitarian" control of life was effectively realized.

The control of education and leisure time activities has been described elsewhere in this study.[18] The monopolization by state and party of the organizations through which the individual could participate was nearly complete. The youth organizations, the school system, and the Italian Dopolavoro and the Nazi Strength through Joy organization of the Labor Front took care of most educational and leisure time activities. Other organizations, or groups, permitted to exist were fascist controlled or supervised. Illustrative of the extent of supervision was the Italian regulation requiring sponsors of scientific, athletic, or philanthropic meetings to secure permits in advance and give assurance that there would be no violation of the "national conscience." [19]

Press, radio, theater, and artistic expression were subject to a variety of controls. In the case of the Italian press, all directors and managers had to have licenses from the Minister of Justice. They had to be politically trustworthy, and licenses could be revoked at the discretion of the Minister. Employees had to be taken from registered journalists, and no journalist was eligible for registration if he had engaged in "public activity contrary to thei nterests of the nation." [20] In

---

[17] See ch. XIII on Religion.
[18] See chs. II on Education and XII on the Use of Leisure Time.
[19] Shotwell, p. 711. See also, Marcelle Breillat-Milhaud, Des Libertés Publiques en Droit Fasciste, Paris, 1939, ch. VI, pp. 127 ff.
[20] Shotwell, pp. 704–705.

addition, there was a severe censorship, the prefect having authority to confiscate any printed matter that was found "false, tendentious or misleading," or calculated "to inspire class hatred or contempt of the government."[21]   Finally, the Ministry of Popular Culture in later years gave directions and suggestions to the press as to what it should print.   The control of all printing and publishing was along similar lines, with stringent licensing and censorship provisions.   Radio was a private monopoly, supervised by a board of control under the Ministry of Communications, and programs were provided by the monopoly and the Government.   Motion pictures were subject to political censorship, and the showing of Government films was compulsory.[22]

In Nazi Germany the Reich Chamber of Culture was the counterpart of the Labor Front and the Food Estate.   It had seven subdivisions, covering writers and authors, journalists and editors, musicians, artists, personnel of theaters, films, and radio.   The basic law provided that "all persons who participate in the production or reproduction, in the intellectual or technical elaboration, the distribution, the preservation, in the sale or as middlemen in the distribution of cultural goods," [23] must be members of one of these organizations. They could be removed from membership for professional misconduct, that is, generally, for political reasons, and were thus barred from their profession.   This regulation made censorship relatively unimportant. In addition, there were specific statutes for each cultural profession. All journalists of editorial rank had to be licensed and had to be personally and politically qualified.   They could be removed by the Press Honor Courts or for "reasons of public welfare" [24] by the Minister of Propaganda.   Broadcasting was a Government monopoly, and was the chief instrument for propaganda activities of the party.

In Germany, as in Italy, and to an even greater extent, the control of cultural expression came to be more and more exerted in positive fashion, through the dissemination of propaganda.   The Ministry of Propaganda, under Goebbels, functioned primarily not as a censorship agency, although it had and used that function, but for the purpose of providing the cultural material which was to be distributed to the public.   In its long-run effects, this was an even more significant restriction of free expression than licensing and censorship controls.

RACIAL DISCRIMINATION

National Socialism rejected the democratic concept of equality of all persons before the law.   It developed an elaborate racial theory, but in practical operation the race most discriminated against was the Semitic.[25]   Antisemitism was never a significant aspect of Italian Fascism, though some attempt was made in later years to imitate Nazi policies.[26]

The first official action against the Jews by the Nazis was their removal from public office in 1933.   Exceptions for veterans were removed in 1935.   The Public Official Act of 1937 also disqualified gentiles married to Jewish wives.

[21] Shotwell, p. 705.
[22] Shotwell, pp. 704–709.
[23] Shotwell, p. 538.
[24] Shotwell, p. 539.
[25] For a brief summary of National Socialist anti-Semitic policies see Shotwell, pp. 500 ff.   See also Franz S. Neumann, Behemoth, the Structure and Practice of National Socialism, New York, 1942, pp. 111 ff.
[26] Breillat-Milhaud, pp. 50–54.

The next step was the exclusion of Jews from all professions "affected with a public interest," which came to include virtually all of the trained professions. Moreover, through the system of licensing in guild and professional association, Jews as well as politically unreliable persons were excluded from the cultural professions.

Next came the deprivation of citizenship and political rights, under the Reich Citizenship Act of 1935, and the prohibition of sexual intercourse between Jews and Aryans, the latter to protect "German blood and honor." The term "Jew" was defined with great precision in the Citizenship Act.

Propaganda, boycotts, and other devices were used to expel Jews from trade and industry, but final expulsion here came later than in other areas. In 1938, all Jewish property had to be registered under the 4-year plan. Following the murder of an employee of the German legation in Paris by a Polish Jew, there was a systematic destruction of Jewish property, and a large number of Jews were thrown in concentration camps. Other measures were taken, including the levying of an atonement fine, which in effect brought about a partial confiscation of Jewish property. Then came the provision that after January 1, 1939, no Jew could own or operate a retail or wholesale business or pursue the occupation of independent artisan.

CONCLUSION

Many aspects of fascist control of individual conduct are not touched on in the above account. Illustrative of the "totalitarian" nature of the fascist state were the programs for checking the declining birthrate in Germany and Italy. Various privileges, rewards, and bounties were offered for large families, and abortion laws were made more rigorous. The Nazi program was concerned with quality of offspring as well as quantity. Racial, physical, mental, and moral standards had to be met before marriage was permitted. S. S. members were required to have special permits to marry. The propagation of physically and biologically "unfit" persons was prohibited, in part through the marriage laws but also by provision for the sterilization of hereditary defectives.

The dominant note in the fascist organization of life, particularly in Germany, was the concept of status or place. Each individual had his role or mission, which was determined by the state. This made for a highly regimented life. As has been pointed out,[27] the individual's leisure time, as well as his working time, was thoroughly organized. In return, however, an effort was made to give him a sense of importance by making him feel that he had a part in the larger role of the groups and associations to which he belonged, and through them a part in the role of the Volk itself. Moreover, he was kept so busy fulfilling his assigned tasks that he found little time for complaint or opposition.

---

[27] See ch. XII, Use of Leisure Time.

PART IV—CONCLUSION

Fascism is manifested in many different ways, but it always assigns an overwhelming importance to the state. Some writers have called it statism or etatism, which, in the extreme form is state worship or statolatry.

Summarizing the preceding chapters, and limited by the examples used, fascism means the following things.

1. Fascist government is rule by a leader possessed of dictatorial powers supported by a single political party, and an elite class. It is characterized by the centralization of political power, and the regimentation of everyone and everything in terms of the purposes of the state.

2. Education and thought control are used to condition the mind of the masses at home for the fascist struggle by all the devices which create, mold or influence, ideas, beliefs, and impressions. Abroad, fascism tries to create a friendly environment in which to spread fascist ideas; and if this is impossible, to soften opposition in anticipation of future attack.

3. Fascist foreign policies are dynamic and aggressive. They concentrate largely on the search for living space and empire, and try to make gains by creating crises from which they hope to profit.

4. Finance and fiscal policies direct banking and private investment decisions in accord with general fascist policies. While fiscal policies play a comparatively minor domestic role, they prescribe heavy occupation levies and banking control as major tools for the exploitation of defeated enemies.

5. Foreign trade is no longer simply an economic phenomenon but becomes one of the many instruments through which the state achieves its political objectives.

6. The economy generally favors big business, strengthens the position of heavy industries, retains enough of the profit system to permit the elite to build up personal fortunes, emphasizes self-sufficiency, institutes higher tariffs, facilitates cartellization, and spends huge sums for military purposes. At the same time it disregards the greatest of all human drives and energies, individual freedom reflected in freedom of occupation, free self-seeking enterprise, free movement of goods and services as well as capital to places most needed, free investments, free markets, free managerial economy and the avoidance of marginal wastes, free competition with survival to the lowest cost product, and free use of all labor whatever its race or color may be.

7. Labor is regimented with the result that free collective bargaining and self-government by labor organizations is abolished.

8. Agriculture is intensively developed with the aim of making the fascist country self-sufficient and able to feed its own population with the products of its soil.

9. Transportation, in addition to furnishing a means of carrying passengers and goods, is developed for strategic, prestige, and unemployment relief purposes.

10. Living standards tend to improve under the impetus of the armaments programs. To date no fascist government has been long enough in existence to determine how lasting these benefits may be; nor do these improvements approach the American standard. The improvement is conditioned by the demands for such militarily important items as fats and butter, which were severely curtailed in the later '30s in Germany.

11. Use of leisure time is carefully supervised and directed by the state with a view to controlling the individual in all his waking thoughts and actions.

12. Religion becomes the object of attack, when it prescribes loyalty and obedience to anyone else before the state, or insofar as it emphasizes the dignity of the individual. If religion gives primacy to the state, or if it agrees with the program of fascism, it may be tolerated and encouraged.

13. Freedom in the democratic sense of the word is nonexistent. In its place are to be found a host of duties and obligations. The life of the individual has small value.

FASCISM IS INTERNALLY CONSISTENT

Contrary to popular belief, fascism is not wholly a perversion nor does it always require a criminal frame of mind. Such a view condemns wholesale millions of well-intentioned, law-abiding people who live in fascist countries. Fascism is an internally consistent mode of life and Government, if its bases are recognized and conceded. Fascism builds everything around the purposes of the state and makes the state preponderant, while democracy holds the individual and his freedoms and rights as primary and would build the welfare of society upon his freedom. From this division flow most of the differences between the two ideologies. Fascism is not peculiar to any people or to any government.

The transition to fascism from any other form of government is deceptively easy, for it progresses by steps and stages; but the change from fascism to other forms of government to date has been destructive and violent, as is testified by the fate of most fascist countries during the last generation. This is not surprising, for the fascist doctrine is couched in violence, and its program is one of conflict, violence, and aggressive prejudice openly espoused and approved. It is this element of violence, when coupled with the overwhelming preponderance of the state in all matters, that distorts fascist culture and limits its intellectual activities and perspective.

EARLY SUCCESS OF FASCISM

There can be no question but that fascist governments exhibited notable strengths. They succeeded in mobilizing and rationalizing the full national effort upon specific programs and according to a set of specific objectives. In the initial stages they gave employment to thousands and millions as the armament programs were stepped up. (This has been challenged as a spurious improvement, whose benefits would have disappeared eventually to be followed by more serious unemployment than that which it corrected.) They gave the "in-groups" a powerful emotional "lift" by making them feel that the fascist members were a group united in one great, common effort.

They could act quickly in a crisis and left little to chance, but gave everyone specific tasks and duties to perform, and these were made to count for the most. Totalitarian ideology, propaganda, and readiness to act gave fascism exceptional strength when pitted against disunited and disorganized states and philosophies.

SOME WEAKNESSES OF FASCISM

Without ascribing them as causes for the defeat of the fascist states in the Second World War, certain weaknesses were revealed by fascism in action. Basically, fascism was a war order, which could survive only as long as it was successful and for which defeat meant extinction. It made no allowance for correlative and competing orders in the world, oversimplifying the international world by dividing it into friendly and enemy states, and making no allowance for any intermediary position.

A popular impression is that fascisms were efficient, because, like all dictatorships, they centralized government, which supposedly meant better coordination of social, economic, and political efforts. This study, however, shows that such a view is erroneous. Chapter IV on Foreign Policy has demonstrated that several agencies and leaders were trying to cover the same field, and thus were working at cross-purposes with each other, vieing with each other, spying on each other, and withholding important information from each other. In industry and trade the same duplication and working at cross-purposes has been revealed. In spite of the fact that Goering was supposed to be the head of civilian and military aviation, the Four-Year Plan, and all airplane production in the Third Reich and its territories, Himmler acquired and operated the Manfred Weiss airplane works in Rumania so as to build up his own air fleet. Fascist governments seem to be full of incipient leaders, whose struggles for power create governmental inefficiency.

By feeding upon and fanning the hatred of groups both at home and abroad, fascisms built up such hatred in the world that they were ultimately consumed by it.

Because fascism failed to permit the individual to develop to his fullest capacity, it failed to make the fullest use of individual ideas and activities. By placing a premium on the individual conforming to the regulations prescribed by the state, it made the state little or great in direct proportion to the ability of the leaders to think and to act. Or, to state the proposition in reverse, the state was limited by the intellectual, physical, and emotional capacities of its leaders. Thus even in the military field, where fascism was supposedly strongest, the democracies were able ultimately to achieve victory. Hitler's intuition was a poor substitute for military science and generalship.

Finally, fascist intolerance of human values refused to recognize that in the last analysis it is the human being who gives the state existence. But most significant of all was the weakness which prevented fascisms from consolidating the substantial gains they had made prior to the Second World War. Their intolerance of opposition prevented them from making fundamental and necessary political and economic compromises.

O

CPSIA information can be obtained
at www.ICGtesting.com
Printed in the USA
LVHW090416040121
675639LV00002B/186